SOCIAL ISSUES AND SOCIAL PROBLEMS INFORMATION GUIDE SERIES

Series Editors: Kenneth D. Sell, Chairman, Department of Sociology, Catawba College, Salisbury, North Carolina and Betty H. Sell, Director, Catawba College Library, Salisbury, North Carolina

Also in this series:

CHILD CARE ISSUES FOR PARENTS AND SOCIETY—*Edited by Andrew Garoogian and Rhoda Garoogian*

SUICIDE—*Edited by David Lester**

*in preparation

The above series is part of the

GALE INFORMATION GUIDE LIBRARY

The Library consists of a number of separate series of guides covering major areas in the social sciences, humanities, and current affairs.

General Editor: Paul Wasserman, Professor and former Dean, School of Library and Information Services, University of Maryland

Managing Editor: Denise Allard Adzigian, Gale Research Company

Divorce in the United States, Canada, and Great Britain

Divorce in the United States, Canada, and Great Britain

A GUIDE TO INFORMATION SOURCES

Volume 1 in the Social Issues and Social Problems Information Guide Series

Kenneth D. Sell

*Professor of Sociology
and
Chairman of the Department
Catawba College
Salisbury, North Carolina*

Betty H. Sell

*Director of the Library
Catawba College
Salisbury, North Carolina*

Gale Research Company
Book Tower, Detroit, Michigan 48226

Library of Congress Cataloging in Publication Data

Sell, Kenneth D
    Divorce in the United States, Canada, and Great Britain.

    (Social issues and social problems information guide series; v. 1)
    Includes indexes.
        1. Divorce--Bibliography. 2. Divorce--Information services. 3. Divorce--United
States--Statistics--Bibliography. 4. Divorce--Canada--Statistics--Bibliography. 5.
Divorce--Great Britain--Statistics--Bibliography. I. Sell, Betty H., joint author. II.
Title. III. Series. Z7164.M2S4 [HQ814]   016.30142'84   78-15894
ISBN 0-8103-1396-0

To our son Peter and daughter Rebecca
who hopefully have understood us
all of these years, with love

VITAE

Kenneth D. Sell is professor of sociology and chairman of the department at Catawba College, Salisbury, North Carolina. He received his Ph.D. in sociology from The Florida State University through its interdivisional program in marriage and the family, in 1968. He also has leadership training and experience in various marital enrichment programs, and is a member of the American Association of Marriage and Family Counselors. He has recently completed a bibliography on DIVORCE IN THE 1970S, and has published articles in the FAMILY COORDINATOR and RQ. He is a past president of the North Carolina Family Life Council, and an officer of the Southeastern Council on Family Relations.

Betty H. Sell is director of the library at Catawba College, Salisbury, North Carolina, since 1970, and previously served as a librarian at The Florida State University Library and at Livingstone College in North Carolina. She is a doctoral candidate in the School of Library Science at The Florida State University, where she received her M.S. and Advanced Masters degrees in library science. Mrs. Sell also earned an M.R.E. from the Lancaster Theological Seminary, Lancaster, Pennsylvania. She is a member of the Beta Phi Mu International Library Science Honor Society. She has held offices in professional library organizations in North Carolina, and with her husband, has leadership training and experience in various marital enrichment programs.

CONTENTS

Contents

Contents

Contents

PREFACE

This volume on divorce in the United States, Canada, and Great Britain, is the first of a series of information guides on current social problems and social issues. This interdisciplinary guide directs the general user, graduate or undergraduate student, scholar, educator, clinician, or researcher to retrospective, current, and continuing sources of information on divorce. Divorce is broadly defined in this guide to include the related topics of child custody, maintenance, one-parent families created by divorce, remarriage of divorced persons, separation, and annulment.

Information on divorce is elusive, being scattered throughout the literature of many disciplines, in a variety of formats. Because, at the same time, information on divorce is expanding rapidly in this decade, it is very difficult to maintain currency in the field, or indeed in any aspect of the field. This difficulty is compounded in that the acquisition of information retrieval techniques is not stressed sufficiently at the graduate and undergraduate levels. It is the hope and expectation of the authors that this guide may aid the individual in more effectively searching the literature for information on divorce.

An earnest attempt was made to systematically examine all of the potentially useful research and nonresearch sources of divorce information in whatever format. Hence, not only are book and periodical sources included in this guide but dissertations, other nontraditionally published materials, statistics, data bases, public opinion polls, films, and other nonprint media are also listed. Sources for locating divorce organizations as well as research centers and funds are also included. All major areas of knowledge relevant to divorce are represented, including the social and behavioral sciences, law, medicine, religion, philosophy, and literature. To facilitate locating in libraries the sources described in this guide, these are cited according to the verified Library of Congress entries.

The results of several special surveys and analyses conducted by the authors were included in this volume when no published source for a specific type of information was identified. These consisted of: a survey of the 150 largest current daily U.S. newspapers to determine which had published subject in-

Preface

dexes; a survey of state vital statistics bureaus to ascertain what state vital statistics reports are currently published and to receive examination copies to verify the type of divorce information contained in the reports; a search to prepare a checklist of dissertations on divorce; and a citation analysis to provide a listing of the most useful current scholarly periodicals.

The majority of the sources described in this volume were examined at the Robert Manning Strozier Library and the Law Library of The Florida State University, with additional sources examined at the Duke University libraries, the libraries of the University of North Carolina at Chapel Hill, the New York Public Library, and the Library of Congress.

The authors wish to express their gratitude to the following librarians on the Strozier Library staff for their cheerful and able assistance: Violet Cottingham, Alice Moore, Sharon Gleim, Mary Jo Kennedy, and Lois Burdick. Our thanks go to our neighbor, Patsy Stubbs, who typed the manuscript with dispatch and good humor. Our special appreciation is expressed to our daughter Becky, who, in the midst of her college program, kept the household functioning smoothly.

Kenneth D. Sell

Betty H. Sell

INTRODUCTION

Over the centuries, divorce has touched ever increasing numbers of couples, their children, and other family members. Through the years, there has been continuing debate and lack of consensus concerning the desirability or the undesirability of divorce, whether or not divorce is or is not detrimental to the institution of the family, and even whether divorce is or is not a problem. Nevertheless, divorce has been, and still is, generally considered a social problem. No adequate definition of a social problem exists, but one widely used definition states that a social problem is a condition that affects a significant number of people in ways deemed adverse by society about which something can be done through collective social action.

As a result, for more than a century, laws have been enacted to make divorce easier to obtain, or more difficult to obtain, depending upon the prevailing social views. Solutions to the problem have been proposed, none of which seem to deal justly with all parties involved. Since no equitable and painless resolution has been devised, the literature on divorce continues to grow.

Books and essays have been published on divorce for many centuries. In England, publications on divorce began to appear soon after the introduction of printing. THE CENSURE AND JUDGEMENT OF ERASMUS, WHYTHER DYUORCEMENT BETWENE MAN AND WYFE STONDETH WITH THE LAWE OF GOD, a translation of Erasmus's treatise, was printed in 1555. In the next century, John Milton was at least as well known for his divorce tracts as for his poetry.

The debate continued and spread. In 1788 in Philadelphia, an anonymous author wrote an exceptional treatise on divorce entitled AN ESSAY ON MARRIAGE OR THE LAWFULNESS OF DIVORCE IN CERTAIN CASES CONSIDERED, ADDRESSED TO THE FEELINGS OF MANKIND. In this essay the author argued for the primacy of individual rights as opposed to custom, tradition, and social stability, with respect to divorce. Apparently the author of these unorthodox views wanted to remain anonymous rather than risk the ostracism suffered by Milton in the previous century. In the same year, Benjamin Trumbull, a pastor in New Haven, Connecticut, published an essay that stressed

Introduction

the priority of family and social stability over individual rights and happiness. It is interesting to note in the literature that this type of dialogue continues to this day.

Through the centuries, continuing expression of concern and even alarm at the rapid increase in the number of divorces can also be noted. For example, Trumbull in his essay discussed with concern the divorce rate in Connecticut in 1788:

> No divorce was given by virtue of the law, till the year 1692. After this divorces were, for many years, very sparingly given. But as they became more customary, as there were no punishments for delinquents, and as the shame decreased with the growth of the practice, they have, within this few years, had a rapid increase. In less than a century 439 pair, 878 persons, have been separated by divorce . . . . About twenty times as many are now divorced annually, as were in almost sixty years after the first settlement of the state. . . . How unlike Connecticut is to her former self?[1]

Nearly two hundred years later, in 1975, the citizens of New Haven were still being warned about the alarming increases in the divorce rate in Connecticut:

> The number of divorces in the state last year totaled 10,748, representing an increase of more than one-third over the previous year. The chief court justice attributed the mounting number of divorces partially to the new no-fault law and a breakdown in all of the sub-cultures, "such as the community, the church, the family, all wars and all permissiveness."[2]

The growth of the literature on divorce appears to parallel the increasing divorce rates. For example, the authors have identified over three hundred English-language books on divorce published prior to the twentieth century. About the same number of books on divorce will be written in the decade of the 1970s!

Research on divorce, as on family relations in general, appeared to gain momentum about the turn of the twentieth century and thereafter increased rather slowly. The growth in the number of doctoral dissertations is probably indicative of the growth of divorce research. In the United States, the first reported dissertation on divorce was completed in 1891 at Columbia University. In the next eighty-five years, about one hundred additional dissertations were completed, with nearly one-half of these accepted since 1970. It is hoped that this guide will aid and expedite effective research and other study on divorce, thereby contributing to greater understanding and resolution of divorce as a social problem.

To use this information guide on divorce effectively, several of its characteristics and features should be kept in mind. The guide will not give the user a prepared list of all publications written on the subject of divorce to date, or even a list of selected publications. In this respect it is not a bibliography per se. It is however a guide which leads the user to identify for himself information on divorce published or "unpublished," in whatever format desired, according to his specific requirements. If comprehensiveness is required, by using and following the entire guide, this can be accomplished to a very high degree. If only a certain type of information on divorce is desired, or information on only a certain aspect of divorce, or information from a certain time span, or information in a certain format, the user can select, as indicated, certain of the suggested sources described in the guide and proceed to search these sources. In this way he can identify publications and other materials that, upon examination, will provide the information he desires. The user thus becomes skilled in independently searching the literature, in all of its variety, for himself, and thereby selecting items deemed significant for his own purposes. A few items and listings are cited and described in this guide, however, in cases where it would be very difficult, time consuming, or otherwise costly, for individual searchers to find and examine these items themselves. Likewise, information in certain areas for which no compilations previously existed has been brought together by the authors.

The sources of information described in this guide are for both retrospective and current information. The methodology is also provided whereby the user, by means of periodically checking suggested ongoing sources or by being able to find new sources as they appear, may in the future keep up with divorce information in his special area of interest. In this respect, a guide such as this is more valuable than an ordinary bibliography which cites publications only up to the date of the completion of the bibliography.

This information guide includes several other features of which the user should be aware. The relevant subject headings in current usage in the sources annotated are indicated after the annotations in order to facilitate searching of the source by the user. Also, subject headings used in card catalogs are indicated at certain points in the guide to aid the user in identifying publications and new information sources that are in library collections. The user should be aware that by examining the table of contents carefully, and by making extensive use of the three indexes at the back of the guide, particularly the subject index, the user can efficiently and effectively find information on a specific aspect, type, or format desired. It is also recommended that, whatever approach is decided upon by the user in searching for the exact information he needs, the search be carefully planned and systematic.

---

[1]Benjamin Trumbull, AN APPEAL TO THE PUBLIC ESPECIALLY TO THE LEARNED WITH RESPECT TO THE UNLAWFULNESS OF DIVORCES, IN ALL CASES EXCEPTING INCONTINENCY (New Haven, Conn.: J. Meigs, 1788), p. 46.

[2]REGISTER (New Haven, Conn.), 19 March 1975.

Chapter 1

SUBJECT BIBLIOGRAPHIES ON DIVORCE

To do intensive study or research on a subject, such as divorce, a large quantity of the literature on the subject needs to be gathered and examined. The researcher must aim for comprehensiveness in his search for specific information on the subject. An effective way to begin to amass pertinent citations or references to books, periodical articles, newspaper articles, reports, documents, or pamphlets on divorce is to locate reliable and appropriate bibliographies on divorce, on subjects closely related to divorce, or which include a significant amount of materials on divorce. This type of subject bibliography, in addition to being specific, is often selective, sometimes limiting the subject, such as divorce, to a particular geographic area or time period, to materials published only in the English language, or to a certain type of publication, such as books.

When using a subject bibliography on divorce, one should determine what parameters or limitations the compiler admittedly or inadvertently followed in compiling the bibliography. Also it is well to determine, if possible, the sources and the subject headings that the compiler searched or consulted in compiling the bibliography. In this way the user can identify what areas, types of materials, and time periods are not included in the bibliography. Often the bibliography may not be as up-to-date as the user requires. With this information one can then determine exactly what additional specific sources should be searched to meet the requirements of the study or research. These specific sources are described in the remaining chapters of this information guide.

Part A of this chapter describes well-known sources for locating subject bibliographies as described above. Parts B and C of this chapter describe the most significant current and retrospective bibliographies to date which are useful for divorce information.

A. LOCATING SUBJECT BIBLIOGRAPHIES ON DIVORCE

An important source for locating subject bibliographies is the library card catalog. Library holdings of bibliographies on divorce in book form can be found under subject headings such as the following:

Divorce--Bibliography
Divorce--Bibliography--Catalogs
Divorce--U.S.--Bibliography
Divorce--Canada--Bibliography
Divorce--Great Britain--Bibliography

Also, since most college, university, and research libraries in the United States use subject headings adopted by the Library of Congress, any of the subject headings listed in item 2-5 can be searched in these libraries, when they are followed by the word "bibliography"; for example, Desertion--Bibliography.

Other sources are the following:

1-1   Besterman, Theodore. A WORLD BIBLIOGRAPHY OF BIBLIOGRA-
PHIES AND BIBLIOGRAPHICAL CATALOGUES, CALENDARS, AB-
STRACTS, DIGESTS, INDEXES, AND THE LIKE. 4th ed., rev.
5 vols. Lausanne, Switzerland: Societas Bibliographica, 1965.

Although this work is broad in scope and attempts uni-
versal coverage, it has somewhat limited usefulness for a
subject as specific as divorce. The long time lag since
the date of publication is also a limitation for those
seeking current information. The bibliographies are arranged by subject in the first four volumes. Volume 5
is an author-title index. A new edition is forthcoming.

Consult: Alimony   Family
          Divorce   Marriage

1-2   BIBLIOGRAPHIC INDEX: A CUMULATIVE BIBLIOGRAPHY OF BIB-
LIOGRAPHIES, 1937-- . New York: H.W. Wilson Co., 1938-- .
Three issues per year cumulated annually, with triennial cumulative
volumes.

The best source of information on new bibliographies
each year, this work is a subject listings of books, periodical articles, and pamphlets that include bibliographies
of fifty or more citations, as well as a subject listing of
separately published bibliographies. Over twenty-two
hundred American and European periodical titles are examined regularly for such bibliographies.

Consult: Broken homes   Domestic-relations courts
          Children of divorced   Father-separated children
            parents   Husband and wife
          Divorce   Marriage
          Divorcées   Remarriage
          Domestic relations   Single-parent family

Persons interested in the study of divorce will be able to identify by means of the above sources a very high percentage of the significant bibliographies published. These will include bibliographies published as separate works or pamphlets, as well as those which are presented at the end of periodical articles and chapters in books. The researcher might be interested in searching, in addition, several U.S. government publications which, since 1976, are including more information on divorce. Citations and abstracts of a few bibliographies already have appeared in these. These sources are: the GOVERNMENT REPORTS ANNOUNCEMENTS AND INDEX (item 5-21), RESOURCES IN EDUCATION (item 5-22), and the MONTHLY CATALOG OF UNITED STATES GOVERNMENT PUBLICATIONS (item 6-183).

B. SIGNIFICANT CURRENT BIBLIOGRAPHIES ON DIVORCE OR RELATED TO DIVORCE

1-3   Aldous, Joan, and Dahl, Nancy S. INTERNATIONAL BIBLIOGRAPHY OF RESEARCH IN MARRIAGE AND THE FAMILY. Vol. 2, 1965-72. Minneapolis: University of Minnesota Press, in association with the Institute of Life Insurance, for the Minnesota Family Study Center, 1974. xviii, 1,530 p.

> In this basic bibliography, which attempts to list all of the empirical research in the family field published throughout the world, a total of 12,870 studies are indexed, most of which were published during the period 1965-72. There are 130 English-language references on divorce. No theses or legal articles are included. This bibliography is arranged by title in a keyword-in-context index, a subject index, and an author index. For the uninitiated, this work is difficult to use. The preceding volume, Aldous and Hill's INTERNATIONAL BIBLIOGRAPHY OF RESEARCH IN MARRIAGE AND THE FAMILY, volume 1 (item 1-10), covers the period 1900-1964. Volume 2 is succeeded by Olson and Dahl's INVENTORY OF MARRIAGE AND FAMILY LITERATURE, 1973-74 (item 1-7).

> Consult: Marriage and divorce--divorce--divorce and separation (052)

1-4   Israel, Stanley, comp. and ed. A BIBLIOGRAPHY ON DIVORCE. New York: Bloch Publishing Co., 1974. xiv, 300 p.

> This selective bibliography lists approximately 500 books on divorce. About 150 of these books, published from the early 1940s to the early 1970s, are annotated. Some of the annotations are good summaries and critiques of the books, some appear to be publishers' comments about the books, and others are the verbatim table of contents of each book. The annotated works are arranged under three broad categories: legal,

religious, and sociological aspects of divorce. Approximately 115 earlier books published in the United States are listed without comment. A third list contains about 175 foreign books without comment. Although the coverage and annotations are incomplete, this work does list a large number of books on divorce.

1-5   McKenney, Mary. DIVORCE: A SELECTED ANNOTATED BIBLIOGRAPHY. Metuchen, N.J.: Scarecrow Press, 1975. vi, 157 p.

Emphasizing divorce reform, this selective bibliography lists over six hundred books, articles, statistical sources, pamphlets, films, and other materials related to divorce published before 1973. The quality of the annotations varies and the author's political sentiments are reflected in the annotations. The items are listed alphabetically by author under the following topics: historical, legal, financial, psychological, sociological, religious, and moral aspects of divorce, statistics, divorcées, children of divorcées, adult and children's literature and films about divorce, and resource persons and organizations concerned about divorce. Although the emphasis of this work is mostly on U.S. materials, there is a highly selected list of foreign works on divorce. A subject and author index is included.

1-6   National Council on Family Relations. Task Force on Divorce and Divorce Reform. TASK FORCE REPORT: DIVORCE AND DIVORCE REFORM; OCTOBER 1973. Emily M. Brown, Chairperson. Minneapolis, Minn.: National Council on Family Relations, 1974. vii, 70 p.

The appendix of this report contains a thirty-page highly selective bibliography of books, articles, children's books, newspaper articles, and government reports on divorce for the period 1960-73.

1-7   Olson, David H.L., and Dahl, Nancy S. INVENTORY OF MARRIAGE AND FAMILY LITERATURE (1973-1974). St. Paul: Family Social Science, University of Minnesota, 1975. vii, 376 p. Annual.

A successor to the INTERNATIONAL BIBLIOGRAPHY OF RESEARCH IN MARRIAGE AND THE FAMILY (item 1-3), this work is somewhat broader in scope than its predecessor in that the articles indexed are not restricted to empirical or theoretical studies on the family. The scope is narrower in that only English-language articles are indexed. There are 60 references on divorce out of a total of 2,413 books and journal articles cited. The contents are arranged by title in a keyword-in-context index, by subject and by author. A list of the 484 periodical titles indexed is also included.

Consult: Divorce and separation (052)
Separation due to divorce in the family (097D)

1-8   Sell, Kenneth D., comp. DIVORCE IN THE 1970S; A SUBJECT GUIDE TO BOOKS, ARTICLES, DISSERTATIONS, GOVERNMENT DOCUMENTS, AND FILM ON DIVORCE IN THE UNITED STATES, 1970-76. Preliminary edition. Salisbury, N.C.: By the author, 1977. 22 p.

Over 560 items are cited in this subject bibliography which deal with the social, psychological, psychiatric, economic, legal, religious, historical, and literary aspects of divorce-related topics. An attempt was made to find all of the books, articles, dissertations, films, and project reports which have been published to date in the United States or are about divorce in the United States in the 1970s. Twenty-seven indexes, abstracts, and bibliographic sources (listed in the guide) were searched systematically from 1970 to the end of 1976. The popular and legal literature were not systematically searched. This work is being continued by supplements.

1-9   Vanier Institute of the Family. AN INVENTORY OF FAMILY RESEARCH AND STUDIES IN CANADA, 1963-67. Ottawa: 1967. xiv, 161 p.

This interdisciplinary listing of over two hundred family studies includes a few studies on divorce. There is no index to the work.

C. SIGNIFICANT RETROSPECTIVE BIBLIOGRAPHIES ON DIVORCE OR RELATED TO DIVORCE

The subject bibliographies described below are earlier works that are important for the study of divorce from a historical perspective.

1-10   Aldous, Joan, and Hill, Reuben. INTERNATIONAL BIBLIOGRAPHY OF RESEARCH IN MARRIAGE AND THE FAMILY. Vol. 1, 1900-1964. Minneapolis: University of Minnesota Press, for the Minnesota Family Study Center and the Institute of Life Insurance, 1967. 508 p.

A total of 12,850 research studies on the family are listed in this comprehensive and basic bibliography which attempts to list all of the empirical research conducted throughout the world in the family field, published in the twentieth century. Of these studies cited, 225 pertain to divorce. No theses or legal works are included. The contents are arranged by title in a keyword-in-context index, and also by a subject index and an author index.

Consult: Marriage and divorce--divorce and separation--desertion

1-11   McDonald, Michael, of Toronto. "Bibliography on the Family from the Fields of Theology and Philosophy." Ottawa: Vanier Institute of the Family, 1964. vi, 95 p. Mimeographed.

Of limited value for the study of divorce, this work annotates books and articles on religious and philosophical themes relevant to the family. There are no indexes.

Consult: Official documents relating to marriage
Theological views of divorce

1-12   New York (City) Public Library. "List of Works in the New York Public Library Relating to Marriage and Divorce." BULLETIN 8 (November 1905): 466-513.

This worldwide bibliography of books and articles contains approximately fifteen hundred citations of which about 150 pertain to divorce in the United States, Canada, and Great Britain. Included are references to nineteenth-century state vital statistics in the United States, as well as 250 references to the nineteenth-century BRITISH PARLIAMENTARY PAPERS at the time when England was in the process of enacting its first divorce law. This bibliography was also issued as a separate work with the same title.

1-13   U.S. Library of Congress. Division of Bibliography. "List of References on Marriage and Divorce, with Special Reference to Uniform Divorce Legislation." W.A. Slade, bibliographer. Washington, D.C.: 1926. 9 p. Typewritten.

Containing mostly articles and documents printed in the United States from the preceding two decades, this unannotated list of 108 references overlaps somewhat the 1925 "List of References on Uniform Divorce Laws" (item 1-14). Photocopies of this document are available from the Library of Congress.

1-14   _____. "A List of References on Uniform Divorce Laws." Washington, D.C.: 1925. 7 p. Typewritten.

This unannotated list of eighty-two U.S. articles, pamphlets, and documents from 1884 to 1925 focuses on the

debate over uniform divorce legislation. Photocopies of
this list are available from the Library of Congress.

1-15 _____. LIST OF REFERENCES SUBMITTED TO THE COMMITTEE
ON THE JUDICIARY, U.S. SENATE, 63RD CONGRESS, 3RD SES-
SION, 1915, IN CONNECTION WITH S.J. RES. 109, RESOLU-
TION PROPOSING AN AMENDMENT TO THE CONSTITUTION OF
THE UNITED STATES RELATING TO DIVORCES. Hermann H.B.
Meyer, comp. Washington, D.C.: 1915. 110 p. Y4.J89/2:D64.

Emphasizing the U.S. and British Commonwealth writings
on divorce in the nineteenth and early twentieth centuries, this bibliography contains 957 unannotated references to books and articles from around the world.
Special sections on uniform divorce laws, the church and
divorce, Jews and divorce, and divorce fiction, are accompanied by a good subject index and an author index.

1-16 _____. "Marriage and Divorce, with Special Reference to Legal
Aspects: A Selected Bibliography." Helen F. Conover, comp.
Washington, D.C.: 1940. 55 p. Mimeographed. LC 2.2:M34/
940.

Of these 574 books, articles, and pamphlets on marriage
and divorce published in the 1930s and held by the Library of Congress, approximately 135 of the references
are general, 172 refer to the national and state legal
systems in the United States, and 234 refer to foreign
works. Also included is a short section on canon,
Jewish, and Mohammedan law concerning divorce.

1-17 _____ "References on Divorce, 1915-1930." D.G. Patterson,
bibliographer. Washington, D.C.: 1930. 17 p. Mimeographed.

A total of 322 foreign- and English-language books and
articles on divorce are included in this unannotated bibliography. The list does not cite legal articles or government documents. Photocopies of this work are available
from the Library of Congress.

1-18 _____. "A Selected List of References on Alimony." Florence S.
Hellman, bibliographer. Washington, D.C.: 1935. 12 p. Mimeographed.

References to 131 periodical articles dealing with the
legal and general aspects of alimony in the United States,
Canada, and Great Britain in the twentieth century are
included in this unannotated selective bibliography. Also
included are a few books, nineteenth-century periodical
articles, and a few foreign periodical articles. Photocopies of this list are available from the Library of Congress.

7

Chapter 2

LOCATING BOOKS ON DIVORCE IN GENERAL
BIBLIOGRAPHIC SOURCES

In addition to the specific subject bibliographies on divorce described in chapter 1, books on divorce may be identified through more general bibliographic sources. These general sources, described in this chapter, are usually arranged by subject, have subject indexes, or are subject indexes. Subject headings useful for locating books on divorce in each source are listed, where possible, after the description of that source.

Books on divorce which can be located through these general sources may be on all aspects of divorce, including historical, legal, religious, psychological, and sociological aspects. They may range from research studies to personal narratives and self-help manuals.

The card catalogs of local libraries as well as the printed catalogs of large libraries such as the Library of Congress and the British Library, now including the library of the British Museum, are excellent general bibliographic sources for identifying books on divorce. These are described in part A of this chapter. Some of these printed library catalogs are considered national bibliographies in that they contain complete bibliographic entries for the books copyrighted and/ or cataloged in that country. They are very accurate and authoritative.

Trade bibliographies, described in part B of this chapter, are lists of books in print which have been compiled from publishers' listings and brochures. For this reason, these works are often not as accurate as the national bibliographies. These trade bibliographies are mainly concerned with "trade" books, that is, books that are of general interest to the reading public. Some smaller publishers in more specialized fields, as well as some university presses and association publishers, may not be included in these works. However, trade bibliographies are very useful for quick information on current publications.

The retrospective book sources, described in part C of this chapter, are listings of earlier works and vary in accuracy. Since these sources often lack any kind of subject approach, much patience is required to scan the items listed in them in order to find even a limited amount of material on divorce. For historical research on divorce, however, this material may be very important.

Sources for finding reviews of books on divorce are described in part D. Some of these sources, those with subject indexes, can also be used to locate additional books on divorce.

The problem of finding the relevant chapters on divorce in books that are not specifically about divorce is treated in part E.

A. SUBJECT INDEXES TO LIBRARY CATALOGS AND NATIONAL BIBLIOGRAPHIES

An important source for locating books on divorce are library card catalogs, especially those of the larger university and research libraries. In this way the researcher has the advantage of examining the books on location without going through the process of interlibrary borrowing. Since most college, university, and research libraries in the United States use subject headings adopted by the Library of Congress, any of the subject headings listed in item 2-5 are appropriate to use when searching for books on divorce in these library catalogs, keeping in mind that these headings may change over time and new ones may be added. Printed library catalogs in book form and national bibliographies are also good sources. The most significant of these are described below.

2-1   British Museum. Department of Printed Books. SUBJECT INDEX
           OF MODERN BOOKS ACQUIRED. London: Trustees of the British
           Museum, 1902-- .

           This index is an alphabetical subject listing of the books
           added since 1881 to the collection of the British Museum,
           now part of the British Library. This collection is world-
           wide in scope. The first cumulation covers the period
           1881-1900.

           Subsequent cumulations have been issued every five years.
           Although the subject index is not highly developed, it
           has the longest run of any existing subject index. At
           present, there is a fifteen-year time lag. The earlier
           title of this work was SUBJECT INDEX OF THE MODERN
           WORKS ADDED TO THE LIBRARY OF THE BRITISH MU-
           SEUM, FROM 1881 TO 1900. For a subject approach to
           works on divorce, with a British emphasis, before 1881,
           the selective indexes by R.A. Peddie (item 2-35) are
           somewhat useful.

           Consult: Marriage--divorce--Canada
                     Marriage--divorce--Great Britain
                     Marriage--divorce--United States

2-2   THE BRITISH NATIONAL BIBLIOGRAPHY. London: British Library
           Bibliographic Services Division, 1950-- . Weekly, with quarterly,

annual, and quinquennial cumulations.

A basic reference source for British copyrighted materials, this work essentially lists and describes bibliographically every new book published in Great Britain. It also includes an author index, a title index, and, at the end of each month, a subject index.

Consult: Desertions   Motherless families
          Divorce   Remarriage
          Fatherless families   Separation, married persons
          Marriage   Single-parent families

2-3 CANADIANA: PUBLICATIONS OF INTEREST RECEIVED BY THE NATIONAL LIBRARY, 1950-- . Ottawa: National Library, 1951-- . Monthly, with annual cumulations.

A basic source for Canadian materials on divorce, this bibliography lists all of the materials cataloged at the National Library of Canada, which serves as a depository for Canadian books and other materials. The work is divided into eight sections: (1) monographs and microfilms, (2) theses in microform, (3) serials, (4) pamphlets, (5) sound recordings, (6) films and filmstrips, (7) publications of the government of Canada, and (8) publications of the provincial governments. There is a subject index in English, a subject index in French, and a general index in English only. Because this set is difficult to use, CANADIAN REFERENCE SOURCES: A SELECTIVE GUIDE (item 3-23) and its SUPPLEMENT should be consulted. CANADIANA was preceded by the CANADIAN CATALOGUE OF BOOKS PUBLISHED IN CANADA, ABOUT CANADA, AS WELL AS THOSE WRITTEN ABOUT CANADIANS, 1921-1949, published by Toronto Public Libraries, 1959. There were two decennial cumulations of this earlier work.

Consult: Divorce

2-4 LONDON BIBLIOGRAPHY OF THE SOCIAL SCIENCES. London: London School of Economics, 1931-- . 32 vols. include supplements, to date. Irregular.

This important and extensive bibliography in the social sciences represents the holdings of a number of libraries in London. The first four volumes alone contain references to 600,000 items. The entire work to date contains references to a considerable number of historical materials on divorce, especially in the British Commonwealth, although the work is international in scope. Books, pamphlets, and documents are cited. This work is of above average usefulness for locating materials on divorce.

Consult: Desertion and non- Marriage
        support Marriage Law
      Divorce Marriage--annulment
      Domicile Husband and wife

2-5   U.S. Library of Congress. LIBRARY OF CONGRESS CATALOGS--
SUBJECT CATALOG. Washington, D.C.: 1950-- . Quarterly,
with annual and quinquennial cumulations.

A subject guide to all of the books cataloged by the
Library of Congress since 1950, with imprints since 1945,
this basic index is worldwide in scope. It lists government documents and serials, in addition to books. Each
citation is bibliographically complete, accurate, and
authoritative. The subject headings are quite detailed
and follow the Library of Congress's SUBJECT HEADINGS
USED IN THE DICTIONARY CATALOGS OF THE LIBRARY
OF CONGRESS. There is a time lag of several months
to more than a year before a new book appears in this
index. Prior to 1975, this work was entitled LIBRARY
OF CONGRESS CATALOG. BOOKS: SUBJECTS. A
CUMULATIVE LIST OF WORKS REPRESENTED BY LIBRARY
OF CONGRESS PRINTED CARDS. The following
subject headings are used in this subject listing. Any
book may appear under more than one heading. It should
be noted that these headings are subject to change and
that new headings may be added from time to time.

Consult: Alimony   Divorcées
      Broken homes   Domestic relations
      Children of divorced Domestic-relations courts
        parents   Father-separated children
      Conflict of laws--   Guardian and ward
        divorce   Legal cruelty
      Custody of children   Marriage
      Desertion and non-   Marriage--annulment
        support   Marriage--law
      Divorce--(by state   Parent and child (law)
        or country)   Paternal deprivation
      Divorce--Biblical   Remarriage
        teachings   Separate maintenance
      Divorce--juvenile   Separate property
        literature   Separation (law)
      Divorce--law   Settlements (law)
      Divorce--personal   Single-parent families
        narratives   Stepchildren
      Divorce (canon law) Stepmother
      Divorce in literature Support--domestic rela-
      Divorce suits   tions
      Divorced fathers   Trials (divorce)

B. GENERAL TRADE BIBLIOGRAPHIES

2-6   AMERICAN BOOK PUBLISHING RECORD. New York: R.R. Bowker
        Co., 1960-- . Monthly, with annual and quinquennial cumulations.

> Often referred to as the BPR, this publication is a record
> of the books published each month in the United States.
> Generally excluded are government publications, serial
> publications including periodicals, and dissertations. This
> monthly record is compiled from the WEEKLY RECORD
> (item 2-16), an author listing published by the R.R. Bow-
> ker Company. The BPR is arranged by Dewey Decimal
> Classification numbers, as cataloged by the Library of
> Congress, with author and title indexes. The BPR AN-
> NUAL CUMULATIVE started in 1965. Several quinquen-
> nial cumulations have appeared. Since the listings are
> arranged by the Dewey Decimal numbers under the cor-
> responding subject headings, one must know the Dewey
> number in order to find books in a subject area. This
> makes the subject approach somewhat difficult. It also
> has the added disadvantage of listing each bibliographic
> entry only once, under one specific subject heading and
> one Dewey Decimal number, when there are additional
> secondary subject headings under which it could be
> listed as well. The limitations of this arrangement should
> be taken into consideration. If one is not able to ascer-
> tain the appropriate Dewey Decimal Classification number
> for the subject of his search, many books may be missed
> when searching.

> Consult: Divorce (301.428)   Remarriage (301.427)
>   Divorcées (301.4284)   Single-parent family
>   (301.427)

2-7   BRITISH BOOKS IN PRINT: THE REFERENCE CATALOGUE OF CUR-
        RENT LITERATURE. London: J. Whitaker and Sons, 1874-- . An-
        nual.

> Information on over 260,000 books currently marketed in
> any given year in England is included in this listing of
> books. The books are arranged by subject, author, and
> title. Publication data included are the price, place,
> and date of publication. This trade publication has a
> long history, dating back to the REFERENCE CATALOGUE
> OF CURRENT LITERATURE, founded by Joseph Whitaker
> in 1874.

> Consult: Divorce
>   Marriage

2-8   CUMULATIVE BOOK INDEX: A WORLD LIST OF BOOKS IN THE
ENGLISH LANGUAGE. New York: H.W. Wilson Co., 1898-- .
Monthly (except August), cumulated quarterly, annually since 1969,
and at least biennially since 1957.

> As the title indicates, this very useful publication at-
> tempts to list all of the U.S., British, Canadian, and
> other English-language books published throughout the
> world. Before 1928 it was mainly a list of books pub-
> lished in the United States. The contents are alphabet-
> ized by subject, author, and title in one list. Gov-
> ernment documents, pamphlets, and inexpensive paper-
> bound books are generally not included. Since this is
> a monthly index, it gives rapid access to new books in
> many fields and it is easy to use. Although the bibli-
> ographic information provided may not be as complete as,
> or concur with, that of the Library of Congress catalogs,
> inaccuracies are very few. The CBI was issued for 1899-
> 1928 under the title of UNITED STATES CATALOG:
> BOOKS IN PRINT.

Consult:	Alimony	Domicile
	Children of divorced	Marriage
	parents	Marriage--annulment
	Conflict of laws	Marriage--annulment
	Custody of children	(canon law)
	Desertion	Marriage--law
	Divorce	Parent and child (law)
	Divorce--	Remarriage
	bibliography	Separate maintenance
	Divorce--fiction	Separation (law)
	Divorce--laws	Single-parent family
	Divorce (canon law)	Stepchildren
	Divorce in literature	Stepparents
	Divorced men	Support (domestic
	Divorcées	relations)
	Domestic relations	

2-9   Jacobstein, J. Myron, and Pimsleur, Meira G., eds. LAW BOOKS
IN PRINT; BOOKS IN ENGLISH PUBLISHED THROUGHOUT THE
WORLD AND IN PRINT THROUGH 1974. 4 vols. Dobbs Ferry,
N.Y.: Glanville Publishers, 1976.

> Refer to item 8-133.

2-10   PAPERBACKS IN PRINT. London: J. Whitaker and Sons, 1960-- .
Annual.

> Over forty-three thousand paperbacks for sale in Great
> Britain are listed by author, title, and some fifty-two
> subject headings in this guide. The subject index ap-

pears to be a keyword-in-title index.

Consult: Divorce
Separation

2-11   PAPERBOUND BOOKS IN PRINT. New York: R.R. Bowker Co.,
1955-- . Annual, with supplements in May and September.

Over 130,000 titles of paperbound books currently sold
by American publishers are listed each year by subject,
title, and author in this publication. The subject index
is difficult to use because the headings are very broad
and general. The main use for this work appears to be
for personal purchase of inexpensive books.

Consult: Home economics--family relations
Sociology--marriage and family

2-12   Pimsleur, Meira G., comp. and ed. LAW BOOKS PUBLISHED.
Dobbs Ferry, N.Y.: Glanville Publishers, 1969-- . Quarterly
with annual cumulations.

Refer to item 8-134.

2-13   PUBLISHERS' TRADE LIST ANNUAL. SUBJECT GUIDE TO BOOKS
IN PRINT; AN INDEX TO THE PUBLISHERS' TRADE LIST ANNUAL.
2 vols. New York: R.R. Bowker Co., 1957-- . Annual, with
a mid-year supplement.

Over 367,000 book titles from U.S. publishers are listed
under 62,000 subject headings, including subdivided
headings, that generally conform to the Library of Congress subject headings. Legal books, fiction, drama,
juvenile fiction, and government documents are usually
not included. This is a good source of information for
new U.S. books on divorce, and is easy to use. The
price, date of publication, and the publisher are given
for most titles. Since this guide at times contains in-
accurate bibliographic information, the CUMULATIVE
BOOK INDEX (item 2-8) and preferably the NATIONAL
UNION CATALOG compiled by the Library of Congress,
should be consulted for accuracy.

Consult: Alimony   Marriage (annulment)
Desertion and non-   Parent and child (law)
  support   Remarriage
Divorce   Separation (law)
Divorce--juvenile   Single-parent families
  literature   Stepchildren
Divorcées   Support (domestic
Domestic relations   relations)

2-14   SUBJECT GUIDE TO CANADIAN BOOKS IN PRINT. Toronto:
        University of Toronto Press, 1973-- . Annual.

        Essentially all of the books in print in Canada are listed
        annually by subject in this work. Most of the books are
        in the English language. A list of subject headings and
        cross-references is included.

        Consult: Family law
                  Marriage

2-15   SUBJECT GUIDE TO FORTHCOMING BOOKS; A BIMONTHLY
        SUBJECT FORECAST OF BOOKS TO COME. New York: R.R.
        Bowker Co., 1967-- . Bimonthly, each issue revising and updating
        the previous issue.

        A companion to FORTHCOMING BOOKS by the same
        publisher, this work announces books that are scheduled
        to be published in the United States within the next five
        months. The expected title, author, month of publica-
        tion (if set), the price, and the publisher are given for
        each book. Entries are arranged by title under subject
        headings, which were revised in 1976. A title may ap-
        pear under several headings. Care should be exercised
        in using this work because listed titles may be changed
        upon publication and some books may never be published.
        It is a useful work however in that it alerts the reader
        to new books forthcoming in his area of interest.

        Consult: Alimony   Remarriage
                  Divorce   Single-parent family
                  Divorcées

2-16   WEEKLY RECORD. New York: R.R. Bowker Co., 1974-- .
        Weekly.

        With a time lag of only one week, this work is the
        only weekly general listing of books published in the
        United States. New books and pamphlets of at least
        fifty pages are arranged in this publication alphabeti-
        cally by author, with no subject index. The list, how-
        ever, can be used in conjunction with the SUBJECT
        GUIDE TO FORTHCOMING BOOKS (item 2-15). It
        also is the basis upon which the monthly and annual
        AMERICAN BOOK PUBLISHING RECORD (item 2-6) is
        formed. Prior to September of 1974 this listing appeared
        for many years as part of the PUBLISHERS' WEEKLY, a
        journal by the same publisher.

C. GENERAL BIBLIOGRAPHIES AND CHECKLISTS OF EARLY WORKS

Books on divorce written prior to 1875 are difficult to locate. No comprehensive bibliography for the period has been found by the authors. Some of the special bibliographies on divorce described in part C of chapter 1 do include works on divorce prior to 1875, but these bibliographies were compiled for specific purposes other than that of general comprehensiveness. However, these should be scanned for early works.

The general retrospective bibliographies and checklists of early works described below are those that are considered most useful to the researcher compiling a bibliography of books on divorce for a given period. Most of these, however, are difficult to use because they lack subject indexes. Fortunately many of the early books on divorce cited in these bibliographies are available in several types of microform. The general bibliographies which follow are arranged by country and then listed chronologically by period.

1. United States

1639-1800

2-17   Evans, Charles, comp. AMERICAN BIBLIOGRAPHY. 1903-34. Reprint. 12 vols. New York: Peter Smith, 1941-42.

> Over thirty-nine thousand early American imprints from 1639 to 1800, including books, pamphlets, and periodicals, are arranged in chronological order in this basic work. Each volume contains an author list and a very general, as well as inadequate, subject list. This bibliography of Americana is incomplete (refer to item 2-18). It also contains some books that were never published. About thirty thousand of the works included in this bibliography are available on microcards in the collections of many large university libraries, grouped under the title of "Early American Imprints 1639-1800. First Series (Evans)." The inadequate subject index in this work makes it difficult to estimate the number of works published on divorce in the United States during this period.
>
> Consult: Marriage

2-18   Bristol, Roger P., comp. SUPPLEMENT TO CHARLES EVANS' AMERICAN BIBLIOGRAPHY. Charlottesville: University of Virginia Press, 1970. xix, 636 p.

> This supplement to Evans's bibliography (item 2-17) contains an additional 11,000 imprints for the years 1646-1800. The author attempted to locate all of the works missed by Evans. The books are arranged in chronologi-

cal order. There is a separate author and title index,
but no subject index, thereby requiring much persever-
ance in searching for books on divorce. Over ten thousand of these additional works are also available in many
large university libraries on microcards, grouped under the
heading of "Early American Imprints 1639-1800. First
Series (Evans)."

1801-19

2-19   Shaw, Ralph R., and Shoemaker, Richard H., comps. AMERICAN
        BIBLIOGRAPHY: A PRELIMINARY CHECKLIST. 19 vols. New
York: Scarecrow Press, 1958-63.

> This checklist, which lists books from American presses
> for the first two decades of the nineteenth century, con-
> tains over fifty thousand titles. Each volume lists the
> books produced for a single year. The works are listed
> by author, with separate cumulated author and title in-
> dexes, but no subject index. This makes searching for
> books on divorce very difficult. The accuracy of the
> work may be somewhat questionable in that only second-
> ary sources were used in compiling this checklist. The
> majority of these titles are now available on microcards
> in many large university libraries under the heading
> "Early American Imprints 1801-1819. Second Series
> (Shaw-Shoemaker)."

1820-30

2-20   Shoemaker, Richard H., comp. A CHECKLIST OF AMERICAN IM-
        PRINTS, FOR 1820-1829. 11 vols. New York: Scarecrow Press,
1964-73.

> Over forty-seven thousand titles are contained in this
> continuation of the AMERICAN BIBLIOGRAPHY (item
> 2-17) for the years 1820-30. The titles are listed
> chronologically by author. As with the preceding vol-
> umes, this set does not contain a subject index, which
> makes it very difficult to use. There are separate cumu-
> lative author and title indexes. Locations for the works
> are indicated. This checklist was also compiled from
> secondary sources; that is, the original works were not
> examined, which may result in occasional inaccuracies.
> Refer to item 2-21.

2-21   Cooper, Gayle. A CHECKLIST OF AMERICAN IMPRINTS FOR
        1830. Metuchen, N.J.: Scarecrow Press, 1972. 493 p.

> This volume completed Shoemaker's project (item 2-20)
> which was incomplete at the time of his death.

1831--

2-22   Bruntjen, Scott, and Bruntjen, Carol. A CHECKLIST OF AMERICAN
        IMPRINTS, 1831-- . Metuchen, N.J.: Scarecrow Press, 1975-- .

        About five thousand books printed in 1831 are listed in
        the 1975 volume by author and title, using secondary
        sources. No indexes are included. The authors plan
        to continue this series.

1820-61

2-23   Roorbach, Orville A., comp. BIBLIOTHECA AMERICANA: CATA-
        LOGUE OF AMERICAN PUBLICATIONS, INCLUDING REPRINTS
        AND ORIGINAL WORKS, FROM 1820 TO JANUARY 1861. 1849-
        61. Reprint. 4 vols. New York: Peter Smith.

        Although Roorbach's record of American book production
        from 1820 to 1861 is very incomplete, it is the only work
        covering most of the period. Books are listed by author.
        The lack of a subject index makes searching for books on
        divorce very difficult.

1861-71

2-24   Kelly, James, comp. THE AMERICAN CATALOGUE OF BOOKS
        PUBLISHED IN THE UNITED STATES FROM JAN. 1861 TO JAN.
        1871. 1866-77. Reprint. 2 quinquennial vols. New York: Peter
        Smith.

        Kelly's work, like its predecessor by Roorbach (item 2-23),
        is also incomplete. Especially lacking are books pub-
        lished in the South during the Civil War. Books are
        listed by author only, which makes searches for books on
        divorce in this source very tedious.

1876-1910

2-25   THE AMERICAN CATALOGUE, 1876-1910. 1880-1911. Reprint.
        8 vols. New York: Peter Smith.

        This valuable work attempts to list all of the books that
        were printed in the United States from 1 July 1876 to
        31 December 1910. The listings are by author and title;
        after 1900, subject listings are included. Prior to 1900
        the subject index was published as a separate work (item
        2-26).

        Consult: Divorce   Marriage
                   Husband and wife

2-26   THE AMERICAN CATALOGUE: SUBJECTS. 1880-1900. Reprint.

5 vols. New York: Peter Smith.

This work represents the only adequate subject index to American books in the nineteenth century. By the turn of the century the CUMULATIVE BOOK INDEX (item 2-8) took over this task and is much superior.

Consult: Divorce   Marriage
         Husband and wife

2. Canada

The following general bibliographic works, listing books published in Canada, are without adequate indexing. Thus they are of little use in locating books on divorce unless one is willing to tediously examine them item by item.

1534-1867

2-27   Toronto. Public Library. A BIBLIOGRAPHY OF CANADIANA: BEING ITEMS IN THE PUBLIC LIBRARY OF TORONTO, CANADA, RELATING TO THE EARLY HISTORY AND DEVELOPMENT OF CANADA. Edited by Frances M. Staton, and Marie Tremaine. Toronto: 1934. 828 p.

This author catalog of 4,646 annotated references from the Toronto Public Libraries has no general subject index. A supplement contains 1,640 additional references.

1751-1800

2-28   Tremaine, Marie. A BIBLIOGRAPHY OF CANADIAN IMPRINTS, 1751-1800. Toronto: University of Toronto Press, 1952. xxvii, 705 p.

This list of 1,204 early imprints is arranged in chronological order with good bibliographic descriptions of each work. It appears to contain very few items on divorce. Entries are made by author, title, and subject. Books, newspapers, and magazines are described.

1791-1897

2-29   Haight, Willet R. CANADIAN CATALOGUE OF BOOKS. 1791-1897. 1896-1904. Reprint. 3 vols. Vancouver: Devlin; London: H. Pordes, 1958.

As an incomplete listing of Canadian books from the nineteenth century, arranged alphabetically by author with no subject index, this work is probably of very little value for locating books on divorce.

2-30   Tod, Dorothea, and Cordingley, Audrey. A CHECKLIST OF CANA-
        DIAN IMPRINTS, 1900-25. Ottawa: Canadian Bibliographic Centre,
        Public Archives of Canada, 1950. 370 p.

> This work lists books and pamphlets of more than fifty
> pages. No government documents are included. Entries
> are by author, with no title or subject indexes.

3. Great Britain

2-31   British Museum. Department of Printed Books. CATALOGUE OF
        BOOKS IN THE LIBRARY OF THE BRITISH MUSEUM PRINTED IN
        ENGLAND, SCOTLAND, AND IRELAND, AND OF BOOKS IN
        ENGLISH PRINTED ABROAD TO THE YEAR 1640. 3 vols. London:
        Trustees of the British Museum, 1884.

> Arranged alphabetically by author, this work has a sub-
> ject index. Title and form (plays, poems, etc.) indexes
> are also included. A few books on divorce are included.

> Consult: Divorce
>   Marriage

2-32   Pollard, Alfred W., and Redgrave, G.R., comps. A SHORT-TITLE
        CATALOGUE OF BOOKS PRINTED IN ENGLAND, SCOTLAND
        AND IRELAND, AND OF ENGLISH BOOKS PRINTED ABROAD,
        1475-1640. London: Bibliographical Society, 1926. xvi, 609 p.

> Approximately 26,500 titles are arranged in this work by
> author with no subject index. This listing represents
> most of the known books for the period. Locations in
> 133 British libraries and 15 American libraries are noted.
> Many of these titles, however, are available in micro-
> form in many large university libraries, grouped into a
> series entitled "Early English Books, 1475-1640."

2-33   Watt, Robert. BIBLIOTHECA BRITANNICA, OR A GENERAL INDEX
        TO BRITISH AND FOREIGN LITERATURE. 4 vols. Edinburgh:
        Printed for Archibald Constable and Co., 1824.

> This subject index cites over thirty works on divorce
> published in English between 1527 and 1812. Additional
> works in Latin are also cited.

> Consult: Divorce

2-34   Wing, Donald G. SHORT-TITLE CATALOGUE OF BOOKS PRINTED
        IN ENGLAND, SCOTLAND, IRELAND, WALES, AND BRITISH
        AMERICA, AND OF ENGLISH BOOKS PRINTED IN OTHER COUN-
        TRIES, 1641-1700. 3 vols. New York: Published for the Index
        Society by the Columbia University Press, 1945-51.

> Some fifty thousand titles are listed in this standard work,
> which was published as a continuation of Pollard and
> Redgrave's SHORT-TITLE CATALOGUE (item 2-32). No
> subject index is included. These titles are gradually
> being microfilmed and included in the series "Early Eng-
> lish Books, 1641-1700," available at many large univer-
> sities. A revised and enlarged edition of Wing's SHORT-
> TITLE CATALOGUE is in preparation by the Modern Lan-
> guage Association of America.

Before 1880

2-35   Peddie, Robert Alexander. SUBJECT INDEX OF BOOKS PUBLISHED
        BEFORE 1880. 4 vols. London: Grafton, 1933-48.

> A valuable reference that provides a subject approach to
> nearly 200,000 books in the British Museum and elsewhere,
> this work is an important source for locating, by subject,
> books published prior to the publication of the British Muse-
> um's SUBJECT INDEX OF MODERN BOOKS ACQUIRED
> (item 2-1). Under each subject heading, the titles are
> listed in chronological order from the late 1400s to 1880.

> Consult: Divorce
>   Marriage

D. LOCATING REVIEWS OF BOOKS ON DIVORCE

Book reviews are useful sources of critical opinion on books, usually appearing
within a year or two of a book's publication. In addition to providing favor-
able or unfavorable contemporary impressions about a book, reviews often summarize the contents of the book.

The main reference sources for finding reviews of books on divorce in the
United States, Canada, and Great Britain are described below. These review
sources, when subject indexes are included, may also serve as finding aids for
books on divorce.

2-36   BOOK REVIEW DIGEST. New York: H.W. Wilson Co., 1905--
        Monthly (except February and July). Annual cumulations, with five-
        year cumulative indexes.

> Selected reviews from approximately seventy-five Ameri-
> can and British general periodicals are indexed by this

ongoing work. In addition to citing reviews of a book in the various periodicals, excerpts from several of the reviews are included. The reviews are selected for inclusion according to the publisher's stated criteria, noted in the preface: "To qualify for inclusion a book must have been published or distributed in the United States. A work of non-fiction must have received two or more reviews and one of fiction four or more reviews in the journals selected." Generally, this statement on number of reviews applies to a time period of within eighteen months of publication of the book. This may eliminate some scholarly books because of the time lag in reviewing in the major professional journals. The books reviewed are arranged by author, with title and subject indexes. This latter is very important when this work is used to identify books on divorce. The citations of the reviews in the BOOK REVIEW DIGEST are cumulated in the NATIONAL LIBRARY SERVICE CUMULATED BOOK REVIEW INDEX (item 2-39), the use of which results in a great reduction in searching time.

When using the subject index, consult:
Child welfare   Fiction--divorce
Divorce   Vital statistics
Divorce--personal
narratives

2-37   BOOK REVIEW INDEX. Detroit: Gale Research Co., 1965-- .
Bimonthly, with annual cumulations.

About 35,000 reviews from 225 popular and scholarly American periodicals are cited annually by this work, making it a more comprehensive source for locating reviews than is the BOOK REVIEW DIGEST (item 2-36). The citations are arranged by the authors of the books. This index is particularly useful for the researcher who is looking for reviews of a specific book on divorce. Since reviews for any particular book may appear over a period of several years, several volumes of this work may have to be consulted to locate all of the reviews indexed by this work. Excerpts from the reviews are not included in this work, only the abbreviated citations to the reviews printed in the various periodicals. There is a time lag of generally less than six months from the time that the review is published until it is indexed.

2-38   CURRENT BOOK REVIEW CITATIONS. New York: H.W. Wilson
Co., 1976-- . Monthly, except August.

This excellent book review index has broad coverage, indexing reviews from over twelve hundred American and foreign periodicals for fiction, nonfiction, and children's books. The reviews are simply cited, with no excerpts, and are indexed by author and title.

2-39   National Library Service Corporation. NATIONAL LIBRARY SERVICE CUMULATED BOOK REVIEW INDEX, 1905-1974. 6 vols. Princeton, N.J.: 1975.

This work is a cumulative index to all of the reviews cited in the BOOK REVIEW DIGEST (item 2-36) for the seventy-year period. There is one listing for authors and one for titles, with no subject listing.

In addition to the above sources for locating reviews of books on divorce, several of the periodical indexes and abstract journals noted in parts A and B of chapter 4 may be consulted. For a review of a book on divorce which has been published too recently for any review of it to be indexed and cited in the above sources, the reader is advised to consult recent issues of the periodicals listed in part D of chapter 4.

E. LOCATING CHAPTERS ON DIVORCE IN COMPOSITE BOOKS

The previous parts of this chapter deal with the identification of whole books on divorce or closely related to divorce. As can be seen, there is little difficulty in identifying these if one systematically searches for them as described in this chapter. However, when it comes to identifying significant chapters in books, particularly in composite books, there is very little bibliographic aid available. As a result much relevant information is often lost.

Composite books are of several types. There are those in which the author of the book deals in each chapter with a fairly distinctive topic, one of which may be some aspect of divorce. Such a chapter on divorce may have information and insight not found elsewhere. But since it is only one chapter in a book covering a fairly broad range of topics, the subject of divorce will not usually be noted in library catalogs or in the other general bibliographic indexes listed above. The latter indexes only whole books. For this reason, a subject heading must be ascribed which is broad enough to cover the entire work, for example, "Social Problems," "United States--Social Conditions," or "United States--Social Life and Customs," with no mention of divorce as a subject.

There is another type of composite book, often on a broad general theme, in which each chapter is written by a different individual on some distinctive aspect of the general theme, and often only loosely related to the theme. This may be the case with conference proceedings and the like. Again, in the general bibliographic system, only a broad subject heading is assigned to the book, and thus a chapter specifically on divorce may be lost bibliographically.

The researcher has limited recourse in his efforts to identify significant chapters in these types of books. Several abstract journals, such as PSYCHOLOGICAL ABSTRACTS (item 4-50), cite selected chapters in composite books. These abstract journals are described in chapter 4, part B.

The only other aids available are the selective works described in part E of chapter 11. Of particular importance for current studies are items 11-31 and 11-32. Although these works have not to date cited many chapters on divorce, they are worth watching in the future, as more attention, discussion, and writing centers on this topic.

Chapter 3

DIVORCE INFORMATION IN BASIC REFERENCE BOOKS

Several types of basic reference works are especially convenient sources of divorce information. Among these are encyclopedias, almanacs, yearbooks, and handbooks. Fortunately many of these basic reference works are readily available to the public in libraries and bookstores. These are useful because they provide divorce information in succinct form for a wide cross-section of the general public, from the relatively uninformed person wanting a short general overview of the subject to the specialist wanting a quick update on recent data or research on some aspect of divorce.

This chapter will describe the most useful basic reference works for divorce and the type of divorce information provided by each. Sources for more detailed and extensive information on divorce are described in later chapters of this information guide. Following the description of each work cited below is a listing of subject headings under which information on divorce may be found in that work. This can potentially save the user considerable time. However, he should be aware that subject headings for later editions of the works may change or new relevant headings may be added.

The last section, part E, of this chapter describes means by which the person particularly interested in being able to identify new reference works specifically on the subject of divorce, as they are published, can do so.

A. ENCYCLOPEDIAS

For persons relatively uninformed in the area of divorce, articles from some of the general encyclopedias listed below can provide very good points of entry into the subject. Some of the encyclopedias listed, however, are more specialized and contain very useful summaries for the student or the researcher in the area.

3-1   CHAMBER'S ENCYCLOPAEDIA. New rev. ed. 15 vols. Oxford and New York: Pergamon Press, 1967.

This well-known British encyclopedia has two short articles on divorce. The one on family law focuses on the legal aspects of divorce in Great Britain and is somewhat dated.

Consult: Divorce
Family law

3-2   COLLIER'S ENCYCLOPEDIA. 24 vols. New York: Crowell-Collier Educational Corp., 1949-- .

The 1975 edition contains a good article on divorce, although it was written about 1970. Information on divorce is provided for other countries as well as for the United States.

Consult: Divorce
Marriage

3-3   ENCYCLOPEDIA AMERICANA. 30 vols. New York: Grolier Educational Corp., Americana Divisions, 1829-- . New editions issued annually under a policy of continuous revisions. Annual supplements.

The article on divorce in the 1976 edition provides a very good general historical background on divorce from ancient societies to the present. The article appears to have been written about 1968, and hence is somewhat dated especially in the light of new no-fault divorce law trends. American and European divorce laws are discussed. Some statistical data on divorce are given. A useful bibliography is included.

Consult: Annulment of marriage   Divorce
Civil law   Marriages, law of
Common law

3-4   ENCYCLOPAEDIA BRITANNICA. 30 vols. Chicago: Encyclopaedia Britannica, 1929-- . New editions issued annually under a policy of continuous revision. The 1974 edition was radically different in format and content. Annual supplements.

The 1975 edition entitled THE NEW ENCYCLOPAEDIA BRITANNICA, contains a very general, somewhat dated treatment of divorce, with little specific information on divorce in the United States, Canada, or Great Britain. The information centers on the problems of divorced persons.

Consult: Family and marriage
Family law

3-5   ENCYCLOPEDIA CANADIANA; THE ENCYCLOPEDIA OF CANADA. 10 vols. Toronto: Grolier of Canada, 1975.

A good article on divorce in Canada, with a description of the development of Canadian divorce law, some statistics, and a bibliography, is provided by this work.

Consult: Divorce

3-6   ENCYCLOPAEDIA JUDAICA. 16 vols. Jerusalem and New York: Macmillan, 1971-72. Annual supplements.

This specialized Jewish encyclopedia has a seven-page article on divorce in the Old Testament and in later Jewish law, followed by a bibliography. Some statistics on Jews and divorce are included. The index of this encyclopedia includes about seventy-five additional references to divorce in the various volumes of the set. The yearbooks which update this set contain very little additional information on divorce.

Consult: Divorce

3-7   ENCYCLOPEDIA OF SOCIAL WORK. 17th ed. 2 vols. New York: National Association of Social Workers, 1977.

This reference work contains lengthy articles by scholars, with bibliographies emphasizing current research and theory.

Consult: Family breakdown

3-8   ENCYCLOPAEDIA OF THE SOCIAL SCIENCES. 15 vols. New York: Macmillan, 1930-35.

This classic work contains scholarly articles on divorce and related topics from the first quarter of the twentieth century, accompanied by good bibliographies. Although this work is over forty years old, it is still very valuable for the historical aspects of divorce.

Consult: Alimony   Family desertion and
          Divorce   nonsupport
          Domestic-relations   Marital property
             courts

3-9   INTERNATIONAL ENCYCLOPEDIA OF THE SOCIAL SCIENCES. 17 vols. New York: Macmillan, 1968.

A nine-page article on family dissolution which focuses on divorce from a sociological perspective constitutes the main information contained in this work. Research on family disorganization is presented from various perspectives. A bibliography is included.

Consult: Divorce
Family: disorganization and dissolution

3-10   NEW CATHOLIC ENCYCLOPEDIA. Prepared by an editorial staff
at the Catholic University of America. 15 vols. New York:
McGraw-Hill, 1967. Supplements published irregularly.

This work contains general articles on divorce, divorce
in the Bible, moral aspects of divorce, divorce law in
the United States, and shorter articles on related topics.
Short bibliographies are included.

Consult: Divorce   Marriage, canon law of
          Marriage   Separation

3-11   WORLD BOOK ENCYCLOPEDIA. 22 vols. Chicago: Field Enterprises Educational Corp., 1917-- . New editions issued annually
under a policy of continuous revision. Annual supplements.

A good up-to-date article on divorce, including no-
fault divorce, giving the pros and cons is provided for
younger readers in the 1976 edition. Useful to adults
as well, the information also includes divorce statistics
and rates for the United States.

Consult: Alimony   Desertion
          Annulment   Divorce

B. ALMANACS AND YEARBOOKS

Almanacs and yearbooks provide quick, fairly recent factual information on
specific subjects but with little interpretation of the facts. There are a number
of these general reference works available, and each contains some distinctive
information on divorce. In addition to these works, which are described below,
basic divorce statistical information is provided in the following annuals:
CANADA YEAR BOOK (item 7-1); DEMOGRAPHIC YEARBOOK (item 6-2);
ANNUAL ABSTRACT OF STATISTICS (published by Great Britain's Central
Statistics Office, item 7-3); and STATISTICAL ABSTRACT OF THE UNITED
STATES (published by the U.S. Bureau of the Census, item 6-6).

3-12   AN ALMANACK . . . BY JOSEPH WHITAKER. London: J. Whitaker & Sons, 1868-- . Annual.

This annual provides discussion on divorce, separation,
annulment, reconciliation, custody of children, maintenance, and legal aid in Great Britain. No statistical
information is included. The general index is located
at the beginning of this work.

Consult: Divorce

3-13   CANADIAN ALMANAC AND DIRECTORY. New York: Pitman
         Publishing Co., 1848-- . Annual.

> Information is provided by this annual on the grounds
> for divorce in Canada, as well as references to other
> sources of information on divorce and divorce statistics
> for the provinces and the nation. No statistics are in-
> cluded in the almanac itself.

Consult: Divorce

3-14   CBS NEWS ALMANAC. Maplewood, N.J.: Hammond Almanac,
         1976-- . Annual.

> This annual contains the following divorce information:
> the number of divorces and rates from 1910 to the
> present, for selected years; grounds for divorces in the
> United States; residence requirements and waiting periods
> for remarriage; median duration of marriages in selected
> states of the United States for selected years from 1950
> to 1970. There is a time lag of approximately one to
> two years in the published data. From 1969 to 1972 this
> work was published as the NEW YORK TIMES ENCYCLO-
> PEDIC ALMANAC and from 1973 to 1975 as the OFFICIAL
> ASSOCIATED PRESS ALMANAC.

Consult: Divorce

3-15   INFORMATION PLEASE ALMANAC. New York: Simon & Schuster,
         1947-- . Annual.

> Data on the total number of divorces, the divorce rates,
> and the number of divorces by state in the United States
> for selected years from 1900 to the present are provided
> by this source. It also contains the grounds for divorce,
> as well as the residency requirements and waiting period
> required for remarriage, for each state. There is gen-
> erally a two-year time lag on information at the time of
> its publication.

Consult: Divorce

3-16   READER'S DIGEST ALMANAC AND YEARBOOK. Pleasantville,
         N.Y.: Reader's Digest Association, 1966-- . Annual.

> This source provides information on the number of divorces
> and the divorce rate by state in the United States. Also
> included is information on federal tax law governing ali-
> mony and child support.

Consult: Divorce

3-17   WHAT THEY SAID: THE YEARBOOK OF OPINION. Beverly Hills,
        Calif.: Monitor Book Co., 1969-- . Annual.

> Approximately twenty-five hundred quotations from notable
> Americans in all fields on topics from abortion to Zionism,
> taken mostly from newspapers and periodicals, are col-
> lected and indexed annually by this reference work. It
> is probably not an accurate reflection of American public
> opinion per se but it does represent the opinions Ameri-
> cans were reading for the year in question.

> Consult: Divorce   Marriage
>   Family

> Other reference sources of quotations on divorce can be
> located in libraries by searching under the heading "Quo-
> tations" in the subject card catalog.

3-18   WORLD ALMANAC AND BOOK OF FACTS. New York: News-
        paper Enterprise Associates, 1868-- . Annual.

> This source provides the following information on divorce
> in the United States: current grounds for divorce for
> each state; the number of divorces and divorce rates in
> the United States for selected years from 1890 to the
> present; and the number of divorces by state for the cur-
> rent year. It should be kept in mind, however, that
> there is a two-year time lag in regard to the information
> at the time of publication. Divorce information provided
> for Canada includes current grounds for divorce for Cana-
> da; the number of divorces and the divorce rates for Cana-
> da for selected years from 1936 to the present; and the
> number of divorces and the divorce rate by province since
> 1961. There is a three-year time lag in the information
> provided for Canada. The general index is located at
> the beginning of this work.

> Consult: Divorce

C. ANNUAL REVIEWS

Annual reviews are special types of yearbooks which consist of useful summaries
and evaluations of research conducted as well as other developments and ad-
vances in a specific field during the previous year. Unfortunately, none of
the annual reviews such as THE ANNUAL REVIEW OF PSYCHOLOGY, or THE
ANNUAL REVIEW OF SOCIOLOGY, both published by Annual Reviews Inc.,
have supplied to date significant information on divorce. Since the latter is
a new review, perhaps this type of information on divorce may be forthcoming
within a few years. Undoubtedly, more of this type of information analysis on
divorce will be available in the future.

D. HANDBOOKS

Handbooks present concisely, usually in one volume, the essential substance and information on a specific topic. They may be issued at regular intervals of at least two years. They are often helpful as an introduction to a field, at the same time providing bibliographies for further study. Several handbooks of particular importance for the subject of divorce are described here.

3-19   AMERICAN HANDBOOK OF PSYCHIATRY. Editor-in-chief, Silvano Arieti. 2d revised and expanded edition. 6 vols. New York: Basic Books, 1974-75.

> Volume 1 of this work contains a major article on divorce. Scattered throughout the set, as well, are references to divorce and children, divorce and retirement, divorce and suicide, divorce and drug use, divorce and homosexuality, and divorce and psychological states.

> Consult: Divorce

3-20   Christensen, Harold T., ed. HANDBOOK OF MARRIAGE AND THE FAMILY. Chicago: Rand McNally and Co., 1964. 1,028 p.

> This somewhat dated work views the family from theoretical, historical, research, and legal perspectives. It contains a moderate amount of information on divorce.

> Consult: Annulment   Divorce
>   Desertion   Remarriage

3-21   Goode, William J.; Hopkins, Elizabeth; and McClure, Helen M. SOCIAL SYSTEMS AND FAMILY PATTERNS: A PROPOSITIONAL INVENTORY. Indianapolis and New York: Bobbs-Merrill, 1971. xxix, 779 p.

> This handbook presents propositions relating the family to other social units in society. The propositions were gleaned from previous research. All of the propositions are cross-indexed. An extensive bibliography is included.

> Consult: Alimony   Remarriage
>   Broken homes   Separation
>   Custody   Stepchildren
>   Desertion   Stepparents
>   Divorce

E. IDENTIFYING NEW REFERENCE BOOKS

Completely new reference books are being published each year, some of which may become important for divorce information. One way to find out about these, as they are acquired in library collections, is to periodically search in library card catalogs under subjects such as:

Divorce--Handbooks, manuals, etc.
Divorce--Dictionaries
Divorce--Yearbooks

or any of the subject headings listed in item 2-5, followed by the above subdivisions.

Reference books on divorce may be identified also by keeping up with the following general guides to reference books as they are supplemented or as new editions are published.

3-22   AMERICAN REFERENCE BOOKS ANNUAL. Edited by Bohdan S. Wynar. Littleton, Colo.: Libraries Unlimited, 1970-- . Annual. Quinquennial cumulative index.

> Each annual volume describes and evaluates reference books which have been published the previous year. Citations to other reviews of the reference books are included. This carefully prepared work is arranged by subject areas with subdivisions. An author, specific subject, and title index is very helpful.

3-23   Ryder, Dorothy E., ed. CANADIAN REFERENCE SOURCES: A SELECTIVE GUIDE. Ottawa: Canadian Library Association, 1973. x, 185 p. Supplement.

> This well-annotated guide to specifically Canadian reference works is arranged in five general areas with subdivisions and with full indexing.

3-24   Sheehy, Eugene Paul; Keckeissen, Rita G.; McIlvaine, Eileen. GUIDE TO REFERENCE BOOKS. 9th ed. Chicago: American Library Association, 1976. xviii, 1,015 p. A revised, expanded and updated version of the 8th ed., by Constance M. Winchell.

> This annotated worldwide basic listing of selected reference works is an essential source for locating new reference works which may contain information on divorce. Supplements and forthcoming editions of this work should be watched for.

3-25   Walford, Albert John, ed. GUIDE TO REFERENCE MATERIAL. 3d ed. 3 vols. London: Library Association, 1973-75.

A worldwide, carefully annotated listing of important reference books, this work emphasizes materials published in Great Britain. The annotations often include citations to reviews of the works.

New works such as those described above may be watched for in the future under subject headings in library card catalogs such as:

Reference Books--Bibliography

An additional source for identifying new reference books which may contain divorce information is the following index:

3-26   LIBRARY LITERATURE; INDEX TO LIBRARY AND INFORMATION SCIENCE, 1921/32-- . New York: H.W. Wilson Co., 1934-- Bimonthly, with annual cumulative volumes. Subtitle varies.

In addition to indexing library and information science materials, this work also selectively indexes nonlibrary science periodicals of reference and research value. In this manner basic reference books of all types, and periodical articles on the literature of special subjects, as well as book lists, are included.

Consult: Book lists--special subjects--family life
          Reference books--bibliography
          Reference books--reviews
          Research materials--special subjects--marriage

Chapter 4

PERIODICAL ARTICLES ON DIVORCE

For study and research on divorce, periodical articles have certain characteristics that make them more useful than books. First, if timeliness is of utmost importance, the periodical article is usually more current, since the time between writing and publication is usually shorter for periodicals. Second, the article may contain succinct information on a specific aspect, a current trend, or a recent finding on divorce not easily found elsewhere. Third, the length of a periodical article may be adequate and sufficient to describe the methodology and findings of a research project or other investigation without need for the more lengthy format of a book. One of the main disadvantages in using periodical articles, however, is the difficulty that the uninformed person may have in identifying pertinent articles on divorce from the thousands of periodicals published each year.

It is not possible to locate pertinent articles efficiently in periodicals without the aid of standard periodical indexes and abstract journals which index a number of different periodicals at one time. In parts A and B of this chapter, the most important of these standard indexes and abstract journals are described and evaluated according to their usefulness in locating articles on divorce. Current subject headings useful for locating the articles in each source are listed after the description. It should be remembered, however, that these headings may change with time and new headings may be used in the future.

Most of the periodical indexes and abstract journals must be searched manually for relevant articles. Some, however, may also be computer searched. This option is noted in the description of each source where applicable.

For the researcher, educator, clinician, or other specialist in divorce, a discussion of current awareness services is provided in part C. For those who wish to keep an even closer watch on the current output of information on divorce in the periodical literature, a listing of periodicals which most frequently publish articles on divorce is provided. Information is also provided, in part D, on how to identify new periodicals on divorce or older related periodicals which may start emphasizing divorce in the future.

A. INDEXES TO PERIODICALS

Periodical indexes, unlike abstract journals, in general simply provide citations to periodicals. They do not provide abstracts of the contents of the articles in addition to the citations, as do the abstracting journals. Indexes are thereby generally more current than abstract journals due to the increased time consumed in the abstracting process of the latter. A citation of a periodical article usually includes the author of the article, the title of the article, the title, volume number, and issue number of the periodical in which the article was found, as well as the page numbers.

One of the most important indexes for research articles on divorce is the SOCIAL SCIENCES CITATION INDEX (item 4-33). On the other hand, one of the most important indexes for periodical articles of more general interest on divorce is the READERS' GUIDE TO PERIODICAL LITERATURE (item 4-31). Other indexes of above average usefulness include: ACCOUNTANTS' INDEX (item 4-2), CATHOLIC PERIODICAL AND LITERATURE INDEX (item 4-7), CUMULATED INDEX MEDICUS (item 4-13), LONDON BIBLIOGRAPHY OF THE SOCIAL SCIENCES (item 4-24), Public Affairs Information Service Bulletin (item 4-30), and the SOCIAL SCIENCES INDEX (item 4-34). In addition to indexes from the social sciences, other useful indexes are described here from such areas as business, law, medicine, and religion. The subject headings used in èach index to locate articles on divorce are indicated after the description of each work in order to save the user considerable time. A real attempt has been made to provide all of the pertinent subject headings for divorce used in each index. However, the user should be aware that subject headings may change over time and new relevant headings may also be added at any time.

4-1   ACCESS; THE SUPPLEMENTARY INDEX TO PERIODICALS. Syracuse, N.Y.: J.G. Burke, distributed by Gaylord Bros., 1975-- . Irregular.

> Access to the contents of about 125 popular periodicals, not previously indexed but widely held by public libraries, is supplied by this new index. An author and a subject index are provided. However, the latter is time consuming to use because it indicates only the author, periodical, and date, with the author index having to be consulted also in order to find the title and pages of the article. Reviews of books and films are included. Average usefulness for this topic.

> Consult: Children of divorced parents
> Divorce

4-2   American Institute of Certified Public Accountants. ACCOUNTANTS' INDEX; A BIBLIOGRAPHY OF ACCOUNTING LITERATURE, 1912-- . New York: 1921-- . Quarterly, with annual cumulations starting in 1973.

Information on the tax and accounting aspects of divorce is a unique aspect of this index. Books, pamphlets, and government documents, as well as articles from over 280 English-language periodicals published since the turn of the century are cited here and include information from the fields of accounting, auditing, data processing, financial reporting, financial management and investments, management, and taxation. The index consists of a subject, title, and author index and has an average time lag of approximately one year. Only about one-fifth of the periodical titles indexed are also indexed in the BUSINESS PERIODICALS INDEX (item 4-5). Above average usefulness for the financial aspects of divorce.

Consult: Divorce settlements
Taxation, United States--divorce settlements and separation agreements

4-3   American Theological Library Association. INDEX TO RELIGIOUS PERIODICAL LITERATURE, 1949/52-- . Chicago: 1953-- . Semi-annual, with biennial cumulations.

Approximately two hundred scholarly Protestant, Roman Catholic, and Jewish periodicals mainly in the English language are indexed by author and subject. About eighty of these periodicals are abstracted in the RELIGIOUS AND THEOLOGICAL ABSTRACTS (item 4-51). There is a time lag of six to nine months for current listings. Average usefulness.

Consult: Divorce   Marriage
Divorcées   Remarriage

4-4   BRITISH HUMANITIES INDEX. London: Library Association, 1915-- . Quarterly, with annual cumulations.

Nearly four hundred periodicals in the social sciences and humanities published principally in England, Australia, and New Zealand are presently indexed by means of separate subject and author indexes. The time lag for current listings is from three to six months. This work was formerly entitled the SUBJECT INDEX TO PERIODICALS, 1915-1961. Average usefulness.

Consult: Children, custody of Divorce
Children, custody of--law Families, fatherless
Children of divorced parents Families, one-parent
    Property--law

4-5   BUSINESS PERIODICALS INDEX. New York: H.W. Wilson Co., 1958-- . Monthly (except August), with annual cumulations.

> Dealing with the topic of divorce as it affects and is influenced by business and economics, this index cites articles and book reviews from over 170 English-language periodicals in accounting, advertising and public relations, automation, banking, communications, economics, finance and investments, insurance, labor, management, and taxation. It is essentially a subject and author index. The time lag for current listings is approximately four months. This index is one of the successors, according to the scope listed above, to the INDUSTRIAL ARTS INDEX, 1913-57. Approximately one-third of the periodical titles indexed are also indexed in the ACCOUNTANTS' INDEX (item 4-2). Average usefulness.

> Consult: Alimony   Divorce
>   Broken homes   Separation (law)
>   Desertion and non-   Support (domestic rela-
>   support   tions)

4-6   CANADIAN PERIODICAL INDEX. Ottawa: Canadian Library Association, 1948-- . Monthly, with annual cumulations.

> Articles and book reviews from English and French-Canadian periodicals in the social sciences and humanities are indexed by this work. Coverage was expanded to nearly one hundred periodical titles in 1976. Indexing is essentially by author and subject. For current listings there is a six-month time lag. This work was formerly entitled CANADIAN INDEX TO PERIODICALS AND DOCUMENTARY FILMS, 1948-1963. Average usefulness.

> Consult: Children of divorced   Marriage
>   parents   Single-parent families
>   Divorce
>   Domestic relations

4-7   CATHOLIC PERIODICAL AND LITERATURE INDEX, vol. 14-- , 1967/68-- . Haverford, Pa.: Catholic Library Association, 1968-- . Bimonthly, with biennial cumulations.

> Articles and book reviews from approximately 135 Catholic periodicals, about 2,500 selected adult books each year by and about Catholics, as well as papal, diocesan, conciliar, and other official church documents are indexed by this work. Most of the above indexed materials originate in the United States, with some, however, from Europe and Latin America. Access is provided by means

of author, title (books only), and subject indexes. A
directory of publishers is included. The time lag for
current listings is approximately six months. This index
was formed from two previous works: the CATHOLIC
PERIODICAL INDEX, 1930-67, and the GUIDE TO
CATHOLIC LITERATURE, 1888-1967. Above average
usefulness.

Consult: Broken homes   Marriage--annulment
        Divorce   Marriage--annulment
        Divorce--laws   (canon law)
        Divorcées   Marriage--indissolubility
                           Remarriage

4-8   CHRISTIAN PERIODICAL INDEX. West Seneca, N.Y.: Christian
Librarians' Fellowship, distributed by Houghton College, 1958-- .
Quarterly, with annual and quinquennial cumulations.

Approximately thirty-five conservative evangelical
Protestant periodicals, from the United States, Canada,
and England, not usually indexed elsewhere, are indexed
by author and subject in this work. The time lag for
current listings is approximately one year. Average usefulness for those interested in divorce from the conservative Protestant viewpoint.

Consult: Divorce
        Marriage

4-9   CUMULATIVE INDEX TO NURSING LITERATURE. Glendale, Calif.:
Seventh-Day Adventist Hospital Association, 1956-- . Bimonthly,
with annual cumulations.

Occasional references pertaining to patients involved in
divorce are cited in this index. A total of 175 journals
are wholly or partially indexed, including all major
nursing journals in English, with selective indexing of
some general medical journals, including journals not
indexed in INDEX MEDICUS. References to pamphlets,
films, filmstrips, recordings, and book reviews are also
included. Access is through separate author and subject
indexes. The time lag for current listings is from six to
nine months. Marginal usefulness.

Consult: Divorce

4-10   EDUCATION INDEX. New York: H.W. Wilson Co., 1929-- .
Monthly (except July and August), with annual cumulations.

The principal contribution of this index in regard to the
subject of divorce is that of the education and guidance
of children of divorced and one-parent families. Only

occasional references can be found regarding divorce in
the areas of higher, adult, and continuing education.
By means of a subject-author index, articles from approximately 225 education periodicals, proceedings of
conferences and other meetings, yearbooks of national
education organizations, monographs, and U.S. government documents are cited. This index has a broader
coverage of nonperiodical materials than the CURRENT
INDEX TO JOURNALS IN EDUCATION (item 4-45).
For current listings there is a time lag of less than six
months. Average usefulness.

Consult: Broken homes   Divorce
          Children of divorced One-parent family
            parents   Remarriage

4-11   GUIDE TO SOCIAL SCIENCE AND RELIGION IN PERIODICAL
        LITERATURE. Flint, Mich.: National Periodical Library, 1964/
        65-- . Quarterly, with annual and triennial cumulations.

        General information on the religious aspect of divorce
        can be located by this work, which indexes more than
        eighty denominational and interdenominational Protestant,
        Roman Catholic, and Jewish periodicals of a general
        rather than a more scholarly nature. The work is essen-
        tially a subject index. Most of the periodicals indexed
        are not covered by the INDEX TO RELIGIOUS PERIODI-
        CAL LITERATURE (item 4-3). The GUIDE TO SOCIAL
        SCIENCE AND RELIGION IN PERIODICAL LITERATURE
        was formerly entitled the GUIDE TO RELIGIOUS AND
        SEMI-RELIGIOUS PERIODICALS. There is a time lag of
        about one year for current listings. Above average use-
        fulness for religious views on divorce as reflected in
        denominational publications.

        Consult: Christianity and society/social
                    responsibility/divorce
                  Divorce
                  Roman Catholic church/divorce
                  Roman Catholic church/marriage and the
                    family
                  Social science/divorce
                  Social science/family/divorce

4-12   HUMANITIES INDEX. New York: H.W. Wilson Co., 1974-- .
        Quarterly, with annual cumulations.

        A recently expanded index covering at least 260 English-
        language periodicals in archaeology, classical studies,
        folklore, history, language and literature, literary and

political criticism, performing arts, philosophy, religion, and theology, this work can be anticipated to provide information on divorce from some of the various aspects represented, although to date very few articles have been cited on divorce. This index and the SOCIAL SCIENCES INDEX (item 4-34), since 1974, are successors to the SOCIAL SCIENCES AND HUMANITIES INDEX, 1965-1974, which in turn succeeded the INTERNATIONAL INDEX, 1907-1965. A marginal source.

Consult: Divorce
Divorce in literature

4-13   INDEX MEDICUS. Bethesda, Md.: National Library of Medicine, National Institutes of Health, 1960-- . Monthly, cumulates annually into the CUMULATED INDEX MEDICUS.

References to the medical and psychiatric aspects of divorce are provided by this massive index, which cites nearly a quarter of a million research articles and books annually from the general medical and psychiatric literature, including approximately 3,400 related journals. Access is by separate subject and author indexes. There is a time lag of three to nine months for current listings. A computerized search service is available through the library's MEDLINE network. The time lag is greatly shortened by using the on-line MEDLINE service or its continuing SDILINE service for current listings. The CUMULATED INDEX MEDICUS supersedes the CURRENT LIST OF MEDICAL LITERATURE, 1941-59. Above average usefulness for medical and psychiatric aspects of divorce.

Consult: Divorce
Family characteristics

4-14   INDEX TO CANADIAN LEGAL PERIODICAL LITERATURE. Montreal: Canadian Association of Law Libraries, 1961-- . Bimonthly, with annual cumulations.

Refer to item 8-114.

4-15   INDEX TO JEWISH PERIODICALS. Cleveland Heights, Ohio: College of Jewish Studies Press, 1963-- . Semiannual.

Approximately forty scholarly and general periodicals in the English language are indexed by author and subject in this work. Book reviews are also included. There is a time lag of more than one year for current listings. Marginal usefulness.

Consult: Divorce

4-16   INDEX TO LEGAL PERIODICAL LITERATURE, 1888-1937. Edited by Leonard A. Jones (vols. 1-2) and Frank E. Chipman (vols. 3-6). 6 vols. Boston: Boston Book Co., 1888-1937.

        Refer to item 8-115.

4-17   INDEX TO LEGAL PERIODICALS. New York: H.W. Wilson Co., in cooperation with the American Association of Law Libraries, 1908-- . Monthly (except September), with annual cumulations.

        Refer to item 8-116.

4-18   INDEX TO PERIODICAL ARTICLES BY AND ABOUT NEGROES. Compiled by the staff of Hallie Q. Brown Memorial Library, Central State University, Wilberforce, Ohio. Boston: G.K. Hall & Co., 1950-- . Annual. Decennial cumulations.

        Information on divorce with special emphasis on the black population is provided by this work. It indexes by author and subject approximately twenty-five black-oriented journals, some of which are not indexed or are only incompletely indexed elsewhere. The index cannot by considered comprehensive, however, since the journals indexed represent only those received by one library. A three-year time lag for current listings exists at the present time. Marginal usefulness.

        Consult: Broken homes   Father-Separated Children
                  Children of Divorce Parents Marriage
                  Divorce   Remarriage

4-19   INDEX TO PERIODICAL ARTICLES RELATED TO LAW. Dobbs Ferry, N.Y.: Glanville Publications, 1958-- . Quarterly with annual cumulations. Ten-year index, 1958-68.

        Refer to item 8-117.

4-20   INDEX TO PERIODICALS OF THE CHURCH OF JESUS CHRIST OF LATTER-DAY SAINTS. Provo, Utah: Brigham Young University, Library, 1966-- . Annual.

        Information on divorce from five official church periodicals is indexed by subject and author in this work. Considerably more articles on divorce are being indexed in recent years, with a time lag for annual listings of approximately five months. Marginal usefulness.

        Consult: Divorce

4-21   INDEX TO U.S. GOVERNMENT PERIODICALS, 1972-- . Chicago: Infordata International, 1975-- . Quarterly. Annual cumulations.

        This index to over 140 U.S. government periodicals,

many of which are not indexed elsewhere, is easy to use.
Back volumes are in preparation to 1970. There are
currently not many references to divorce. For further
information, refer to item 8-118.

Consult: Divorce   Family services
          Family   Marriage
          Family life

4-22   INTERNATIONAL BIBLIOGRAPHY OF SOCIAL AND CULTURAL
        ANTHROPOLOGY, 1951-- . Paris: UNESCO, 1951-59; Chicago:
        Aldine, 1960-- ; London: Tavistock Publications, 1960-- . Annual.

    This worldwide index provides author and subject indexing
    to over eight hundred anthropological journals. The two-
    to three-year time lag, and the small number of articles
    on divorce make this a marginal source.

    Consult: Divorce

4-23   INTERNATIONAL BIBLIOGRAPHY OF SOCIOLOGY, 1951-- .
        Paris: UNESCO, 1951-60; Chicago: Aldine, 1961-- ; London:
        Tavistock Publications, 1962-- . Annual.

    Many of the one thousand periodicals in this basic index
    of the sociological literature are indexed elsewhere.
    Books, pamphlets, and government publications are also
    indexed. Items are arranged within eleven subject areas.
    The two- to three-year time lag, plus the repetition,
    makes this a marginal source.

    Consult: Divorce
              Family disorganization

4-24   LONDON BIBLIOGRAPHY OF THE SOCIAL SCIENCES. London:
        London School of Economics, 1931-- . 32 vols. include supple-
        ments, to date. Irregular.

    Refer to item 2-4.

4-25   NINETEENTH CENTURY READERS' GUIDE TO PERIODICAL LITERA-
        TURE, 1890-1899, WITH SUPPLEMENTARY INDEXING, 1900-1922.
        2 vols. Edited by Helen Grant Cushing and Adah V. Morris. New
        York: H.W. Wilson Co., 1944.

    This easy to use author-subject index to fifty-one scholarly
    and general periodicals of the 1890s, including seven peri-
    odicals not indexed by POOLE'S INDEX TO PERIODICAL
    LITERATURE (item 4-26), also lists drama criticism and
    book reviews under the name of the author of such works.
    The main emphases of the materials included in the index
    are those of history, religion, education, geography, and

economics, and thereby divorce information as related
to these emphases.

Consult: Divorce
          Marriage law

4-26   POOLE'S INDEX TO PERIODICAL LITERATURE. By William Frederic
         Poole . . . with the assistance as associate editor of William I.
         Fletcher, and the cooperation of the American Library Association
         and the Library Association of the United Kingdom. Revised volume
         1802-1881. Supplements. Reprint. New York: Peter Smith.

         Nearly five hundred general, rather than essentially
         scholarly, British and American periodicals and book
         reviews from the nineteenth and early twentieth centuries
         are indexed by this basic subject index. Novels, poems,
         and plays are indexed by title as well. This work is
         somewhat difficult to use because of the lack of dates in
         the citations to the periodical articles. A special table
         must be referred to in order to find the year of publica-
         tion of each article cited.

         Consult: Deserted   Divorcées
                   Desertion   Family
                   Divorce   Marriage

4-27   POPULAR PERIODICAL INDEX. Camden, N.J.: Camden Library,
         Rutgers University, 1973-- . Semiannual, noncumulative issues.

         Approximately twenty popular periodicals such as MONEY,
         TV GUIDE, PLAYBOY, are indexed in this work by
         title and subject. The time lag for current listings is
         about four months. Average usefulness.

         Consult: Children of divorced parents
                   Divorce

4-28   POPULATION INDEX. Princeton, N.J.: Office of Population
         Research, Princeton University, and the Population Association of
         America, 1935-- . Quarterly.

         An index to periodical articles, books, proceedings,
         charts, and statistics on broad demographic topics,
         this work also contains summaries of demography, and
         lists the official statistical publications in demography.
         The index is arranged under nineteen broad topics, one
         of which includes information on divorce. The time
         lag for current listings is about one year. This work
         was formerly entitled POPULATION LITERATURE.
         Average usefulness.

         Consult: Section G. 1.--Marriage and divorce

4-29   Princeton University. Office of Population Research. POPULA-
        TION INDEX BIBLIOGRAPHY; CUMULATED BY AUTHORS AND
        GEOGRAPHICAL AREAS. 9 vols. Boston: G.K. Hall and Co.,
        1971.

        One section of this index and book catalog provides
        references on divorce. The entire work is composed of
        photostatic copies of library cards displaying bibliograph-
        ic information on periodical articles, government docu-
        ments, monographs, and pamphlets on demographic topics.
        The contents are arranged by author and by country;
        within countries the items are arranged by subject. This
        worldwide source covers the period 1935-68. Average
        usefulness.

        Consult: Section 5--Marriage and divorce

4-30   Public Affairs Information Service. BULLETIN. New York:
        1915-- . Weekly. Cumulated quarterly and annually. CUMULA-
        TIVE SUBJECT INDEX, 1915-1974. Arlington, Va.: Carrollton
        Press, 1976-- . In progress; 3 vols. to date.

        Much information on divorce can be secured through this
        selective index of current books, pamphlets, government
        publications, periodical articles, and reports of private
        agencies published in English throughout the world.
        Over one thousand periodical titles are indexed selec-
        tively. The prices and sources of materials cited are
        given when applicable. Photocopies of out-of-print
        pamphlets and reports are available from the New York
        Public Library. A list of new subject headings is printed
        annually. Computer searching is available since 1976.
        There is a time lag of three to nine months for current
        listings. Above average usefulness.

        Consult: Alimony   Parent and child (law)
                  Desertion and non-   Remarriage
                     support   Single-parent family
                  Divorce   Support (domestic rela-
                  Father-separated   tions)
                     children

4-31   READERS' GUIDE TO PERIODICAL LITERATURE, 1900-- . New
        York: H.W. Wilson Co., 1905-- . Semimonthly, except monthly in
        July and August. Cumulated quarterly and annually.

        This basic author-subject index to articles from approxi-
        mately 160 periodicals of general interest also indexes
        reviews of books, theatrical productions, and motion
        pictures. There is a time lag of only one to two months
        for current listings. Basic for nonresearch articles on
        divorce.

Consult:

Alimony	Marriage
Broken homes	Marriage--annulment
Children of divorced	(canon law)
parents	Marriage counseling
Desertion and Non-	Parent and child (law)
support	Remarriage
Divorce·	Single-parent family
Divorce (canon law)	Stepchildren
Divorcées	Stepparents
Insurance, divorce	Support (domestic relations)

4-32   SEVENTH-DAY ADVENTIST PERIODICAL INDEX. Riverside, Calif.:
Loma Linda University Libraries, 1971-- . Semiannual.

This work is a selective index to fifty-eight Adventist
publications, with a time lag of approximately two years
for current listings. Photocopies of the articles cited are
available from the publisher. Marginal usefulness.

Consult: Divorce   Remarriage
Marriage

4-33   SOCIAL SCIENCES CITATION INDEX: AN INTERNATIONAL
MULTIDISCIPLINARY INDEX TO LITERATURE OF THE SOCIAL, BE-
HAVIORAL, AND RELATED SCIENCES, 1969-- . Philadelphia:
Institute for Scientific Information, 1974-- . Three issues per year,
with annual cumulations.

For the person who has found a periodical article on
divorce that is very pertinent for his research, the
SOCIAL SCIENCES CITATION INDEX provides citations
to related articles and reviews that may also be pertinent. These articles and reviews have cited the same
article that the user has found to be so valuable. The
user can then read these additional articles which may
perhaps have expanded upon the original research.
Thus the user is able to follow the development of research in a very specific area. This particular function
is performed by the first and second main parts of this
work: (1) the Citation Index, and (2) the Source Index,
which is arranged by author cited, providing full bibliographic information and even the current address of
the author, when possible, for consultation if desired.
Corporate authors, such as agencies, universities, and
research centers are handled in the same way. The
third main part of this work is the Permuterm Subject
Index. This uses a technique of subject indexing which
pairs every keyword, in the title of an article with every
other keyword, and then connects the name of the author
with each pair of keywords. To find an article on divorce the user must anticipate all the possible words that
might be used in a title of an article that might be of

interest to him. This index is somewhat difficult to use
for the first time and the instructions given in the index
itself should certainly be studied carefully. Book reviews
are also indexed. This basic work presently covers over
twelve hundred journals in anthropology, business, criminology, education, history, law, philosophy, psychiatry,
psychology, sociology, social work, and theology from
forty-five countries. In addition, two thousand journals
in the physical and biological sciences are selectively
indexed when relevant to the social scientist. There is
a time lag of less than one year for current listings. A
computerized search service is available since 1972 directly from the publisher, or at libraries and other information centers that provide facilities for this type of
searching. Reprints of the articles can also be obtained
from the publisher. Although this index has very broad
coverage of the periodical literature, it should be noted
that other indexes and abstract journals provide citations
to articles in journals not indexed by this work. A basic
source for research articles.

Consult:
Alimony	Married
Annulment(s)	One parent
Broken homes	Post divorce
Custody	Post marital
Deserted	Property
Desertion	Reconstituted
Divorce(s)	Remarriage(s)
Divorced	Remarried
Family breakdown	Separate maintenance
Family disorganiza-	Separated
tion	Separation(s)
Family dissolution	Single parent
Father absent	Stepchild
Homes, broken	Stepchildren
Husband(s)	Stepfather(s)
Marital	Stepmother(s)
Marital status	Wife
Marriage	Wives

4-34   SOCIAL SCIENCES INDEX. New York: H.W. Wilson Co., 1974-- .
Quarterly, with annual cumulations.

Indexing over 260 scholarly English-language social
science journals in the areas of anthropology, economics,
geography, law, criminology, medical science, political
science, psychology, public administration, and sociology,
this author-title index provides information on divorce
from these disciplines. Book reviews are also indexed at
the end of each volume. There is a time lag of nine
months to one year for current listings. Many journals

not indexed in SOCIOLOGICAL ABSTRACTS (item 4-53) are covered by this work. This index was formerly part of the SOCIAL SCIENCES AND HUMANITIES INDEX, April 1965–March 1974, during which period the social science coverage was not as extensive. From 1907 to 1965 this latter index was entitled the INTERNATIONAL INDEX, with added coverage of many foreign-language journals. Above average usefulness.

Consult:

Alimony	Father-separated children
Broken homes	Legal cruelty
Children of divorced parents	Marriage
	Parent child (law)
Desertion and non-support	Remarriage
	Single-parent family
Divorce	Stepchildren
Divorce suits	Stepfathers

4-35   SOUTHERN BAPTIST PERIODICAL INDEX. Nashville, Tenn.: Historical Commission of the Southern Baptist Convention, 1965-- . Annual.

Approximately forty-five periodicals published by the Southern Baptist Convention are comprehensively indexed by author and subject in this work, which is the only index for many of these periodicals. The time lag for current listings is at least one year. A computer search is available on a limited basis. Average usefulness for Baptist views on divorce.

Consult: Divorce

4-36   SUBJECT INDEX TO CHILDREN'S MAGAZINES. Madison, Wis.: 1949-- . Monthly (except June and July). Semiannual cumulations.

Refer to item 11-36.

4-37   UNITED METHODIST PERIODICAL INDEX: AN INDEX TO SELECTED UNITED METHODIST PERIODICALS. Nashville, Tenn.: Methodist Publishing House, 1961-- . Quarterly.

Approximately sixty Methodist periodicals are indexed for general use of this denomination by this author-subject index, which includes book reviews. From 1961 to 1968 this work was entitled the METHODIST PERIODICAL INDEX. Marginal usefulness for divorce information published by this denomination.

Consult: Divorce   Marriage
           Family

4-38   U.S. Air University. Library. AIR UNIVERSITY LIBRARY INDEX
        TO MILITARY PERIODICALS. Maxwell Air Force Base, Ala.:
        1949-- . Quarterly, with annual cumulations. Title varies.

        Nearly seventy English-language military and aeronautical
        periodicals, not generally indexed elsewhere, are included
        in this subject index. Significant news articles, news
        items, and editorials are also indexed. This index is pre-
        ceded by the AIR UNIVERSITY PERIODICAL INDEX, 1949-
        1962. Marginal usefulness unless interested in divorce
        among military personnel.

        Consult: Marriage and divorce

4-39   VERTICAL FILE INDEX: A SUBJECT AND TITLE INDEX TO SE-
        LECTED PAMPHLET MATERIALS, 1932/34-- . New York: H.W.
        Wilson Co., 1935-- . Monthly (except August). Quarterly cumula-
        tions since 1973.

        This index, devoted exclusively to pamphlet materials,
        includes few references to divorce materials. Its former
        title was VERTICAL FILE SERVICE CATALOG, 1932-54.
        Marginal usefulness.

        Consult: Divorce
                 Single-parent family

4-40   WRITINGS ON AMERICAN HISTORY, 1902-- . Washington, D.C.:
        Kraus-Thomson Organization Press, for the American Historical Asso-
        ciation, 1903-- . Annual.

        This basic work from the 1902 volume through the 1960
        volume each year formed volume 2 of the ANNUAL
        REPORT OF THE AMERICAN HISTORICAL ASSOCIA-
        TION. These earlier volumes included abstracts for
        periodical articles and books, providing also author,
        title, and subject indexing. The publication of an-
        nual volumes was at least twelve years behind in 1974,
        with the volume for 1961 still in preparation, when the
        series took on a new format, starting with the 1974 vol-
        ume as a pilot project. These newer volumes have a
        classified arrangement, with only an author index, which
        makes specific subject searching on divorce much more
        difficult. The new format provides citations, not ab-
        stracts, of articles from over four hundred periodicals,
        many of which are local and state publications. Ap-
        proximately 350 dissertations were included also in the
        1975 volume. The gap from 1962 to 1973 was filled
        by a four-volume set compiled and edited by James J.
        Dougherty et al., with the same title and publisher as
        the main series. Dougherty has continued as compiler-
        editor of the series since that date.

For the earlier volumes through 1961 consult:
Divorce.

For the later volumes, 1962 to date, consult:
The section entitled "Social History:
Demography, the Family, Social Structure,
Mobility, and the History of Professional
and other Similar Social Groups."

B. ABSTRACT JOURNALS

Abstracts are very useful to the researcher because they summarize in a succinct manner the methodology and often the major findings of published research within specific subject areas. They are thus great time savers for researchers in selecting materials pertinent to their information needs. However,
the extra time required in the preparation of the abstracts generally increases
the time lag from the original appearance of the published article or report to
the time it is cited and abstracted in the secondary source. The main sources to
be consulted for locating abstracts of published research on divorce are SO-
CIOLOGICAL ABSTRACTS (item 4-53), PSYCHOLOGICAL ABSTRACTS (item
4-50), and CURRENT INDEX TO JOURNALS IN EDUCATION (item 4-45).

4-41   ABSTRACTS FOR SOCIAL WORKERS. New York: National As-
        sociation of Social Workers, 1965-- . Quarterly, with annual
        cumulated author and subject indexes. Since 1977, entitled SO-
        CIAL WORK RESEARCH and ABSTRACTS.

        Abstracting articles from about 187, mostly American,
        journals on social work and related fields in the social
        and behavioral sciences, this source provides divorce
        information useful for social workers and persons in re-
        lated helping services. The abstracts are arranged alpha-
        betically by author in six main subject areas and thirty-
        two subareas. There is a time lag of approximately one
        year for current listings. Marginal general usefulness.

        Consult: Divorce   Father Absence
                  Families   Marriage

4-41A   ABSTRACTS OF POPULAR CULTURE (See addendum 4-41A.)

4-42   ABSTRACTS ON CRIMINOLOGY AND PENOLOGY. Leiden, The
        Netherlands: Criminologica Foundation, 1961-- . Quarterly, with
        annual cumulated author and subject indexes.

        Divorce information related to crime, treatment and re-
        habilitation of criminals, law enforcement, and adminis-
        tration of justice is provided by this international source.
        Abstracts of articles from over 450 journals published in
        thirty-five countries are arranged under thirteen broad
        topics, with access by author and subject. This work

was entitled EXCERPTA CRIMINOLOGICA from 1961
to 1968. Marginal general usefulness.

Consult: Broken home   Divorce
          Custody

4-43   AMERICA, HISTORY AND LIFE. Santa Barbara, Calif.: Clio Press
        for the American Bibliographical Center, 1964-- . In 4 parts: part
        A, 3 issues per year; part B, two issues per year; part C, annual;
        and part D, annual cumulation.

        Over 125 U.S. and Canadian history journals are ab-
        stracted in this source. Since 1974, "divorce" has been
        used as a subject heading, which makes the use of this
        work much less time consuming than it was prior to the
        adoption of this heading. At the present time this is a
        marginal source.

        Consult: Divorce   Marriage
                  Family

4-44   CHILD DEVELOPMENT ABSTRACTS AND BIBLIOGRAPHY, June-
        December, 1927-- . Chicago: University of Chicago Press, for the
        Society for Research in Child Development, 1927-- . Three issues
        per year, with annual cumulative indexes.

        Some divorce information as it relates to the biological,
        medical, psychological, educational, and social aspects
        of the development of children can be located through
        this source. Abstracts of articles from approximately 150
        periodical titles, and numerous books cited with annota-
        tions, are arranged by author in eight broad categories.
        Subject and author indexing is also provided. Marginal
        usefulness.

        Consult: Custody   Father absence
                  Divorce   One-parent family

4-45   CURRENT INDEX TO JOURNALS IN EDUCATION. New York:
        Macmillan Information, 1969-- . Monthly, with annual cumulations.

        This source, prepared by the U.S. Educational Resources
        Information Center (ERIC), although privately printed,
        indexes and abstracts research articles appearing in
        over seven hundred English-language journals on educa-
        tion and related areas. Contents are arranged in four
        parts: main entries, subject index, author index, and
        journal contents. The main entry, arranged by accession
        number, cites the article from the journal issue in which
        it appeared, and provides an abstract of the article,
        along with assigned subject descriptors and identifiers.
        The descriptors are those used by ERIC for its RESOURCES
        IN EDUCATION as listed in its regularly updated THE-
        SAURUS OF ERIC DESCRIPTORS. Refer to RESOURCES

IN EDUCATION (item 5-22) for more information.
Since February 1976, "divorce" has become one of the
descriptors, not just an identifier, which will make this
source much easier to use. The time lag for current
listings is from six to twelve months. Reprints of the
articles abstracted are not available from the publisher
or the center. Computer searches are available at libraries or other information centers which provide facilities for this type of data base searching or directly by
mail from the center itself. Above average usefulness.

Consult: Divorce   Marital instability
          Family problems   Marital status
          Fatherless family   One-parent family

4-46   EXCERPTA MEDICA: Section 32, PSYCHIATRY. Amsterdam, The
        Netherlands: Excerpta Medica, 1948-- . 20 issues forming 2 vols./
        year, with a separate annual cumulative author and subject index
        for each volume. Section 32 was formerly 8B.

        Abstracts of articles on this topic from over thirty-five
        hundred worldwide biomedical journals are arranged in
        thirty-five general categories on psychiatry and related
        areas. Since two volumes are produced per year with
        a separate author and subject index for each volume,
        care must be taken when searching so as not to miss any
        volume. There is a time lag of about one year for cur-
        rent listings. A computerized search service is available
        for materials published since 1968. Average usefulness.

        Consult: Broken home   Remarriage
                  Divorce

4-47   EXCERPTA MEDICA: Section 17, PUBLIC HEALTH, SOCIAL MEDI-
        CINE, AND HYGIENE. Amsterdam, The Netherlands: Excerpta
        Medica, N.V., 1955-- . 20 issues forming 2 vols./year, with a
        separate annual cumulative author and subject index for each volume.

        Approximately eight thousand articles per year on this
        topic are abstracted as a result of scanning over thirty-
        five hundred biomedical and chemical journals. A listing
        of the periodicals indexed is not included. The abstracts
        are arranged under twelve broad headings. Since two
        volumes are produced each year with a separate author
        and subject index for each volume, care must be taken
        so as not to miss any volume. There is a time lag of
        about one year for current listings. A computerized
        search service is available for materials since 1968.
        Average usefulness.

        Consult: Broken home
                  Divorce

4-48   HISTORICAL ABSTRACTS. Santa Barbara, Calif.: Clio Press for
the American Bibliographical Center, 1955-- . Quarterly, with
annual and quinquennial indexes.

Abstracts from over two thousand history periodicals from
around the world are published in this source. Since
1964, however, articles on the United States and Canada
have been omitted from this work. For these two countries, refer to AMERICA, HISTORY AND LIFE (item 4-43).
Also, since 1964, the abstracts are arranged in two
parts: the modern period 1450-1914, and the twentieth
century since 1914. Since 1974, "divorce" has been
used as a subject heading which makes searching much
less time consuming. This is a marginal source.

Consult: Divorce   Marriage
          Family

4-49   INTERNATIONAL POLITICAL SCIENCE ABSTRACTS. Paris: International Political Science Association, 1951-- . Bimonthly, with
annual cumulative author and subject indexes.

Information on divorce laws and the political process can
be located from over six hundred journals in political
science and related fields by this source. Abstracts of
the journal articles are arranged in six broad categories,
with access by author and subject. Marginal general
usefulness.

Consult: Divorce

4-50   PSYCHOLOGICAL ABSTRACTS. Washington, D.C.: American
Psychological Association, 1927-- . Monthly with annual and triennial cumulated indexes.

Research articles from over 850 American and foreign
journals in psychology and related areas are abstracted,
and at least 1,500 books; also chapters in books, as well
as dissertations, are indexed annually by this basic source
for research information on the psychological aspects of
divorce. The abstracts and citations are arranged in each
issue under sixteen topics, alphabetically by author.
Following these sections in each issue are brief·author
and subject indexes, which are expanded and cumulated
semiannually. A two-volume CUMULATED SUBJECT
INDEX TO PSYCHOLOGICAL ABSTRACTS, 1927-60,
published by G.K. Hall of Boston in 1966, has been
followed by triennial supplements for 1961-65, 1966-68,
1969-71, 1972-74, all of which are very helpful. Care
should be taken in the use of the subject indexing, as
the subject headings are not consistent over time. A
THESAURUS OF PSYCHOLOGICAL TERMS used in the

subject indexing system is provided as an aid for the user. Computerized literature searches are available since 1967 at libraries or other information and research centers that provide facilities for this type of data base searching, or the user can arrange searches directly by mail with the publisher. The final pages of each monthly issue provide information on this latter service. The time lag for current listings in the monthly issues varies, perhaps averaging one year, but can be shortened by use of the computerized search service. A basic source.

Consult: Desertion   Marital problems
         Divorce   Marital relations
         Family--broken   Marital separation
         Father absence   Marriage--broken
         Marital conflict   Stepparents

4-51   RELIGIOUS AND THEOLOGICAL ABSTRACTS. Myerstown, Pa.: 1958-- . Quarterly, with annual cumulative author and subject indexes.

Abstracts of articles from approximately eighty U.S. and fifty European scholarly religious journals from the Protestant, Catholic, Orthodox, and Jewish traditions are provided by this source. Divorce information found here is mostly from the Biblical, theological, and historical perspectives. The time lag for current listings is over one year. Average usefulness.

Consult: Divorce

4-52   SOCIAL SCIENCE ABSTRACTS. 5 vols. New York: Social Science Abstracts, Columbia University, 1929-33.

Some information on divorce can be found in this work which includes over fifty thousand abstracts from worldwide periodicals in the social sciences for the period 1928-32. A cumulative author and subject index is provided. Marginal usefulness.

Consult: Divorce
         Family desertion

4-53   SOCIOLOGICAL ABSTRACTS. Jan.-Oct. 1953-- . New York, 1953-- . Bimonthly with annual cumulated indexes.

Research articles from over 250 journals in sociology and related areas are abstracted and arranged under sixty broad subject headings by this basic source for divorce research information. A few books are abstracted, as are, on an irregular basis since 1968, papers presented at regional and national sociological meetings. Approxi-

mately one-fourth of the abstracted articles are taken
from foreign-language periodicals. About 30 percent of
the periodicals abstracted, mostly foreign and regional,
are not indexed by the SOCIAL SCIENCES CITATION
INDEX (item 4-33). On-line computer searching is
available from 1962 to 1971 for index citations only.
Starting in 1977, on-line searching is available by which
the complete record, with abstracts, may be retrieved,
from 1972 to date. These search services are available
at libraries or other information centers that provide computer facilities of this type. A basic source for research
articles on divorce.

Consult: Custody   Separation
         Divorce

4-54   WOMEN STUDIES ABSTRACTS. Rush, N.Y.: Rush Publishing Co.,
        1972-- . Quarterly, with annual cumulative indexes.

        Divorce information, with a special focus on women,
        from a variety of types of publications can be located
        by means of this source. Several thousand abstracts of
        journal articles, pamphlets, reports and papers are pub-
        lished annually often giving the source and purchase
        price of the pamphlets, reports, and the unpublished
        materials. Extensive lists of unabstracted articles, book
        reviews, and film reviews are also provided. Special
        issues of journals that are devoted to the subject of
        women are noted. Many of the books cited are also
        annotated. Each quarterly issue of this work contains a
        bibliographic essay on some aspect of women's studies.
        Author and subject indexing facilitates the use of this
        source. There is a time lag for current listings of less
        than one year. Average usefulness.

        Consult: Alimony   Father absence
                 Child custody   Marriages--second
                 Children of divorced   Separated women
                    parents   Single-parent families
                 Desertion   Single parents
                 Divorce

4-55   WORK RELATED ABSTRACTS. Detroit, Mich.: Information Coordi-
        nators, 1951-- . Monthly, with monthly, quarterly, and annual
        cumulative subject indexes. Loose-leaf.

        Information regarding the effects of divorce on work, and
        vice versa, is provided by this source. It abstracts sig-
        nificant information from over 250 management, government,
        professional journals, and dissertations mainly from the
        United States. Many of these periodicals are not indexed
        elsewhere. This work was formerly entitled LABOR
        PERSONNEL INDEX, 1951-58, and EMPLOYMENT RE-

LATIONS ABSTRACTS, 1959-72. Marginal general use-fulness.

Consult: Family relationships
Marital status

4-56   In addition to the above sources, the New York Times Company has been marketing at a substantial fee, since 1973, its New York Times Information Bank. This is a fully automated on-line retrieval system designed to offer fast access to information on current events reported in the NEW YORK TIMES and more than sixty other newspapers and journals. Abstracts are included with the citations retrieved. The data base presently starts with 1969 for the NEW YORK TIMES it-self, and with 1971-72 for the other newspapers and journals. This is a very rapid method of obtaining current information on divorce.

C. CURRENT AWARENESS SERVICES

Published current awareness services are especially prepared for researchers, educators, or clinicians who may need to identify relevant periodical articles in an area of interest, such as divorce, as soon as they are published. Several effective services are described in this section.

4-57   CONTENTS OF CURRENT LEGAL PERIODICALS. Los Angeles: Law Publications, 1972-- . Monthly.

Refer to item 8-119.

4-58   CURRENT CONTENTS: SOCIAL AND BEHAVIORAL SCIENCES. Philadelphia: Institute for Scientific Information, 1969-- . Weekly issues.

This weekly service provides very rapid information on the contents of the most current issues of over one thousand journals in the social and behavioral sciences, often within two weeks of the publication of the issues. The tables of contents of the periodical issues are reproduced. Subject access to the articles listed is through a keyword-in-title index. There is also an author index with addresses provided. This indexing cumulates into the SOCIAL SCIENCES CITATION INDEX (item 4-33) by the same publisher. The subject headings listed in item 4-33 may also be consulted when using this current awareness service.

Another fast way to keep up with current periodical articles related to divorce, as soon as possible after they are published, is to establish an arrangement with one or more of the computer searching services, such as those noted in parts A and B of this chapter. Upon submission of a list of keywords relevant to the researcher's interest, these services may supply printouts of citations, with or without abstracts, to the researcher soon after they enter the data base, thus avoiding the time lag involved in waiting for the published issues of abstract journals.

D. SCHOLARLY PERIODICALS USEFUL FOR CURRENT DIVORCE INFORMATION

4-59   For the person interested in keeping up with developments in the area of divorce to the extent of perusing current issues of selected periodicals as they are published, the following list of periodicals is submitted. The list, which is a result of a citation analysis by the authors, consists of major academic journals publishing at least one or two articles on divorce per year. The most important journals to be consulted are the JOURNAL OF MARRIAGE AND THE FAMILY, the JOURNAL OF DIVORCE, and the FAMILY COORDINATOR, both of which have published an average of about four articles on divorce per year in this decade.

AMERICA
AMERICAN JOURNAL OF
  ORTHOPSYCHIATRY
AMERICAN JOURNAL OF
  PSYCHIATRY
ARCHIVES OF GENERAL
  PSYCHIATRY
CATHOLIC MIND
DEMOGRAPHY
DEVELOPMENTAL PSY-
  CHOLOGY
FAMILY COORDINATOR
FAMILY LAW QUARTERLY

JOURNAL OF DIVORCE
JOURNAL OF FAMILY
  COUNSELING
JOURNAL OF FAMILY
  LAW
JOURNAL OF MARRIAGE
  AND THE FAMILY
JOURNAL OF SOCIAL
  ISSUES
JOURNAL OF TAXATION
SOCIAL PROBLEMS
U.S. CATHOLIC

Since in any field new periodicals are being published each year, and also since some of the more established periodicals may at any time change their emphases, the researcher may need a means by which to keep up with the additions and changes. This is very difficult and, in some ways, almost impossible to do. The following standard publication is suggested as an aid only.

4-60   ULRICH'S INTERNATIONAL PERIODICALS DIRECTORY, 1977-78. 17th ed. New York: R.R. Bowker Co., 1977. Revised biennially. 2,289 p.

This standard directory provides information on approximately fifty-seven thousand periodicals from all over the world. It is arranged alphabetically under 250 subject headings. Information on each periodical includes frequency of issue, name and address of publisher, and year first published. The directory also lists periodicals, within the last two or three years, that have changed their name, that have ceased publication, or that have just begun publication. Even with all of this information it is difficult to identify periodicals which may turn out to be good sources for divorce articles. Subject headings such as "sociology," "law," and "home economics" will have to be used when searching, since there is no heading specifically on divorce. The listing of new periodicals may indicate possibilities to be examined.

For identifying, among the more established periodicals, those changing emphasis and becoming more important for divorce information and research, a quick citation count on the subject in the appropriate indexing and abstracting sources may reveal such trends.

Chapter 5

DISSERTATIONS, THESES, AND OTHER "UNPUBLISHED" RESEARCH REPORTS ON DIVORCE

Some of the most significant information on divorce for the researcher, and yet, in many ways, the most difficult to locate, is found in dissertations, theses, and other research reports. Some of this research gets published as books, or as journal articles in complete or in summary form, or as small monographs which form parts of scholarly series. However, the greater part of these reports on scholarly investigations remain "unpublished," at least not published in the traditional sense. This creates considerable difficulty both in identifying what research of this type has been done on divorce, and then in trying to secure copies of the research as needed. This chapter describes sources for identifying this type of material on divorce and also, when possible, provides information on securing the materials themselves or copies of the same.

A. DISSERTATIONS AND THESES

Dissertations and theses on divorce or related to divorce are very important to the researcher in the field. Some dissertations may be published commercially as books and thus may be located in the ways suggested in chapter 2 of this guide. Others may be published privately. However, many are considered "unpublished," being available only directly from the authors or institutions involved, or by securing a photocopy or microform copy from a source which has been granted rights of reproduction by the authors or institutions. The best sources for locating completed dissertations are described below. Unfortunately, even though it is especially important for the researcher to keep informed of dissertations announced and in progress, there is apparently no regularly published listing of "dissertations in progress" specifically on divorce research. Part C of this chapter suggests aid for the researcher in this regard.

1. Locating Dissertations and Theses on Divorce

5-1   Aslib. INDEX TO THESES ACCEPTED FOR HIGHER DEGREES IN THE UNIVERSITIES OF GREAT BRITAIN AND IRELAND. London: 1950/51-- . Annual.

> This listing of theses, prepared by the Association of

Special Libraries and Information Bureaus, provides the author, title, name of university granting the degree, and the degree granted for each thesis cited. The theses are arranged by broad subject categories, and then by university within each category. No abstracts are provided however. There is an author index and a subject index by broad categories. The rules for lending theses for each university are also included.

5-2 Black, Dorothy M. GUIDE TO LISTS OF MASTER'S THESES. Chicago: American Library Association, 1965. 144 p.

This work contains lists of master's theses arranged by institutions granting the degrees, and by subject or discipline. Unusually detailed annotations are provided for the lists cited.

5-3 COMPREHENSIVE DISSERTATION INDEX, 1861-1972. 37 vols. Ann Arbor, Mich.: Xerox University Microfilms, 1973. Annual supplements.

This work, which indexes over 417,000 dissertations in the main set alone, in addition to 35,400 in the 1973 supplement and an added 39,000 in the 1974 supplement, is an attempt to be a complete inventory of the output of doctoral dissertations accepted by universities in the United States. Since 1970, many Canadian dissertations and some from other countries are included. This index in effect cumulates and supersedes the indexes to DISSERTATION ABSTRACTS INTERNATIONAL (item 5-4), including its RETROSPECTIVE INDEX, 1970, 29 volumes; the Library of Congress's LIST OF DOCTORAL DISSERTATIONS PRINTED IN 1912-38; and DOCTORAL DISSERTATIONS ACCEPTED BY AMERICAN UNIVERSITIES, 1933/34-1954/55, by the Association of Research Libraries. Also included are dissertations never before listed in other published lists. Each dissertation is cited under one of twenty-two major discipline areas. Most of the dissertations relating to divorce are listed under Sociology, Education, and Psychology. A lesser number are listed under Language and Literature, History, Political Science, Law, Religion, Health Science, and Cinema. Within each discipline, the entries are listed by keyword-in-title. A computer-generated index by keyword and author leads the user to specific citations to dissertations. Care should be exercised, however, when the researcher uses the keyword index to try to locate all of the dissertations on his specific area of concern. He must try to search under every possible related word, but may still miss a few pertinent dissertations. This makes the keyword type of index difficult to use effectively for comprehensive searching, as there may be dissertations with titles containing words that are not very likely to come to mind. The citation for each dissertation provides the title, author, degree, institution, date, pagination when available, the citation number by which to locate the abstracts in the DISSERTATION ABSTRACTS INTERNATIONAL, or other listing, and the number for ordering a microform copy or a photocopy of any dissertation held by Xerox University Microfilms. Computer searching of the COMPREHENSIVE DISSERTATION INDEX data base is directly available through the publisher's Datrix service or at libraries and other information centers which provide facilities for this. Through 1976, the following list of nineteen keywords from titles have been identified by the authors as being initially useful in locating divorce dissertations. The number of dissertations found under each keyword through 1976 is indicated. This is only an initial listing; there may be other terms that may be used.

Consult:

Annulment(s)--2	Father absence--3
Broken families--1	Marital disruption(s)--3
Broken homes--8	Marital dissolution--1
Child custody--2	Nonsupport(ing)--2
Deserting--1	Post divorce--1
Desertion(s)--4	Post marital--1
Divorce(s)--58	Reconstituted families--1
Divorced--6	Remarriage(s)--2
Divorcée(s)--2	Separation(s)--4
Family disorganiza-tion--1	Separate(d)--4
	Stepfather--1

5-4   DISSERTATION ABSTRACTS INTERNATIONAL.   Ann Arbor, Mich.: Xerox University Microfilms, 1938-- .   Monthly.

Abstracts of doctoral dissertations which are submitted to Xerox University Microfilms by cooperating universities are included in this extensive compilation, which is a basic source of information on divorce research. These abstracts are arranged alphabetically by subject area and then by the cooperating university. Each listing provides the dissertation title, author, university, date, name of supervisor, abstract, pagination, as well as the number for ordering, from Xerox University Microfilms, microfilm copies (starting in 1976, also microfiche copies) or photocopies of the dissertations. In 1966, with volume 27, this work was divided into two sections: (A) Humanities and Social Sciences and (B) Sciences and Engineering. Both sections should be consulted; for example, psychology is in section B. Part 2 of issue number 12 each year is the annual subject and author index cumulated from the monthly indexes. Issue number 13, which started with volume 16, 1955/56, consists of an annual subject listing of essentially all dissertations accepted in the United States and Canada during that academic year, whether they have been submitted or not to Xerox University Microfilms. An author index is also provided. For volumes 1–11, 1938–51, this work was entitled MICROFILM ABSTRACTS. For volumes 12–29, 1952 to June 1969, it was entitled DISSERTATION ABSTRACTS. After this date as the present title indicates, the publisher has been attempting to extend coverage to foreign dissertations. Also with volume 30, 1969/70, the indexes are now computer generated on the basis of keywords-in-title, with separate indexes for the two sections, A and B. This basic work for information on divorce research is also indexed in the COMPREHENSIVE DISSERTATION INDEX, 1861–1972 (item 5-3).

Consult: The keywords listed in item 5-3 above.

5-5　　MASTERS ABSTRACTS: A CATALOG OF SELECTED MASTERS THESES ON MICROFILM. Ann Arbor, Mich.: Xerox University Microfilms, 1962-- . Quarterly, with annual cumulations.

Only a small proportion of the institutions granting master's degrees are represented in this index. The theses are arranged in broad subject areas with no other indexing. Very few theses on divorce are included in this work. Photocopies and microfilm or microfiche copies of the theses are available from the publisher.

Consult:　Home economics　　Sociology--family
　　　　　Law

5-6　　Ottawa. Canadian Bibliographic Centre. CANADIAN GRADUATE THESES IN THE HUMANITIES AND SOCIAL SCIENCES, 1921-46. Ottawa: E. Cloutier, Printer to the King, 1951. 194 p.

Over three thousand citations of masters' theses and doctoral dissertations granted in Canada from 1921 through 1946 are listed in this source. Entries contain the name of the author, title of the dissertation, the number of pages, the type of degree, the date granted, and the professor directing the research. A brief abstract is sometimes included. The dissertations are arranged by discipline and subdivided by universities, with an author index but no subject index other than by broad discipline.

5-7　　Ottawa. National Library. CANADIAN THESES; A LIST OF THESES ACCEPTED BY CANADIAN UNIVERSITIES. Ottawa:

1952-- . Annual.

> This annual, with a time lag of four years, supplies the author, title, degree, the institution granting the degree, and the year granted for all masters' theses and doctoral dissertations in Canada. The theses are arranged by discipline, with an author index but no subject index. Theses for the years 1947-60 are cumulated in a two-volume work.

5-8 RETROSPECTIVE INDEX TO THESES OF GREAT BRITAIN AND IRE-LAND, 1716-1950. Vol. 1: Social Sciences and Humanities. Edited by Roger R. Bilboul; Francis L. Kent, assoc. ed. Santa Barbara, Calif.: ABC-Clio, 1975-- .

> This multivolume work attempts to list all of the theses written prior to the Aslib annual (item 5-1). A few theses on divorce prior to 1950 are included.

> Consult: Marriage

2. Preliminary Checklist of Doctoral Dissertations on Divorce: Reported 1891-April 1978 .

The following preliminary checklist of U.S., British, and Canadian doctoral dissertations on divorce is submitted here as an aid to the researcher. It is the result of an extensive, manual , and computerized search of the COMPREHENSIVE DISSERTATION INDEX (CDI) (item 5-3) through April 1978, with the purpose of being comprehensive on the subject. As described previously, searching the CDI is difficult and elusive because identification by the researcher of all possible significant "keywords" is required. The list of keywords at the end of item 5-3 were used sucessfully for searching the formulation of this checklist. Conceivably there are other keywords that may have been overlooked (others may be used in the future), and therefore this checklist may not be comprehensive. This is a problem of keyword-in-title indexing and searching.

The list is referred to as a preliminary checklist because the other sources, listed in part A, section 1, above, and which were not incorporated in the CDI, have not as yet been searched in the preparation of this list.

The dissertations below are listed in alphabetical order within broad subject groups. It should be noted that each dissertation appears only once in the checklist, not being listed further under secondary aspects. The author, title, and date of completion are given for each dissertation. When the dissertation is abstracted in the DISSERTATION ABSTRACTS INTERNATIONAL (item 5-4) or its predecessors, the volume and page number is given for locating the abstract. The earlier dissertations that have not been abstracted in the above sources simply indicate the name of the university granting the degree. In cases where earlier dissertations have been published as books or monographs, this has been indicated by an asterisk(*). See also the addendum, p. 251.

5-9   ANNULMENT

Kiernan, Irene R.   "Annulments of Marriage in the Roman Catholic Church: A Study in Social Change." 1958. (19/07, p. 1855).

5-10   CHILD CUSTODY (See also addendum 5-10A.)

Blakeslee, Richard J.   "Characteristics of Families Permanently Deprived of Child Custody, Salt Lake County, 1963." University of Utah, 1963.

Margolin, Frances M.   "An Approach to Resolution of Visitation Disputes Post-divorce: Short Term Counseling." 1973. (34/04B, p. 1754).

Woody, Robert H.   "Child Custody Legal Proceedings: An Investigation of Criteria Maintained by Lawyers, Psychiatrists, Psychologists, and Social Workers." 1975. (36/06B, p. 2739).

5-11   CHILDREN OF DIVORCED PARENTS (See also addendum 5-11A.)

Birnbaum, Louis A.   "A Comparative Study of the Relation of Broken Homes to the Social Class and School Success of Secondary School Boys." 1966. (27/04A, p. 928).

Collins, Maria A.   "Achievement, Intelligence, Personality and Selected School-related Variables in Negro Children from Intact and Broken Families Attending Parochial Schools in Central Harlem." 1969. (30/12A, p. 5280).

Condit, Elroy J.   "The Educational Performance of Students from Non-broken Homes Compared with the Educational Performance of Students from Homes Broken by Death or Divorce." University of Northern Colorado, 1960.

Crescimbeni, Joseph.   "The Effect of Family Disorganization on Academic Achievement of Pupils in the Elementary School." 1964. (25/08, p. 4475).

Engemoen, Bonny L.   "The Influence of Membership in a Broken Home on Test Performance of First Grade Children." 1966.

(27/09A, p. 2726).

McNeal, Robert E. "A Study Comparing the Relationship of Broken Homes to the School Success of Junior High School Students." 1973. (34/05A, p. 2173).

Miller, Carrie E. "The Effect of the Home Broken by Divorce upon the Self Concept of Selected College Women." 1959. University of Denver.

Prewitt, Maryon P.W. "Divorced Mothers and Their Children: Basic Concerns." 1974. (35/05A, p. 5178).

Reinhard, David W. "The Reaction of Adolescent Boys and Girls to the Divorce of Their Parents." 1971. (32/04B, p. 2408).

Santrock, John W. "Family Structure, Maternal Behavior and Moral Development in Boys." 1973. (34/07B, p. 3474).

Sterne, Richard S. "Broken Homes and the Violation of Delinquency Norms--in First Offenders among Juveniles." 1962. (23/05, p. 1822).

Stewart, Robert J. "Effects of Traumatic and Nontraumatic Parental Separation in Clinically Evaluated Children." 1973. (34/04B, p. 1762).

Webb, James B. "A Comparative Study of the Relation of Broken Homes to the School Success of High School Students." 1970. (31/07A, p. 3187).

5-12   DESERTION AND NONSUPPORT (See also addendum 5-12A.)

*Eubank, Earle E. "A Study of Family Desertion." University of Chicago, 1916.

*Patterson, Samuel H. "Family Desertion and Non-support, a Study of Court Cases in Philadelphia from 1916 to 1920." University of Pennsylvania, 1922.

Snyder, Lillian M. "The Impact of the Criminal Justice System in Baltimore on the Deserting Nonsupporting Father in Relation to the ulfillment of his Role as Provider." 1975. (36/12A, p. 8302).

5-13   DIVORCE (See also addendum 5-13A.)

Adams, Harold E. "Divorce in Primitive Societies." Yale University, 1929.

Barrett, Roger K. "The Relationship of Emotional Disorder to Marital Maladjustment and Disruption." 1973. (34/09B, p. 4651).

Bechill, Verne C. "A Comparison of the Role Incongruity in Married and Divorced Couples." 1962. (23/04, p. 1449).

Bostick, Theodora P. "English Foreign Policy, 1528-1534: The Diplomacy of Divorce." 1967. (28/08A, p. 3103).

Brown, Prudence. "Psychological Distress and Personal Growth among Women Coping with Marital Dissolution." 1976. (37/02B, p. 947).

*Cahen, Alfred. "Statistical Analysis of American Divorce." Columbia University, 1932.

Caldwell, Steven B. "Models of First Marriage and Divorce in the United States: Combining Over-time and Cross-section Evidence." 1975. (36/09A, p. 6328).

Da Costa, Derek M. "Divorce in Canada." Harvard University, 1972.

Dean, Gillian. "Impact and Feedback Effects: Divorce Policy and Divorce in the American States." 1974. (35/09A, p. 6205).

de Mestier du Bourg, Hubert J.M. "Etude Comparative des Causes et des Effets du Divorce en droit Canadien." 1974. (35/07A, p. 4572).

Fisher, Esther O. "Education for the Divorced." Columbia University, 1962.

Hackney, Gary R. "The Divorce Process and Psychological Adjustment." 1975. (37/03B, p. 1434).

Heritage, Lena J. "A Study of Selected Factors and Their Effect on Postdivorce Adjustment." 1971. (32/09A, p. 4950).

Hobart, James F. "The Presentation and Empirical Validation of a Conceptual Model of Divorce." 1975. (37/04B, p. 1902).

Keller, Lillian M. "Marriage/family/child/counselors' Attitudes toward Divorce as Related to Selected Social Characteristics." 1976. (37/03A, p. 1806).

Kephart, William M. "A Study of Divorce: Philadelphia County, 1937-1950." University of Pennsylvania, 1951.

Lee, David K. "Marital Disruption among University Physicians and Professors: An Empirical Study of the Relationship between Professional Activities and Evaluations and Marital Disruption." 1968. (29/11A, p. 4121).

*Lichtenberger, James P. "Divorce: A Study in Social Causation." Columbia University, 1910.

Lillywhite, John D. "A Sociological Study of Divorce, Spokane and Whitman Counties, State of Washington, 1927-1947." Washington State University, 1949.

Long, Nathaniel T., Jr. "A Study of Divorce in Davidson County, Tennessee, 1946-1960." 1961. (22/09, p. 3287).

May, Elaine T. "The Pursuit of Domestic Perfection: Marriage and Divorce in Los Angeles, 1890-1920." 1975. (36/01A, p. 484).

Mazur-Hart, Stanley F. "Effects of No-fault Divorce: An Interrupted Time Series Quasi-experiment." 1976. (37/05B, p. 2573).

Oberdorfer, Douglas W. "The Effects of the Depression on Wisconsin's Marriage and Divorce Rates." University of Wisconsin-- Madison, 1941.

O'Brien, John E., Jr. "The Decision to Divorce: A Comparative Study of Family Instability in the Early versus the Later Years of Marriage." 1971. (31/12A, p. 6748).

O'Neill, William L. "The Divorce Crisis of the Progressive Era." 1963. (24/12, p. 5363).

Pascal, Harold J. "Need Interaction as a Factor in Marital Adjustment." 1974. (35/04A, p. 2056).

Pineo, Peter C. "Dyadic and Change Analysis in a Study of Marriage and Divorce." University of Chicago, 1960.

Raschke, Helen J. "Social and Psychological Factors in Voluntary Postmarital Dissolution Adjustment." 1974. (35/08A, p. 5549).

Rodis, Themistocles C. "Morals: Marriage, Divorce, and Illegitimacy during the French Revolution, 1789-1795." 1968. (30/03A, p. 1119).

Rush, Bernard H. "An Investigation of Parent-child Relationships, in Broken Homes and their Relationship to School Behavior." 1956. (16/08, p. 1509).

*Schroeder, Clarence W. "Divorce in a City of 100,000 Population." University of Chicago, 1939.

Sear, Alan M. "Pregnancy Timing, Marital Disruption and Associated Variables: A Record Linkage Analysis." 1971. (32/02A, p. 1098).

Taylor, Patricia A. "Women's Labor Force Participation and Marital Stability in the United States: A Panel Study." 1976. (37/05A, p. 3217).

Thompson, Kendrick S. "The Divorce Profile: Differential Social Correlates in 1952 and in 1972." 1974. (35/08A, p. 5550).

Van Scoyoc, Marthellen R. "Early Marriage: A Comparison of a Divorced and Married Group." 1962. (24/05, p. 2183).

*Waller, Willard W. "The Old Love and the New; Divorce and Readjustment." University of Pennsylvania, 1930.

Wilkening, Howard E. "A Study of Relationships between Certain Selected Variables and Expressed Attitudes toward Marriage and Divorce." New York University, 1942.

*Willcox, Walter F. "The Divorce Problem: A Study in Statistics." Columbia University, 1891.

Williams, John W., Jr. "Divorce in the Population of the United States and in a Homogeneous Subset of that Population (United States Air Force Officers) 1958-1970." 1971. (32/04A, p. 2215).

5-14   DIVORCE COUNSELING (See also addendum 5-13B.)

DIVORCED PERSONS (See addendum 5-14A.)

Blair, Maudine. "Divorcées' Adjustment and Attitudinal Changes about Life." 1969. (30/12A, p. 5541).

Dries, Robert M. "The Divorced Woman: Measurement of Self-Actualization Change and Self Concept." 1975. (35/02B, p. 884).

Polizoti, Leo F. "The Efficacy of Direct Decision Therapy for Decreasing Indecision and Irrational Ideas and Increasing Self-acceptance in Divorce Women." 1976. (36/10B, p. 5236).

Schoicket, Sally G. "Affinal Relationships of the Divorced Mother." 1968. (31/01A, p. 469).

Spinks, William B., Jr. "A Comparison of MMPI Profile Characteristics of Divorcées with those of Marriage Counselees." 1974. (35/10B, p. 5139).

5-15   DIVORCE IN LITERATURE (See also addendum 5-15A.)

Axelrad, Arthur M. "One Gentle Stroking: Milton on Divorce." 1962. (24/01, p. 280).

*Barnett, James H. "Divorce and the American Divorce Novel." University of Pennsylvania, 1939.

Burke, Francis M. "Fellini's 'La Dolce Vita': Marcello's Odyssey to Annulment." 1974. (36/02A, p. 579).

Coolidge, Lowell W. "Milton's 'Doctrine and Discipline of Divorce.'" Case Western Reserve University, 1937.

Halkett, John G. "Milton and the Idea of Matrimony: A Study of Milton's Divorce Tracts and 'Paradise Lost.'" 1964. (25/06, p. 3570).

Huguelet, Theodore L. "Milton's Hermeneutics: A Study of Scriptural Interpretation in the Divorce Tracts and in 'De Doctrina Cristiana.'" 1959. (20/07, p. 2803).

*Koster, Donald N. "The Theme of Divorce in American Drama, 1871-1939." University of Pennyslvania, 1942.

Moody, Lester D. "John Milton's Pamphlets on Divorce." 1956. (17/04, p. 855).

Potts, James B., Jr. "Milton's Deviations from Standard Biblical Interpretation in the Discussion of Divorce." 1968. (29/04A, p. 1213).

Thompson, Claud A. "Milton's 'The Doctrine and Discipline of Divorce': A Bibliographical Study." 1971. (32/03A, p. 1487).

Willis, Gladys J. "The Rule of Charity in John Milton's Discussion of Marriage and Divorce: From the 'Divorce Tracts' to 'Paradise Lost' and 'Samson Agonistes.'" 1973. (34/08A, p. 5129).

FATHER ABSENCE (See addendum 5-15B.)

5-16   LEGAL ASPECTS OF DIVORCE (See also addendum 5-16A.)

Broel-Plateris, Alexander A. "Marriage Disruption and Divorce Law." University of Chicago, 1961.

*Coudert, Frederick R. "Marriage and Divorce Laws in England." Columbia University, 1894.

Fairbanks, James D. "Politics, Economics and the Public Morality: State Regulation of Gambling, Liquor, Divorce and Birth Control." 1975. (36/08A, p. 5509).

Griffin, Ernest R. "The Full Faith and Credit Clause: Its Development and Application to Divorce Decrees." 1966. (27/02A, p. 514).

Groves, Patricia H. "Lawyer-Client Interviews and the Social Organization of Preparation for Court in Criminal and Divorce Cases." 1973. (34/07A, p. 4428).

Millar, John R., Jr. "A Study of the Changes of Divorce Legislation in the State of South Carolina." 1954. (14/11, p. 2151).

Rodman, Karl M. "Jurisdiction in Divorce--a Study in Comparative Law." Northwestern University, 1948.

Sellin, Johan T. "Marriage and Divorce Legislation in Sweden." University of Pennsylvania, 1922.

Skaist, Aaron J. "Studies in Ancient Mesopotamian Family Law

Pertaining to Marriage and Divorce." 1963. (24/04, p. 1586).

5-17   ONE-PARENT FAMILIES (See also addendum 5-17A.)

Barringer, Kenneth D. "Self Perception of the Quality of Adjustment of Single Parents in Divorce Participating in Parents Without
Partners Organizations." 1973. (34/07A, p. 4446).

Clarke, Paul A. "A Study of the School Behavior Effects upon
Boys of Father Absence in the Home." 1961. (25/5, p. 3097).

Steinberg, Marvin A. "Children's Coping Behaviors Related to
Father Absence." 1974. (35/01B, p. 490).

Zold, Anthony C. "The Effects of Father Absence during Childhood
on Later Adjustment: A Long-term Follow-up." 1975. (36/04B,
p. 1648).

5-18   RELIGIOUS ASPECTS OF DIVORCE (See also addendum 5-18A.)

Decker, John W. "Marriage and Divorce in the Early Christian
Church." Southern Baptist Theological Seminary, 1917.

*Emerson, James G., Jr. "The Problem of the Remarriage of Di-
vorced Persons in the United Presbyterian Church of the United
States of America." University of Chicago, 1959.

Evans, David S., Jr. "The Role of the Minister in Marital Counseling in Divorce Situations." 1966. (28/01A, p. 103).

Feldblum, Meyer S. "Studies in Talmudic Law of Divorce." 1958.
(19/08, p. 2170).

Harrell, Pat E. "The History of Divorce and Remarriage in the
Ante-Nicene Church." 1965. (26/10, p. 5988).

Howington, Nolan P. "The Historic Attitude of the Christian
Churches Concerning Marriage, Divorce, and Remarriage." Southern
Baptist Theological Seminary, 1948.

Mohler, Raymond D. "The Attitude of Christianity toward Marriage
and Divorce." Southern Baptist Theological Seminary, 1935.

Petty, Charles V. "Current Attitudes and Practices of Southern Baptists Regarding Divorce." Southwestern Baptist Theological Seminary, 1970.

*Shukri, Ahmed. "Muhammedan Law of Marriage and Divorce." Columbia University, 1916.

Wolodarsky, Meyer. "Divorce in Judaism." Yale University, 1899.

5-19   REMARRIAGE, STEPPARENTS, AND STEPCHILDREN (See also addendum 5-19A.)

Cooper, E. Newbold. "Effect of Step-father Relationship on Behavior and Adjustment to School Life at Girard College." Rutgers University, 1951.

Duberman, Lucile. "Becoming a Family: A Study of Reconstituted Families." 1973. (38/08A, p. 5353).

5-20   SEPARATION (See also addendum 5-20A.)

Cherlin, Andrew J. "Social and Economic Determinants of Marital Separation." 1976. (37/03A, p. 1827).

*Gibbons, Marion L. "Domicile of the Wife Unlawfully Separated from her Husband." Catholic University of America, 1948.

Herman, Sonya J. "The Use of Time Limited Therapy and its Effect on the Self Concept of Separated Single Parents." 1975. (36/03B, p. 1147).

Landgraf, John R. "The Impact of Therapeutic Marital Separation on Spouses in Pastoral Marriage Counseling." 1973. (33/10B, p. 5021).

Meyers, Judith C. "The Adjustments of Women to Marital Separation: The Effects of Sex-role Identification and of Stage in Family Life, as Determined by Age and Presence or Absence of Dependent Children." 1976. (37/05B, p. 2516).

O'Farrell, Timothy J. "Marital Stability among Wives of Alcoholics: Reported Antecedents of a Wife's Decision to Separate from or Endure her Alcoholic Husband." 1975. (36/04B, p. 1927).

Putney, Richard S. "Support Systems of the Separated/Divorced." 1976. (37/01B, p. 529).

B. UNPUBLISHED RESEARCH REPORTS

The major part of basic, applied, and evaluative research reporting is done
through books and periodical articles. However, there also exists a growing
body of literature, more so in the natural and applied sciences than in the
social sciences, which is often referred to as report literature. In the applied
sciences the term "technical reports" is often used. In the social sciences,
the "applied" research reports are often in the form of program evaluation reports. This type of reporting is becoming published less often in book form
because the reports often do not require the lengthy format of books. Also
the time lag in regard to publishing research reports in book form, and even
as articles in periodicals, is not considered tolerable by many researchers.
The U.S. government has taken the lead in establishing reporting services,
with less time lag, which publish the reports in a nontraditional manner. The
government solicits research reports through various clearinghouses and information centers, abstracts them, indexes and cites these abstracts, publishes regularly and speedily the abstracts and indexes, and provides upon request photocopies or microform copies of the original reports. Thus the reports in a sense
cannot really be considered "unpublished" and are sometimes referred to as
"near-print" materials. Two of these government sources, of importance to research on divorce, are described here.

5-21   GOVERNMENT REPORTS ANNOUNCEMENTS AND INDEX. Vol.
        1-- . Springfield, Va.: National Technical Information Service,
        1946-- . Semimonthly, with an annual cumulative index. C51.9/
        3/vol./no.

        This extensive reporting service abstracts and indexes all
        newly released federally funded or sponsored research and
        development reports. Approximately fifty thousand reports
        from 225 U.S. government agencies are abstracted an-
        nually. Although it is heavily oriented toward the physi-
        cal sciences, some behavioral science research is reported,
        including a few reports on divorce research. The index
        has been issued concurrently with the announcement
        volumes which include the abstracts. An annual cumu-
        lated index volume has been provided since 1965. In-
        dexing is done by subject, personal and corporate author
        (agency, etc.), contract number, and the report number.
        Each abstract includes the source and price of purchase
        for each report, and also indicates whether the report
        can be obtained in paper copy or in microfilm. Com-
        puterized searching is available from the NTIS. From
        1946 to 1964, the announcement volumes have been vari-
        ously known as: BIBLIOGRAPHY OF SCIENTIFIC AND
        INDUSTRIAL REPORTS; BIBLIOGRAPHY OF TECHNICAL
        REPORTS; U.S. GOVERNMENT RESEARCH REPORTS.

From 1965 to January 1971, it was entitled U.S. GOVERN-
MENT RESEARCH AND DEVELOPMENT REPORTS. The
title of the index volumes also has varied since 1965 as
follows: GOVERNMENT-WIDE INDEX; U.S. GOVERN-
MENT RESEARCH AND DEVELOPMENT REPORTS; and
since 1965, GOVERNMENT REPORTS INDEX. This abstracting and indexing service is difficult to use.

Consult: Divorce
Family relations

5-22　　RESOURCES IN EDUCATION. Washington, D.C.: U.S. Educational Resources Information Center, November 1966-- . Monthly,
with annual cumulative indexes. HE19.210:vol./no.

Divorce information as related to education and allied
fields can be secured from this extensive source published
by the U.S. government through the sixteen clearinghouses of the Educational Resources Information Center
(ERIC) system. This center acquires, selects, reviews,
abstracts, indexes, and disseminates research reports
in educational and other fields useful to educators.
Most of the research is published for the first time. Individuals may submit unpublished research for consideration. Each entry consists of an ERIC accession number,
the author(s) name, the title of the paper or report, the
organization and/or sponsoring body of the research,
pagination, cost of purchasing upon request a copy of
the report in paper copy or microfiche formats, descriptors and identifiers (see 4-45) of the subject of each report, and an abstract of the contents of the report. The
entries are arranged by the ERIC accession number under
subject descriptors which are alphabetically arranged.
The THESAURUS OF ERIC DESCRIPTORS, regularly updated, contains the official words and phrases used as
descriptors, with references to broader, narrower, and
related terms. Current changes in the descriptor system
are noted in the back of the RESOURCES IN EDUCA-
TION monthly issues. By referring to the thesaurus,
searches can be more efficiently performed. In addition
to the descriptors tagged to each entry in the RIE, the
authors of the abstracts assign other words known as
identifiers to the description of the report. These identifiers thereby provide added information and access. Since
February of 1976, "divorce" has been used as a descriptor, which will facilitate further use of this resource.
This is not the easiest work to use, even though the cross-
reference system is good, and separate author, subject,
and institution indexes are provided. Manual searches
are facilitated by cumulations such as Prentice-Hall's
COMPLETE GUIDE AND INDEX TO ERIC REPORTS,

THROUGH 1969, published in 1970, and the ERIC
EDUCATION DOCUMENTS INDEX, 1966-69. Computer
search services are available either at libraries or other
information centers that provide facilities for this type of
data base searching or directly by mail through the
center itself. Computer tapes are also available for purchase, as well as hard copy and microfiche copies of the
reports as indicated above. Many universities hold complete files of the ERIC microfiche. This work was previously entitled RESEARCH IN EDUCATION, 1966-74.

Consult: Divorce   Marital instability
          Family problems   Marital status
          Fatherless family   One-parent family

C. RESEARCH IN PROGRESS

Research in progress on divorce, not yet regularly reported in the scholarly
literature, is difficult to find and to keep up with. Three possible sources
for becoming aware of research in progress on divorce are listed below.

5-23   The FOUNDATION CENTER, New York, maintains a data bank
        on the research that is supported by grants of $5,000 or more, donated
        by private foundations and reported by the same. An index of recip-
        ients and the corresponding subject categories can be obtained.
        Computer searching is available for organizations associated with the
        Foundation Center. The center publishes FOUNDATION NEWS,
        the FOUNDATION DIRECTORY (item 13-11), and the annual FOUN-
        DATION GRANTS INDEX, 1970/71-- (item 13-12).

        Consult: Associates Program

                  The Foundation Center
                  888 Seventh Avenue
                  New York, N.Y. 10019

5-24   The SMITHSONIAN SCIENCE INFORMATION EXCHANGE main-
        tains a data bank for over thirteen hundred state, local, and federal
        agencies that fund and/or conduct research. The file contains informa-
        tion on approximately two hundred thousand ongoing or recently com-
        pleted research projects. The information includes supporting agency,
        title of the project, principal investigators, and an abstract of the
        project. A current awareness service is also available. A fee is
        charged for these services.

        Consult: Smithsonian Science Information Exchange
                  Room 300
                  1730 M Street, N.W.
                  Washington, D.C. 20036

5-25   Drs. Helen and Vernon Raschke have been maintaining for several years an inventory of divorce research-in-progress, and file of divorce researchers. Computerized summaries of this information are available, for a fee, from them at:

>   3308 Mapleton Cressent
>   Chesapeake, Va.   23321

or they may be contacted through:

>   The National Council on Family Relations
>   1219 University Avenue, Southeast
>   Minneapolis, Minn.   55414

Chapter 6

DIVORCE STATISTICS: UNITED STATES

Basic sources for locating divorce statistics for the United States are described and evaluated in this chapter. First, in part A, general sources of brief or condensed statistical information are described for the user who is interested in data without extensive detail. Then, in parts B and C, the two main sources of extensive and detailed divorce statistics for the United States are carefully described. These two sources are the national censuses and the national and state vital statistics reports.

In part D, sources of additional statistics on divorce provided in studies by other governmental agencies are described. These data in some ways are complementary or supplementary to the census data and vital statistics on divorce. For example, the United States Current Population Survey in a sense updates the national censuses on a sample basis.

The statistics on divorce, referred to above, are available in published form and some also are available in large computer data bases from which they can be retrieved as desired by the researcher for his own investigations. The computer data bases generally contain more detailed, more extensive, and often more up-to-date data than do the published works. Many universities have some of these data available. The tapes and punched cards can also be procured directly from the data gathering agencies.

A special section, part E, describes ways by which the investigator can keep abreast of new published sources of divorce statistics, as well as the increasing number of data bases that contain statistics on divorce in the United States.

When using these statistical compilations, whether in printed or computer stored form, the researcher should evaluate the reliability of the data, as errors may occur because of incomplete reportings, for example, when estimates are included in the totals. Also some data on divorce are derived from samples, and sampling errors are another factor in unreliability. Discussion on the reliability of the data and sources of error is usually found in an appendix or in a technical section of the printed work consulted.

Divorce statistics for the United States have been reported since 1867. In parts B and C, the various sources of these early data are described in considerable detail.

For an excellent discussion on the development of the collection of divorce statistics in the United States, see chapter 1 of MARRIAGE AND DIVORCE: A SOCIAL AND ECONOMIC STUDY, by Hugh Carter and Paul C. Glick. The revised edition of this 500-page work was published by Harvard University Press in 1976.

Statistics on public opinion regarding divorce or related to divorce are discussed in chapter 9, part E.

Throughout this chapter, the document number assigned by the Superintendent of Documents is listed, where possible, after each volume or item for easier location of the materials in libraries which arrange the materials by this classification system.

A. DIVORCE STATISTICS IN BRIEF

The United States, along with other countries, publishes statistics on a wide variety of subjects annually. When reliable and up-to-date data are needed, a few basic annuals, which are described below, are referred to frequently. Although there is only a limited analysis of data on divorce in these works, they may be sufficient for the general user who requires brief, condensed, or summarized data of this nature. Quick access to earlier data may be secured from the retrospective sources described in parts B and C.

6-1   CBS NEWS ALMANAC. Maplewood, N.J.: Hammond Almanac, 1976-- . Annual.

> The number of divorces and rates from 1910 to the present, for selected years, as well as the median duration of marriages in selected states of the United States for selected years from 1950 to 1970 can be found in this almanac and in its forerunners starting in 1969. Refer to item 3-143.

> Consult: Divorce

6-2   DEMOGRAPHIC YEARBOOK. New York: United Nations, 1948-- . Annual.

> This compendium of population data, which contains the official statistics from nearly 250 nations and territories of the world, in 1950 began reporting the number of divorces for each country in which this information was available, including the United States. Crude divorce

rates are also provided, as are annual data on the marital status
of the population, with different analyses each year. An excellent discussion of the reliability of data is provided. In the
1958, 1968, and 1976 yearbooks, special analyses of divorce
data were made which include the age, duration of the
marriage, and the number of dependent children. Statistics
on annulments were also included. This annual is a basic
source for U.S., as well as worldwide, statistics on divorce.

6-3   INFORMATION PLEASE ALMANAC. New York: Simon & Schuster, 1947-- . Annual.

> Data on the total number of divorces, the divorce rates,
> and the number of divorces by state in the United States
> for selected years from 1950 to the present are provided
> by this source. Refer further to item 3-15.

> Consult: Divorce

6-4   READER'S DIGEST ALMANAC AND YEARBOOK. Pleasantville,
N.Y.: Reader's Digest Association, 1966-- . Annual.

> This source provides data on the number of divorces and
> the divorce rate by state for the United States. Refer
> further to item 3-16.

> Consult: Divorce

6-5   U.S. Bureau of the Census. HISTORICAL ABSTRACTS OF THE
UNITED STATES, COLONIAL TIMES TO 1970. Bicentennial Edition.
2 pts. Washington, D.C.: Government Printing Office, 1975.
1,232 p. C3.134/2: H62/1789-1970/pts.

> For earlier U.S. statistics on divorce, this is the best
> quick reference work based on authoritative sources.
> It is essentially a supplement to the STATISTICAL AB-
> STRACT OF THE UNITED STATES (item 6-6) and presents
> historical statistics of the same type. The historical sta-
> tistics include the following data on divorce in the United
> States: the number of divorced persons by age and sex,
> from 1890 to 1970, by decades; the annual number of
> divorces from 1920 to 1970; the divorce rates per 1,000
> population and per 1,000 married females from 1920 to
> 1970; the percentage of spouses separated for 1950 to
> 1970; and the number of divorced persons per 1,000 mar-
> ried persons, spouse present, for the years 1948 to 1970.

> Consult: Divorce   Marriage
>   Divorced persons

6-6   _____. STATISTICAL ABSTRACT OF THE UNITED STATES. Washington, D.C.: Government Printing Office, 1878-- . Annual. C3.134:year.

> A quick, basic source of official government data on divorce since 1908, each annual volume provides divorce data by state and by age, race, and sex for the current year and previous years. There is a two- to three-year time lag in the publication of these data, according to the data in question. Most of the annual divorce data are summarized from the United States Census (items 6-10 to 6-47), the United States Vital Statistics (items 6-54 and 6-57), or the CURRENT POPULATION REPORTS (item 6-113). This basic work thus serves as a guide to further information by citing the exact sources from which the data were gathered. A most useful tabulation of the data from 1890 to 1970 is provided by the HISTORICAL ABSTRACTS OF THE UNITED STATES TO 1970 (item 6-5).

> Consult: Marriage and divorce
>   Marital status

6-7   WORLD ALMANAC AND BOOK OF FACTS. New York: Newspaper Enterprise Associates, 1868-- . Annual.

> This is a quick source of data on the number of divorces and divorce rates in the United States for selected years from 1890 to the present. It also provides statistics on the number of divorces by state in the United States for the current year. There is a two-year time lag from the time the data are gathered until published. Refer to item 3-18.

6-8   WORLD BOOK ENCYCLOPEDIA. Chicago: Field Enterprises Educational Corp., 1917-- . New editions issued annually under a policy of continuous revision. Annual supplements.

> Statistics on number of divorces and divorce rates for the United States are provided by this work. Refer further to item 3-11.

> Consult: Divorce

Although not in itself a primary source of divorce information, the following ongoing index offers a very quick way to pinpoint precise, often brief, and relevant statistics on divorce as needed.

6-9   AMERICAN STATISTICS INDEX . . . A COMPREHENSIVE GUIDE AND INDEX TO THE STATISTICAL PUBLICATIONS OF THE UNITED STATES GOVERNMENT. Washington, D.C.: Congressional Information Service, 1973-- . Annual, with monthly supplements.

Refer to item 6-173.

B. CENSUS STATISTICS: PUBLISHED AND COMPUTER STORED

As divorce becomes more prevalent in the United States, the national census reports provide more tabulations concerning divorced persons. To aid the researcher in finding appropriate data on divorce from these huge national surveys, all of the published tables containing statistics on divorced persons in the latest U.S. census, 1970, are cited and described in detail in the first section which follows. In the second section, divorce data from earlier censuses are described, but in less detail. In the third section, the census statistics stored in computer data bases are described for the researcher.

1. Published Current Census Statistics

The U.S. decennial census has been an important source of data on divorced persons since 1890. The 1970 census contains the most detailed tabulations concerning separation and divorce to date, with nearly one thousand tables containing some data on divorce. In addition to reporting social characteristics of persons who were divorced at the time of the census enumeration, there is considerable information given about persons who had been divorced and subsequently remarried.

A comprehensive and detailed listing of all the tables in the 1970 census containing statistics on divorced persons is presented here in order to eliminate for the researcher the very time-consuming task of searching through the twenty thousand tables of this census to find the approximately one thousand pertinent tables. Although the analytical finding aids in the flyleaves of the census volumes are very useful for finding some of the information on divorced persons presented in the tables, they do not and cannot point the user to every table that contains data on divorce. This extensive listing also calls attention to the fact that the census contains a wealth of detail about the social characteristics of divorced and ever divorced persons that has not yet been fully analyzed.

Volume 1 of the 1970 census, published in fifty-eight parts, is entitled CHARACTERISTICS OF THE POPULATION. The first part of volume 1 forms the U.S. Summary volume and contains eleven tables summarizing national or regional data on divorce. Parts 2-52 are reports for each state and contain twelve identically arranged tables of divorce information. Volume 2, SUBJECT REPORTS, published in thirty-nine parts, is a topical analysis of data on divorced persons for the entire population, or parts of the population, in nearly ninety tables. The Census of Population and Housing gives divorce information on every tract in every Standard Metropolitan Statistical Area.

The description of the divorce data in the 1970 census which follows contains the number of the table, the title of the table, and in parentheses the variables pertaining to divorced persons that are not indicated in the title. The

document number assigned by the Superintendent of Documents is listed after
each census publication for easier location in libraries that arrange the materials by this system.

For more information on how to use the 1970 census more effectively, the
reader should consult the 1970 CENSUS USERS' GUIDE, published by the
Bureau of the Census in 1970. (C3.6/2:C/33/2).

6-10 U.S. Bureau of the Census. 1970 CENSUS OF POPULATION.
   Vol. 1, CHARACTERISTICS OF THE POPULATION, pt. 1, U.S.
   Summary, sections 1 and 2. Washington, D.C.: Government
   Printing Office, 1972-73. Tables. Charts. Graphs. Maps.
   C3.223/9:970/v.1/pt.1, secs. 1 and 2.

> The following tables in the U.S. Summary volume con-
> tain data on divorced persons for the entire nation.
> Listed below are the titles of the tables, with the im-
> portant variables noted in parentheses.
>
> TABLES:
>
> 64.--Marital Status by Sex for the United States, Re-
> gions, and States. (Separated persons; divorced persons.)
>
> 111.--Education, Fertility, and Family Composition by
> Metropolitan and Nonmetropolitan Residence. (Persons
> known to have been divorced, 14-54 years old, by resi-
> dence.)
>
> 203.--Marital Status, Presence of Spouse, and Whether
> Married More Than Once, by Race, Sex, and Age:
> 1960 and 1970. (Separated; divorced; and ever known
> to have been divorced; for 1970 only.)
>
> 206.--Families and Subfamilies by Marital Status, Race,
> and Sex of Head, and Number of Children under 18
> Years Old; and Unrelated Individuals and Inmates of
> Institutions 14 Years Old and Over by Marital Status,
> Race, and Sex. (Separated persons; divorced persons.)
>
> 211.--Persons Ever Married and Mean Age at First
> Marriage of Persons 30 to 49 Years Old, by Social
> and Economic Characteristics. (Separated persons by
> race and sex; divorced persons by race and sex.)
>
> 216.--Labor Force Status by Sex, Marital Status, Race,
> and Age. (Divorced persons.)
>
> 279.--Marital Status, Presence of Spouse and Whether
> Married More Than Once, by Race, Sex, and Age, for
> Regions. (Divorced persons; separated persons; ever di-
> vorced persons.)
>
> 282.--Families and Subfamilies by Marital Status, Race,
> and Sex of Head, and Number of Own Children Under
> 18 Years Old; and Inmates of Institutions, 14 Years Old

and Over by Marital Status, Race, and Sex, for Regions.
(Divorced persons; separated persons.)

288.--Labor Force Status by Sex, Marital Status, Race,
Age, for Regions. (Divorced persons.)

331.--Persons Ever Married by Presence of Spouse,
Whether Married More Than Once, and Sex, for States.
(Divorced persons; ever divorced persons.)

351.--Persons Ever Married by Presence of Spouse,
Whether Married More Than Once, and Sex for
Standard Metropolitan Statistical Areas of 250,000
or More. (Ever divorced persons.)

6-11   _____. 1970 CENSUS OF POPULATION. Vol. 1, CHARAC-
TERISTICS OF THE POPULATION, pts. 2-52. Washington, D.C.:
Government Printing Office, 1972-73. C3.223/9:970/v.1/pts. 2-52.

The following tables contain information on divorced
persons for each of the fifty states. Each state has a
separate volume, but the tables are numbered the same
in each volume. Listed below are the titles of the
tables, with the relevant variables noted in parentheses.

TABLES:

22.--Household and Family Characteristics by Race.
(Divorced persons in urban areas, central cities, other
urban areas, and rural areas; separated persons in urban
areas, central cities, other urban areas, and rural areas.)

26.--Marital Status and Household Relationship by Race
and Sex, for Areas, and Places. (Divorced persons;
separated persons.)

30.--Marital Status and Household Relationship by Race
and Sex for Towns and Places of 10,000 to 50,000.
(Divorced persons.)

37.--Marital Status and Household Relationship by Race
for Counties. (Divorced men and women.)

52.--Education, Fertility, and Family Composition by
Race, for Urban and Rural Residence. (Divorced persons,
black, white, or Spanish language.)

63.--Education, Fertility, and Family Composition by
Size of Place. (Number of ever divorced persons, 14-
54 years old.)

74.--Education, Fertility, and Family Characteristics
by Metropolitan and Nonmetropolitan Residence. (Number of ever divorced persons, 14-54 years old.)

152.--Marital Status, Presence of Spouse, and Whether
Married More Than Once, by Race, Sex, and Age:
1970 and 1960. (Number of ever divorced persons, 14-

54 years of age.)

155.--Families and Subfamilies by Marital Status, Race, and Sex of Head, and Number of Own Children under 18 Years Old; and Unrelated Individuals and Inmates of Institutions 14 Years Old and Over, by Marital Status, Race, and Sex. (Divorced persons; separated persons.)

160.--Persons Ever Married, and Mean Age at First Marriage of Persons 30 to 49 years old, by Social and Economic Characteristics. (Divorced persons; separated persons.)

162.--Number of Children Ever Born per 1,000 Women 35 to 44 Years Old by Social and Economic Characteristics. (Divorced persons; separated persons; by race.)

165.--Labor Force by Sex, Marital Status, Race, and Age. (Divorced persons in the labor force.)

6-12   . 1970 CENSUS OF POPULATION. Vol. 1, CHARAC-
TERISTICS OF THE POPULATION, pt. 53, Puerto Rico. Washington, D.C.: Government Printing Office, 1972-73. C3.223/9:970/
v.1/pt.53.

The following tables contain divorce data on Puerto
Rico: Tables 21, 24, 30, 121, 124, 129, and 132.
These tables contain data on divorced persons by age
groups, sex, residence, the number of own children,
number of children ever born, labor force participation,
and education.

6-13   . 1970 CENSUS OF POPULATION. Vol. 1, CHARAC-
TERISTICS OF THE POPULATION, pt. 55, Virgin Islands. Washington, D.C.: Government Printing Office, 1972-73. C3.223/
9:970/v.1/pt.55.

Table 6 indicates the number of divorced and separated
persons in the Virgin Islands by sex and place.

6-14   1970 CENSUS OF POPULATION. Vol. 2, SUBJECT RE-
PORTS. PC(2)1A-10B. 39 pts. Washington, D.C.: Government
Printing Office, 1972-73. C3.223/10:970/v.2/pts. 1A-10B.

These reports are topical tabulations of data on the entire
population or segments of the population. The reports are
issued in thirty-nine parts, each on a specific subject.
All tables containing divorce data are from twenty-three
of these parts. These are listed below. The important
variables that are not indicated in the title of each report are noted in parentheses. The Superintendent of
Documents number is cited for easier location of these
materials.

6-15 _____. 1970 CENSUS OF POPULATION. Vol. 2, SUBJECT RE-
PORT: PC(2)1A.--National Origin and Language. Washington,
D.C.: Government Printing Office, 1972-73. C3.223/10:970/v.2/
pt. 1A.

TABLES:

2.--Selected Social Characteristics of the Native Population of Native Parentage by Age and Race. (Separated
persons; divorced persons.)

3.--Selected Social Characteristics of the Foreign Stock
by Nativity and Age. (Separated persons by sex; divorced persons by sex.)

11.--Selected Social Characteristics of the Foreign Stock
by Age, Nativity, and Country of Origin. (Separated
persons by sex; divorced persons by sex; from twenty-four
countries.)

17.--Social Characteristics of the Foreign-Born Population by Year of Immigration and Country of Birth.
(Divorced persons by sex, from twenty-four countries.)

6-16 _____. 1970 CENSUS OF POPULATION. Vol. 2, SUBJECT
REPORT: PC(2)1B.--Negro Population. Washington, D.C.: Government Printing Office, 1972-73. C3.223/10:970/v.2/pt. 1B.

TABLES:

5.--Selected Characteristics of the Negro Population 14
Years Old and Over by Age and Urban and Rural Residence. (Divorced persons by sex; separated persons by
sex.)

8.--Social and Employment Characteristics of Negro
Family Heads by Urban and Rural Residence. (Divorced
persons by sex; separated persons by sex.)

12.--Age, Marital Status, Education, and Industry of
the Negro Population for Selected Standard Metropolitan
Statistical Areas, and Cities. (Divorced persons by sex;
separated persons by sex.)

6-17 _____. 1970 CENSUS OF POPULATION. Vol. 2, SUBJECT RE-
PORT: PC(2)1C.--Persons of Spanish Origin. Washington, D.C.:
Government Printing Office, 1972-73. C3.223/10:970/v.2/pt. 1C.

TABLES:

6.--Social Characteristics of Persons of Spanish Origin
14 Years Old and Over, by Age and Urban and Rural
Residence. (Divorced persons by sex; separated persons
by sex.)

11.--Selected Social and Economic Characteristics of
Families with Head of Spanish Origin by Nativity. (Di-

vorced men; divorced women; separated women; Mexican, Cuban, and Puerto Rican heads of families.)

14.--Age, Marital Status, Education, and Industry of Persons of Spanish Origin for Selected Standard Metropolitan Statistical Areas and Places. (Divorced persons by sex; separated persons by sex; Mexican, Cuban, and Puerto Rican origin.)

6-18   . 1970 CENSUS OF POPULATION. Vol. 2, SUBJECT RE-PORT: PC(2)1D.--Persons of Spanish Surname. Washington, D.C.: Government Printing Office, 1972-73. C3.223/10:970/v.2/pt. 1D.

TABLES:

8.--Social Characteristics of Persons of Spanish Surname 14 Years Old and Over by Age and Urban and Rural Residence. (Divorced persons by sex; separated persons by sex; natives or nonnatives; in five southwestern states.)

11.--Families with Head of Spanish Surname by Social and Employment Characteristics and Urban and Rural Residence. (Divorced men; divorced women; separated women; natives and nonnatives; in five southwestern states.)

15.--Age, Marital Status, Years of School Completed, and Industry of Persons of Spanish Surname. (Divorced persons by sex; separated persons by sex; for selected Standard Metropolitan Statistical Areas and places.)

6-19   . 1970 CENSUS OF POPULATION. Vol. 2, SUBJECT RE-PORT: PC(2)1E.--Puerto Ricans in the United States. Washington, D.C.: Government Printing Office, 1972-73. C3.223/10:970/v.2/pt. 1E.

TABLES:

5.--Social Characteristics of Puerto Ricans 14 Years Old and Over by Age. (Divorced persons by sex; separated persons by sex; for selected states.)

8.--Families with Puerto Rican Head by Social and Employment Characteristics for Urban and Rural Residence. (Divorced men; divorced women; separated women; by Puerto Rican birth or parentage; for regions and selected states.)

15.--Age, Marital Status, Years of School Completed, and Industry of Puerto Ricans for Standard Metropolitan Statistical Areas with 25,000 or More Puerto Ricans. (Divorced persons by sex; separated persons by sex; Puerto Rican birth or parentage.)

16.--Age, Marital Status, Years of School Completed, and Industry of Puerto Ricans for Standard Metropolitan

Statistical Areas with 10,000 to 25,000 Puerto Ricans.
(Divorced Persons by sex; separated persons by sex;
Puerto Rican birth or parentage.)

17.--Age, Marital Status, Years of School Completed,
and Industry of Puerto Ricans for Cities with 25,000 or
more Puerto Ricans. (Divorced persons by sex; separated
persons by sex; Puerto Rican birth or parentage.)

18.--Age, Marital Status, Years of School Completed,
and Industry of Puerto Ricans for Cities with 5,000 to
25,000 Puerto Ricans. (Divorced persons by sex; separated persons by sex; Puerto Rican birth or parentage.)

6-20 _____. 1970 CENSUS OF POPULATION. Vol. 2, SUBJECT RE-
PORT: PC(2)1F.--American Indians. Washington, D.C.: Government Printing Office, 1972-73. C3.223/10:970/v.2/pt. 1F.

TABLES:

5.--Selected Characteristics of the Indian population 14
Years Old and Over by Age and Urban and Rural Residence. (Divorced persons by sex; separated persons by
sex; in selected states.)

8.--Social and Employment Characteristics of Indian
Family Heads by Urban and Rural Residence. (Divorced
men; divorced women; separated women; in selected
states.)

12.--Age, Marital Status, Education, and Industry of
the Indian Population for Selected Standard Metropolitan
Statistical Areas, Reservations, and Tribes. (Divorced
persons by sex; separated persons by sex.)

6-21 _____. 1970 CENSUS OF POPULATION. Vol. 2, SUBJECT RE-
PORT: PC(2)1G.--Japanese, Chinese, and Filipinos in the United
States. Washington, D.C.: Government Printing Office, 1972-73.
C3.223/10:970/v.2/pt. 1G.

TABLES:

5.--Selected Characteristics of the Japanese Population
14 Years Old and Over by Age and Urban and Rural
Residence. (Divorced persons by sex; separated persons
by sex; for selected states.)

8.--Social and Employment Characteristics of Japanese
Family Heads by Urban and Rural Residence. (Divorced
men; divorced women; separated women.)

12.--Age, Marital Status, Education, and Industry of
the Japanese Population for Selected Standard Metropolitan Statistical Areas and Cities. (Divorced persons
by sex; Separated persons by sex.)

20.--Selected Characteristics of the Chinese Population 14 Years Old and Over by Age and Urban and Rural Residence. (Divorced persons by sex; separated persons by sex; for selected states.)

23.--Social and Employment Characteristics of Chinese Family Heads by Urban and Rural Residence. (Divorced men; divorced women; separated women; for selected states.)

27.--Age, Marital Status, Education, and Industry of the Chinese Population for Selected Standard Metropolitan Statistical Areas and Cities. (Divorced persons by sex; separated persons by sex.)

35.--Selected Characteristics of the Filipino Population 14 Years Old and Over by Age and Urban and Rural Residence. (Divorced persons by sex; separated persons by sex; for selected states.)

38.--Social and Employment Characteristics of Filipino Family Heads by Urban and Rural Residence. (Divorced men; divorced women; separated women; for selected states.)

42.--Age, Marital Status, Education, and Industry of the Filipino Population for Selected Standard Metropolitan Statistical Areas and Cities. (Divorced persons by sex; separated persons by sex.)

6-22   _____. 1970 CENSUS OF POPULATION. Vol. 2, SUBJECT RE-PORT: PC(2)2B.--Mobility for States and the Nation. Washington, D.C.: Government Printing Office, 1972-73. C3.223/10:970/v.2/pt. 2B.

TABLES:

3.--Mobility Status of Total and Negro Persons 14 Years Old and Over by Marital Status, Age, and Sex. (Divorced black persons; separated black persons; by place of residence.)

32.--Region of Birth of Native White and Native Negro Persons Living in the North by Age, Sex, and Marital Status. (Divorced persons; separated persons.)

33.--Region of Birth of Native White and Native Negro Persons Living in the West by Age, Sex, and Marital Status. (Divorced persons; separated persons.)

34.--Region of Birth of Native White and Native Negro Persons Living in the South by Age, Sex, and Marital Status. (Divorced persons; separated persons.)

6-23   _____. 1970 CENSUS OF POPULATION. Vol. 2, SUBJECT RE-PORT: PC(2)3A.--Women by Number of Children Ever Born.

Washington, D.C.: Government Printing Office, 1972-73. C3. 223/10:970/v.2/pt. 3A.

TABLES:

22.--Marital Status and Whether Husband or Wife was Previously Widowed or Divorced for White Women 15 to 49 Years Old, Ever Married, by Number of Children Ever-born and Age. (Divorced persons; separated persons.)

23.--Marital Status and Whether Husband or Wife was Previously Widowed or Divorced for Negro Women 15 to 49 Years Old, Ever Married, by Number of Children Ever Born and Age. (Divorced persons; separated persons.)

42.--Years of School Completed and Marital Status by Number of Children Ever Born per 1,000 White Women 15 to 49 Years Old and Age of Woman. (Divorced persons; separated persons.)

43.--Years of School Completed and Marital Status by Number of Children Ever Born per 1,000 Negro Women 15 to 49 Years Old and Age of Woman. (Divorced persons; separated persons.)

6-24   _____. 1970 CENSUS OF POPULATION. Vol. 2, SUBJECT RE-PORT: PC(2)4A.--Family Composition. Washington, D.C.: Government Printing Office, 1972-73. C3.223/10:970/v.2/pt. 4A.

TABLES:

4.--Households by Number of Related Children Under 18 Years Old, and Marital Status, Age, Race, and Sex of Head. (Divorced persons.)

8.--Marital Status and Sex of Family Head by Age, Race, and Spanish Origin, and Number of Own or Other Related Children Under 18 Years Old. (Divorced persons; separated persons; in rural or urban areas.)

18.--Characteristics of Families with Own Children Under Specified Ages by Type of Residence, Race, and Spanish Origin of Head. (Divorced female heads of families; separated female heads of families.)

19.--Characteristics of Families with Own Children and Family Members of Specified Ages Other than Head and Wife by Race and Spanish Origin. (Divorced female heads of families; separated female heads of families; and other family members by age.)

22.--Characteristics of Families by Number and Type of Subfamilies and Presence of Nonrelatives by Type Residence and Race of Head. (Divorced female heads.)

6-25 _____. 1970 CENSUS OF POPULATION. Vol. 2, SUBJECT RE-
PORT: PC(2)4B.--Persons by Family Characteristics. Washington,
D.C.: Government Printing Office, 1972-73. C3.223/10:970/v.2/
pt. 4B.

TABLES:

1.--Family Status of Persons under 18 Years Old by
Presence and Marital Status of Parents, Age, and Race.
(Divorced persons; separated persons.)

2.--Marital and Family Status of Persons 14 Years Old
and Over by Age, Race, and Sex, and Whether Married
More than Once. (Divorced persons; separated persons;
ever divorced persons; by living arrangements.)

7.--Marital History of Family Head Ever Married and
Relationship of Family Members to Head by Age, Race,
and Sex. (Divorced persons; remarried persons; in the
United States, and urbanized areas.)

8.--Marital History of Husband and Wife and Children
Living with Both Parents by Age, Race, and Sex. (Divorced persons; remarried persons; in the United States;
and urbanized areas.)

9.--Marital Status of Family Members 14 Years Old and
Over Living with One or Both Parents by Marital Status
of Parents, Age, Race, and Sex. (Divorced parents;
separated parents.)

6-26 _____. 1970 CENSUS OF POPULATION. Vol. 2, SUBJECT RE-
PORT: PC(2)4C.--Marital Status. Washington, D.C.: Government
Printing Office, 1972-73. C3.223/10:970/v.2/pt. 4C.

TABLES:

1.--Age of Persons 14 Years Old and Over, by Marital
Status, Whether Married More than Once, Whether
Known to Have Been Widowed or Divorced, Race, and
Sex. (Divorced persons; separated persons; remarried
persons; in rural or urban areas.)

2.--Years Since First Marriage of Persons Ever Married
14 Years Old and Over by Marital Status, Whether
Married More than Once, Whether Known to Have Been
Widowed or Divorced, Race, and Sex. (Divorced persons;
remarried persons; in urban areas; in the South.)

3.--Years Since First Marriage and Whether Known to
Have Been Widowed or Divorced of Persons Ever Married
14 Years Old and Over by Marital Status, Age, Race,
and Sex. (Divorced persons; separated persons; remarried
persons; in urban areas.)

4.--Years of School Completed of Persons 14 Years Old
and Over by Marital Status, Whether Married More than
Once, Whether Known to Have Been Widowed or Divorced, Age, Race, and Sex. (Divorced persons; separated persons; remarried persons; in urban areas.)

5.--Occupation of Employed Persons 14 Years Old and
Over by Marital Status, Whether Married More than
Once, Whether Known to Have Been Widowed or Divorced, Age, Race, and Sex. (Divorced persons; separated persons; remarried persons.)

6.--Occupation of Employed Persons 35 to 54 Years Old
by Marital Status, Whether Married More than Once,
Whether Known to Have Been Widowed or Divorced, Age,
Race, and Sex. (Divorced persons; separated persons;
remarried persons.)

7.--Income in 1969 of Persons 14 Years Old and Over
by Marital Status, Whether Married More than Once,
Whether Known to Have Been Widowed or Divorced,
Age, Race, and Sex. (Divorced persons; separated persons; remarried persons.)

8.--Social and Economic Characteristics of Persons Ever
Married 14 Years Old and Over by Whether Known to
Have Been Widowed, Divorced, or Widowed and Divorced, Race, and Sex. (Divorced persons by years of
education.)

9.--Occupation, Education, and Earnings of Males 45 to
54 Years Old with Earnings in 1969, by Marital Status,
Whether Married More than Once, Whether Known to
Have Been Divorced, and Race. (Divorced persons.)

6-27   _____. 1970 CENSUS OF POPULATION. Vol. 2, SUBJECT RE-
PORT: PC(2)4D.--Age at First Marriage. Washington, D.C.:
Government Printing Office, 1972-73. C3.223/10:970/v.2/pt. 4D.

TABLES:

4.--Marital Status of Persons Ever Married Who First
Married in 1901 to 1970 by Age at First Marriage, Year
of First Marriage, Whether Married More than Once,
Whether First Marriage Ended in Widowhood or Divorce,
Race, and Sex. (Divorced persons; separated persons.)

6-28   _____. 1970 CENSUS OF POPULATION. Vol. 2, SUBJECT RE-
PORT: PC(2)4E.--Persons in Institutions and Other Group Quarters.
Washington, D.C.: Government Printing Office, 1972-73. C3.
223/10:970/v.2/pt. 4E.

TABLES:

16.--Marital Status and Marital History of Inmates of Institutions 14 Years Old and Over by Age, Race, and Sex. (Divorced persons; separated persons; ever divorced persons.)

24.--Selected Characteristics of Inmates of Correctional Institutions by Type of Control of Institutions and Sex. (Divorced persons; separated persons; ever divorced persons; in state, federal, and local jails.)

25.--Selected Characteristics of Patients in Mental Hospitals by Type of Control of Hospital and in Residential Treatment Centers by Sex. (Divorced persons; separated persons; ever divorced persons; in state, federal, and private mental hospitals.)

26.--Selected Characteristics of Patients in Tuberculosis Hospitals by Type of Control of Hospital and in Chronic Disease Hospitals (except Tuberculosis and Mental) by Sex. (Divorced persons; separated persons; and ever divorced persons; in state, federal, and private hospitals.)

27.--Selected Characteristics of Persons Receiving Care in Homes for the Aged and Dependent by Type of Control of Home, Nursing Care, and Sex. (Divorced persons, separated persons; ever divorced persons; in public or private nursing homes for the aged.)

54.--Selected Characteristics of the Non-institutional Population in Group Quarters by Type Group Quarters. (Divorced persons, separated persons; ever divorced persons; in military barracks; and other group quarters.)

6-29 _____. 1970 CENSUS OF POPULATION. Vol. 2, SUBJECT REPORT: PC(2)6A.--Employment Status and Work Experience. Washington, D.C.: Government Printing Office, 1972-73. C3.223/10:970/v.2/pt. 6A.

TABLES:

3.--Household Relationship and Marital Status by Employment Status, Age, Race, and Sex. (Divorced persons by rural-urban residence.)

15.--Children Ever Born to Women Ever Married 45 Years Old and Over by Marital and Employment Status, Age, and Race. (Divorced women in full or part-time employment.)

19.--Household Relationship and Marital Status by Weeks Worked in 1969, Age, Race, and Sex. (Divorced persons by rural-urban residence.)

20.--Weeks Worked in 1969 and 1959 of Males 14 Years Old and Over by Marital Status, Age, and Race: 1970 and 1960. (Divorced males.)

21.--Weeks Worked in 1969 and 1959 of Females 14 Years Old and Over by Marital Status, Age, Race, and Presence of Own Children: 1970 and 1960. (Divorced women.)

6-30 _____. 1970 CENSUS OF POPULATION. Vol. 2, SUBJECT RE-PORT: PC(2)6B.--Persons Not Employed. Washington, D.C.: Government Printing Office, 1972-73. C3.223/10:970/v.2/pt. 6B.

TABLES:

3.--Marital Status of Persons 16 Years Old and Over not in the Labor Force by Year Last Worked, Age, Race, and Sex. (Divorced persons.)

4.--Household Relationship and Marital Status of the Labor Reserve by Age, Race, Spanish Origin, and Sex. (Divorced persons.)

6-31 _____. 1970 CENSUS OF POPULATION. Vol. 2, SUBJECT RE-PORT: PC(2)6C.--Persons with Work Disability. Washington, D.C.: Government Printing Office, 1972-73. C3.223/10:970/v.2/pt. 6C.

TABLE:

2.--Duration of Work Disability for Persons 18 to 64 Years Old with Disability by Household Relationship, Marital Status, Race, Sex, and Age. (Divorced persons; separated persons; by total or partial disability; length of disability.)

6-32 _____. 1970 CENSUS OF POPULATION. Vol. 2, SUBJECT RE-PORT: PC(2)6E.--Veterans. Washington, D.C.: Government Printing Office, 1972-73. C3.223/10:970/v.2/pt. 6E.

TABLES:

2.--Household Status of Civilian Male Veterans by Relationship, Marital Status, Age, Race, and Spanish Language. (Divorced males by residence.)

11.--Age of Civilian Male Veterans by Income in 1969, Marital Status, Race, and Spanish Language. (Divorced males.)

6-33 _____. 1970 CENSUS OF POPULATION. Vol. 2, SUBJECT RE-PORT: PC(2)7A.--Occupational Characteristics. Washington, D.C.: Government Printing Office, 1972-73. C3.223/10:970/v.2/pt. 7A.

TABLES:

31.--Marital Status of the Experienced Civilian Labor Force

by Occupation and Sex.   (Divorced persons.)

32.--Marital Status of Negroes and Persons of Spanish Origin in the Experienced Civilian Labor Force by Occupation and Sex.   (Divorced persons.)

6-34   _____.   1970 CENSUS OF POPULATION.   Vol. 2, SUBJECT RE-
PORT: PC(2)7B.--Industrial Characteristics.   Washington, D.C.:
Government Printing Office, 1972-73.   C3.223/10:970/v.2/pt. 7B.

TABLE:

46.--Marital Status of the Experienced Civilian Labor
Force by Class of Worker, Agricultural and Non-
agricultural Industries, Race, Spanish Origin, and Sex.
(Divorced persons; government workers; nongovernment
workers; self-employed persons.)

6-35   _____.   1970 CENSUS OF POPULATION.   Vol. 2, SUBJECT RE-
PORT: PC(2)7E.--Occupation and Residence in 1965.   Washington,
D.C.:   Government Printing Office, 1972-73.   C3.223/10:970/v.2/
pt. 7E.

TABLES:

13.--Labor Mobility and Interstate Migration between
1965 and 1970 for Persons 25 to 64 Years Old, by Age,
Sex, and Marital Status.   (Divorced persons; separated
persons.)

14.--Occupational Mobility and Interstate Migration
between 1965 and 1970 for Employed Persons 25 to 64
Years Old by Major Occupation Group, Sex, and Marital
Status.   (Divorced persons; separated persons.)

6-36   _____.   1970 CENSUS OF POPULATION.   Vol. 2, SUBJECT RE-
PORT: PC(2)9A.--Low-income Population.   Washington, D.C.:
Government Printing Office, 1972-73.   C3.223/10:970/v.2/pt. 9A.

TABLES:

12.--Marital Status and Sex of Family and Subfamily
Heads and Unrelated Individuals by Presence and Age
of Own Children, Poverty Status in 1969, Race, and
Spanish Origin.   (Divorced persons; separated persons.)

21.--Selected Characteristics of Persons 16 to 64 Years
Old with Work Disability by Poverty Status in 1969, Age,
Sex, Race, and Spanish Origin.   (Divorced persons; sepa-
rated persons.)

6-37   _____.   1970 CENSUS OF POPULATION.   Vol. 2, SUBJECT RE-
PORT: PC(2)10A.--Americans Living Abroad.   Washington, D.C.:

Government Printing Office, 1972-73. C3.223/10:970/v.2/pt. 10A.

TABLES:

4.--Social Characteristics of United States Civilian Population Abroad by Type. (Divorced persons; separated persons; for federal civilian employees, crews of merchant
vessels; by sex.)

7.--Social Characteristics of Federal Civilian Employees
Abroad, 18 years Old and Over, by Country of Residence.
(Divorced persons; separated persons.)

9.--General and Social Characteristics of Federal Civilian
Employees Abroad, 18 Years Old and Over, by Areas of
Residence, Age, and Sex. (Divorced persons; separated
persons.)

12.--Social and Occupational Characteristics of Federal
Civilian Employees Abroad, 18 Years Old and Over, by
Area of Residence, Year Left the United States, and
Ability to Speak Local Language. (Divorced persons;
separated persons.)

23.--Social Characteristics of Employed "Other Citizens"
Abroad, 14 Years Old and Over, by Country of Residence.
(Divorced persons; separated persons.)

24.--Social Characteristics of Employed "Other Citizens"
Abroad by Country of Residence. (Divorced persons; separated persons.)

26.--General and Social Characteristics of "Other Citizens"
Abroad by Areas of Residence, Age and Sex. (Divorced
persons; separated persons.)

27.--General and Social Characteristics of Employed
"Other Citizens" Abroad, 16 Years Old and Over, by
Area of Residence, Age, and Sex. (Divorced persons;
separated persons.)

30.--Social and Occupational Characteristics of Employed
"Other Citizens" Abroad, 16 Years Old and Over, by
Area of Residence, Year Left the United States, and
Ability to Speak Local Language. (Divorced persons;
separated persons.)

6-38 _____ . 1970 CENSUS OF POPULATION AND HOUSING. CEN-
SUS TRACT REPORTS. 241 pts. Washington, D.C.: Government
Printing Office, 1972. Tables. Maps. C3.223/11:970/pts. 1-241.

TABLE:

P-1.--General Characteristics of the Population. This
table gives the number of separated and divorced males
and females in every census tract in the 241 Standard

Metropolitan Statistical Areas of the United States. Each
CENSUS TRACT REPORT is printed in a separate booklet.

2. Published Retrospective Census Statistics

In this section the divorce statistics that are found in pre-1970 censuses are
described briefly. The censuses are listed in chronological order from the first
census that contains divorce statistics through the censuses of the 1960s. The
most recent censuses, 1970, are described earlier in part B, section 1 of this
chapter.

The 1890 census of population was the first U.S. census to report divorced persons as a separate category of marital status. Although questions were asked
about marital status in the 1880 census, the data on divorced and widowed persons were tabulated together.

The document number assigned by the Superintendent of Documents is listed after
each census publication cited for easier location of these materials in libraries
that arrange census volumes by this system.

6-39   U.S. Census Office. 11th Census, 1890. CENSUS REPORTS.
        ELEVENTH CENSUS: 1890. 25 vols. in 23. Washington, D.C.:
        Government Printing Office, 1892-97. Plates. Maps. Diagrams.
        Tables: I 12.5:1-15.

        Volume 1 of the Population Census contains data on
        divorce in the chapter on conjugal condition. The
        tables 81-85 on pages 829-910 have data on divorce
        by states, cities, age, race, sex, and divorced persons
        of foreign birth.

6-40   U.S. Census Office. 12th Census, 1900. CENSUS REPORTS.
        TWELFTH CENSUS OF THE UNITED STATES, TAKEN IN THE YEAR
        1900. 10 vols. Washington, D.C.: Government Printing Office,
        1901-2. Plates. Maps. Tables. Diagrams. I 13.5:2.

        Volume 2 of the Population Census, in the chapter on
        conjugal condition, pages 251-348, presents data on
        divorce. This section provides statistics on divorced
        persons in 1900 by age, sex, race, foreign and native
        birth, for the states, territories, cities of 25,000 and
        over, and cities of 100,000 and over.

6-41   U.S. Bureau of the Census. THIRTEENTH CENSUS OF THE UNITED
        STATES, TAKEN IN THE YEAR 1910. REPORTS. 11 vols. Washing-
        ton, D.C.: Government Printing Office, 1912-14. Maps. Tables.
        Diagrams. C3.16/1.

        Volume 1 of the Population Census contains information

on divorced persons in the chapter on marital condition.
Tables 1-41, on pages 507-687, give data for 1910 on
sex, race, foreign or native born for states, territories,
and cities.

6-42 _____. FOURTEENTH CENSUS OF THE UNITED STATES, TAKEN
IN THE YEAR 1920. REPORTS. 13 vols. Washington, D.C.:
Government Printing Office, 1921-23. Maps. Diagrams. Charts.
Tables. C3.28/5:2.

Statistics on divorced persons are found in volume 2,
"Population," in the section on marital condition. The
twenty-three tables in this section are located on pages
381-604.

6-43 _____. FIFTEENTH CENSUS OF THE UNITED STATES: 1930.
POPULATION. 6 vols. Washington, D.C.: Government Printing
Office, 1931-34. Maps. Tables. Diagrams. Forms. C3.37/5:
P81/v. 2.

The thirty-four tables on separation and divorce are
printed in volume 2, "General Report, Statistics by
Subjects," on pages 836-1088.

6-44 _____. SIXTEENTH CENSUS OF THE UNITED STATES: 1940.
POPULATION. 17 vols. Washington, D.C.: Government Printing
Office, 1942-43. Maps. Tables. Diagrams. C3.940-5:P81/v.4/
pts. 1-4.

Volume 4, part 1, "U.S. Summary of Characteristics by
Age, Marital Status, Relationship, Education and Citizenship," has data on divorce for the United States, states,
regions, and cities of 100,000 and over, in tables 5-8.
Volume 4, parts 2,3,4, Alabama--Wyoming, contain details on marital status by states in tables 6-10. There
are no data on divorce in the census tract tabulations.
The subject reports for this census should be consulted as
there are five reports which contain information on divorce.

6-45 _____. CENSUS OF POPULATION: 1950. A REPORT OF THE
SEVENTEENTH DECENNIAL CENSUS OF THE UNITED STATES.
Vol. 1. NUMBER OF INHABITANTS. Vol. 2. CHARACTERISTICS
OF THE POPULATION. Vol. 3. CENSUS TRACT STATISTICS.
Vol. 4. SPECIAL REPORTS. Washington, D.C.: Government Printing
Office, 1952-57. Maps. Tables. Diagram. C3.950-7/5:v.2/pts.
1-54.

The data on divorce in this census are organized similarly
to that of the 1970 census, but with less detail. Many

of the tables on marital status statistics combine data on
the widowed and divorced. The 1950 census was the first
to report marital status in the census tract statistics, but
the widowed and divorced are combined into one category.
In volume 1, table 56 has data on the number and percentage of persons divorced by age and sex for each state
and census year since 1890. Table 57 contains data on
divorced persons by sex, race, age groups, residence,
and cities.

6-46   _____. CENSUS OF POPULATION: 1960. THE EIGHTEENTH
DECENNIAL CENSUS OF THE UNITED STATES. Vol. 1. CHARAC-
TERISTICS OF THE POPULATION. 57 parts. Vol. 2. SUBJECT
REPORTS. 33 pts. Washington, D.C.: Government Printing Office,
1961-63. Illus. Maps. Tables. C3.223/10:960/v.1/pts. 1-57.
C3.223/10:960/v.2/pts. 1A-8C.

The tables in the 1960 census are arranged similarly to
those of the 1970 census, but with less detail. Refer to
part B, section 1, of this chapter.

6-47   _____. U.S. CENSUSES OF POPULATION AND HOUSING:
1960. CENSUS TRACTS: FINAL REPORT. 180 parts. Washington,
D.C.: Government Printing Office, 1961-62. Maps. Tables. C3.
224/11:960/pts. 1-180.

Information on divorced and separated persons is recorded
for both census tracts and city blocks of the 180 Standard
Metropolitan Statistical Areas. Other tables are similar
to those of the 1970 Census. Refer to part B, section 1,
of this chapter.

Helpful guides to the large body of published materials, not including computerized data files, from these earlier censuses are the following two sources:

6-48   U.S. Bureau of the Census. Data User Service Office. Statistical
Compendia Staff. BUREAU OF THE CENSUS CATALOG OF PUBLICA-
TIONS: 1790-1972. Washington, D.C.: Government Printing
Office, 1974. Two sections with separate indexes: 320 p. and
591 p. C56.222/2-2:790-972.

This catalog of all printed materials issued by the Bureau
of the Census, since its organization through 1972, is
divided into two parts. Part 1 lists and describes information on the publications of the nineteen earlier censuses of population. The second part lists and describes
other Bureau of the Census publications. No computerized
data files are listed. This work is based on the annual
cumulations of the CATALOG OF UNITED STATES CEN-
SUS PUBLICATIONS, prepared by Henry Dubester, and

published by the Bureau of the Census in 1950.

6-49   U.S. Bureau of the Census.   Library of Congress.   Census Library
         Project.   STATE CENSUSES: AN ANNOTATED BIBLIOGRAPHY OF
         CENSUSES OF POPULATION TAKEN AFTER THE YEAR 1790 BY
         STATES AND TERRITORIES OF THE UNITED STATES.   Prepared by
         Henry J. Dubester.   Washington, D.C.:   Government Printing Office,
         1948.   v, 73 p.

         This booklet lists and describes the known state censuses,
         taken mostly in the nineteenth century, with locations
         indicated for the materials still in existence.   Except in
         a few instances, there is no indication whether or not
         divorce was one of the categories of marital status in the
         state censuses which asked questions on marital status.
         Only by examining the original census reports or the ar-
         chival records can the value of these documents be assured
         as sources of historical statistics on divorce.

3. Census Statistics in Computer Data Bases

With the advent of the electronic computer and more efficient methods of
handling data, the possibility for the researcher to handle large amounts of
data is now a reality.   Consequently, the computerized data bases of census
surveys, or samples from these data, can be analyzed in new ways by researchers in their own specific investigations.

Beginning with the 1960 census, user samples of the state data, as well as of
the national data, were made available, both on tape and on punched cards.
The 1960 CENSUS OF POPULATION AND HOUSING has samples of 0.1 percent,
0.01 percent and 0.001 percent of population with the personal identifications
removed.   Since not all of the possible analyses of the data are made, this
has allowed researchers to make additional tabulations that were not printed in
the published reports.

The 1970 census also has a user sample with the same proportions of the population represented.   In addition, data from six other samples or counts were made
available for purchase by interested parties.   These counts have the following
characteristics:

         First count--Contains data on age, sex, race, marital
         status, relation to household head and family type.   The
         data covers states, counties, and minor civil divisions.
         The coverage is 100 percent.

         Second count--This covers the same characteristics as
         above but includes more social detail and also includes
         census tract enumerations.   This coverage is 100 percent.

Third count--Contains about the same social data as the
first count but includes data for each city block in urbanized areas, in addition to the other civil areas.

Fourth count--These tapes contain social data from the
5 percent, 15 percent, and 20 percent census samples.
Data are available for census tracts, minor civil divisions, and counties, as well as Standard Metropolitan
Statistical Areas and states. The questions asked in the
samples are more extensive than in the full census.

Fifth count--These summary tapes contain housing and
population data for ZIP Code areas.

Sixth count--This summary contains detailed tabulations
for population and housing for states, Standard Metropolitan Statistical Areas, and larger cities and nonmetropolitan counties of 50,000 or more population taken from
the ˙5 percent, 15 percent, and 20 percent samples.

6-50   Additional technical information on these tapes can be found in the
        1970 CENSUS USERS GUIDE, published by the Bureau of the Census
        in 1970. (C3.6/2:C/33/2). For a description of computerized data
        files and special tabulations compiled by the U.S. Bureau of the
        Census for 1958 to 1968, consult its GUIDE TO CENSUS BUREAU
        DATA FILES AND SPECIAL TABULATIONS, 1969 (C3.6/2:D26).

C. VITAL STATISTICS: PUBLISHED AND COMPUTER STORED

Vital statistics, unlike census statistics, are reports of events as they occur
rather than of data collected at a certain point in time. The vital statistics
on divorce contain information about persons at the time when the divorce decree became final. Governments collect and report these data regularly.

1. Entire United States

The federal government collects monthly reports of the divorce statistics from
each state which maintains a central office for collecting vital statistics.
Where the divorce statistics are not collected in a central office, data are
sometimes collected directly from the counties. Where the data are incomplete
for some states, estimates are made when possible. The U.S. vital statistics
(item 6-54) are published monthly and annually as provisional reports, followed
much later by annual final reports. The characteristics of these reports and
computer data bases are described below.

6-51   U.S. Bureau of the Census. MARRIAGE AND DIVORCE, 1867-1906.
        2 vols. Washington, D.C.: Government Printing Office, 1908-9.
        Maps. Charts. Tables.

        The most comprehensive statistical study of divorce in the

United States in the late nineteenth century, these volumes
are the result of extensive studies of the local marriage
and divorce records of nearly every county in the United
States for two twenty-year periods. Part 1 contains a
comprehensive analysis of the data on divorce, showing
rates, legal causes, residence, alimony, duration of the
marriage, children involved, and the person to whom the
divorce was granted. It also contains a brief history of
the development of the divorce laws in the United States,
the proposed Uniform Divorce Law of 1906, and a digest
of the divorce laws of each state. Statistics on divorce
in Canada, Great Britain, and nineteen other countries
are included for the period 1867-1906. A digest of Canadian and British laws is presented. Part 2 contains nineteen extensive tables on divorce in the states for the
period 1867-1906.

6-52   _____. MARRIAGE AND DIVORCE, 1916. Washington, D.C.:
Government Printing Office, 1919. 47 p. Tables.

Comparative data on divorce for 1896, 1906, and 1916
are provided by this publication. It also contains divorce
data for 1916 by states, counties, party to whom the divorce was granted, grounds for divorce, whether contested
or not, alimony granted, and by the number of children
involved.

6-53   _____. MARRIAGE AND DIVORCE . . . 1922-32. 11 vols.
Washington, D.C.: Government Printing Office, 1925-34. Tables.

A series of annual reports similar to, but less detailed
than, the 1867-1906 report (item 6-51), this set contains
data on the number of divorces, legal causes, duration of
the marriage, contested cases, person to whom the divorce
was granted, number of children involved in the divorce,
and annulments for the period from 1922 to 1932. Data are
given for states, counties, and regions.

6-54   U.S. National Center for Health Statistics. MONTHLY VITAL
STATISTICS REPORT. Washington, D.C.: Government Printing Office, 1952-- . Graphs. Tables. Monthly. HE20.6009:vol. & no.

This publication reports the provisional number of divorces
occurring in nearly all of the states for the month, as well
as the monthly cumulation. Data for the same month from
the previous year are also included. There is a time lag of
approximately three months in the publication of the data.
An annual provisional summary report is issued in March of
each year, with a final divorce summary report issued several years later. This monthly report is the best current

source of U.S. divorce statistics.

6-55   _____. STANDARDIZED MICRO-DATA TAPE TRANSCRIPTS. Washington, D.C.: Government Printing Office, 1976. 30 p. HE20. 6202:T68.

Divorce data based on information from samples of divorce certificates from the twenty-nine states in the Divorce Registration Area are now available for the years 1968 to 1973. A 25 percent sample of the divorce certificates has been put on tape. This publication describes the information stored on these tapes. Information on divorce is supplied for the following variables:

Year
Age at decree and at marriage for: husband and wife
Date of birth for (month/year): husband and wife
Age at separation* for 1970-73: husband and wife
Date of marriage (month/year)
Date of separation (month/year) (1970-73)
Education* of: husband and wife (1970-73)
Month of divorce
Number of children under eighteen
Number of this marriage for: husband and wife
Number of previous marriages ended by death* (1970-73): husband and wife
Number of previous marriages ended by divorce* (1970-73): husband and wife
Race of: husband (three categories) and wife (three categories)
State of marriage (1972-73)
State of divorce
Total number of living children* (1970-73)
*Applicable only for those states having information on the certificate.

6-56   _____. VITAL AND HEALTH STATISTICS. Series 1-22. Washington, D.C.: Government Printing Office, 1963-- . Graphs. Maps. Tables. Irregular.

Preceded by the series VITAL STATISTICS--SPECIAL REPORTS (item 6-58), this series includes various special studies of vital statistics which include divorce statistics. Refer to item 6-116 and following for descriptions of the contents of the relevant numbered bulletins.

6-57   _____. VITAL STATISTICS OF THE UNITED STATES, 1937--.

Washington, D.C.: Government Printing Office, 1939-- . Maps.
Tables. 3 vols. annually. HE20.6210:yr./v.

> Some divorce statistics have been reported in this publica-
> tion since 1946. More extensive reporting of information
> on divorce began in 1950. A separate volume, volume
> 3, for marriage and divorce statistics has been published
> since 1960. Statistics on divorce are reported for each
> state and most counties in the United States. These data
> are collected from Divorce Registration Areas, which may
> be cooperating states, the District of Columbia, or terri-
> tories, that report divorce statistics according to federal
> standards. Statistics for the Virgin Islands and Puerto
> Rico are included in some volumes. The technical ap-
> pendix includes a facsimile of the divorce certificate
> used by each DRA, a map showing the DRAs and non-
> DRA areas, the dates when central files on divorce sta-
> tistics were established throughout the country, as well
> as special statistical information appearing on the divorce
> records of some DRAs. Data conforming to federal stan-
> dards are analyzed by race, sex, the number of children
> affected by divorce, duration of the marriage, age of the
> husband and the wife at the time of the marriage and at
> the time of the divorce, and the number of previous mar-
> riages. There is a four-year time lag in publication of
> the data, which reduces the usefulness of this publication.
> However, this is a basic authoritative source of divorce
> vital statistics.

6-58   U.S. National Office of Vital Statistics. VITAL STATISTICS--
        SPECIAL REPORTS. Vol. 1, nos. 1-53. Washington, D.C.: Gov-
        ernment Printing Office, 1936-63. FS2.109:vols.

> A supplementary source of divorce vital statistics for
> the period of publication, this series has been succeeded
> by VITAL AND HEALTH STATISTICS (item 6-56). See
> pages 56-58 in 100 YEARS OF MARRIAGE AND DIVORCE
> STATISTICS--UNITED STATES, 1867-1967 (item 6-154) for
> a detailed list of the issues of VITAL STATISTICS--
> SPECIAL REPORTS that contain divorce statistics.

2. Individual States, Puerto Rico, and the Virgin Islands

Most states publish vital statistics reports which include information on divorce.
There are several advantages in using these state reports. First, they are often
published in advance of the federal vital statistics, and, second, they often
contain information not tabulated in the federal reports. The main disadvantage
in using the state vital statistics reports is that each state analyzes and tabulates
its data somewhat differently from the others, and thus comparable statistics are
not available for all states. Additionally, it is difficult to find complete col-

lections of state vital statistics reports.

Some states publish monthly or quarterly vital statistics reports in addition to their annual reports. Nearly all of these reports may be obtained free of charge from the issuing agencies. Special tabulations of data are occasionally available from some state vital statistics bureaus.

The divorce information published in the state vital statistics reports are described here in detail because it is extremely difficult for any one library, let alone for one individual, to secure a collection of current issues for all of the states. This may be because some have ceased publication indefinitely, or the issuing agency may itself have changed, or it may have changed location, or the agency may not be careful in fulfilling commitments for standing orders, or because the publication schedules are irregular. Because of the difficulty for the researcher to examine all of these current issues, the authors have made the effort to secure and examine the latest issue for each state and describe its contents in regard to divorce statistics. The researcher can thus ascertain whether a particular state report contains the information that he needs. The statistical tabulations for each state tend to be uniform in format from year to year, and are likely to present more data rather than fewer as the years go by.

The state vital statistics reports are often difficult to locate in libraries by means of a subject approach, especially when they are not fully cataloged. When these are fully cataloged, the subject heading is likely to be similar to the following: "Ohio--Statistics, Vital." It is easier to locate reports in libraries when the title or the issuing agency is known.

In the listing which follows, complete bibliographic detail in regard to earlier issues and files of these works cannot be given because titles and agencies vary so much through the years, and runs are often interrupted. Nor has any comprehensive retrospective list of these works been found. For each state, in the citations that follow, the current cover title of its report is given, as well as the state government agency presently responsible for publication of the report, with the address of the agency in case the researcher wishes to order the publication or acquire information on the availability of previous reports. The date of the latest issue examined appears in parentheses.

To keep up with any changes in these state vital statistics publications or new issues as they appear, as well as any special state reports on divorce statistics, consult periodically the MONTHLY CHECKLIST OF STATE PUBLICATIONS (item 8-138). It should be remembered however that this is a listing of publications received at the Library of Congress from the states, and that the participation of the various states is uneven.

ALABAMA

6-59   ALABAMA'S VITAL EVENTS. Division of Vital Statistics, Alabama Department of Health, State Office Building, Montgomery, Ala.

36104. Annual. Charts. Graphs. Maps. Tables. Appendix.
(1974) Fee charged.

The Alabama report contains the following data on divorce:
(1) marriages by previous marital status of the bride and
groom, (2) marriages by age and previous marital status
of the bride and groom, (3) number and rates of divorce
and annulments since 1965, (4) divorces and annulments
by county, (5) duration of marriage by number of children
under eighteen years of age, (6) divorces and annulments
by duration of the marriage, (7) divorces by the month of
occurrence, (8) divorces and annulments by party to whom
granted, and (9) divorces and annulments by legal grounds
for the decree. There is a time lag of over two years
prior to publication of the data.

ALASKA

6-60   ALASKA'S VITAL STATISTICS. Department of Health and Social
Services, Division of Public Health, Health Information System, Pouch
H-06C, Juneau, Alaska 99811. Annual. Graphs. Maps. Tables.
(1974)

The divorce data in this report are: (1) distribution of
marriages by race of the groom and by race of the bride,
(2) distribution of divorces by number of children under
eighteen years, and (3) distribution of divorces by place
of marriage. There is an eighteen-month time lag prior
to publication of the data.

ARIZONA

6-61   ARIZONA VITAL AND HEALTH STATISTICS REPORT. Management
Information Systems, Arizona Department of Health, 1740 West Adams
Street, Room 103, Phoenix, Ariz. 85007. Irregular. Tables. Map.
Graphs. (1974)

The vital statistics summary has information on: (1) the
number of divorces and annulments by month of occurrence,
and (2) divorces and annulments by the county of occurrence. There is a two- to three-year time lag prior to
publication of the statistics.

ARKANSAS

6-62   ARKANSAS VITAL STATISTICS. Arkansas Department of Health,
Division of Health Statistics, 4815 West Markham Street, Little Rock,
Ark. 72201. Annual. Tables. (1973-74)

Arkansas data included in this document are: (1) the
number of divorces and annulments for the state for each
year of the biennium, (2) the crude divorce rate for the

state for 1973–74, (3) the number of divorces and annulments for each county, (4) the divorce rates for each
county, and (5) divorce rates by race (incomplete). There
is a nine-month time lag prior to publication of the data.

CALIFORNIA

6-63   VITAL STATISTICS OF CALIFORNIA. State Department of Health,
714–744 P Street, Sacramento, Calif. 95814. Annual. Graphs.
Tables. Maps. Technical appendix. (1971)

This report contains the following information on divorce:
(1) the number of petitions for dissolution of marriage,
nullity, and legal separations by county, and (2) the
number of final decrees for dissolution of marriage, nullity and legal separations by county. The appendix contains facsimile copies of the certificate of registry of a
final decree of dissolution of marriage, of judgment of
nullity, and of legal separation. There is a five-year
time lag prior to publication of the data.

COLORADO

6-64   ANNUAL REPORT OF VITAL STATISTICS OF COLORADO. Colorado
Department of Health, Division of Administrative Services, Records
and Statistics Section, 4210 East 11th Avenue, Denver, Colo. 80220.
Annual. Map. Tables. (1973)

The only table on divorce contains the number and rate
of dissolution of marriage by county of occurrence and
for the entire state. There is a two-year time lag prior
to publication of the data.

CONNECTICUT

6-65   REGISTRATION REPORT OF BIRTHS, MARRIAGES, DIVORCES AND
DEATHS. Public Health Statistics Section, Department of Health, 79
Elm Street, Hartford, Conn. 06115. Annual. Tables. (1973) Fee
charged.

The following tables on divorce are contained in this
publication: (1) divorces granted, by the duration of
the marriage, (2) divorces by the number of children
under twenty-one years of age, (3) the number of divorces and the divorce rate since 1960, (4) the previous
marital status of the bride and groom by age, (5) the
previous marital status of the bride and groom, and (6)
divorces and annulments by grounds and by county and
sex. There is an eighteen-month time lag prior to publication of the data.

DELAWARE

6-66   ANNUAL REPORT. Delaware State Board of Health, Board of Vital
       Statistics, Department of Health and Social Services, Jesse S. Cooper
       Memorial Building, Dover, Del. 19901. (1969)

> No vital statistics have been published for Delaware
> since 1970. The last report contained the following
> divorce information: (1) the number of divorces and
> annulments by month of occurrence for the previous
> year, and (2) the number of divorces and annulments
> by county for the previous year.

DISTRICT OF COLUMBIA

6-67   VITAL STATISTICS SUMMARY. Department of Human Resources,
       1875 Connecticut Avenue, Washington, D.C. 20009. Annual.
       Charts. Map. Tables. (1973)

> This report to date does not include divorce data for
> the District of Columbia. There is a two-year time
> lag prior to publication of the data.

FLORIDA

6-68   FLORIDA VITAL STATISTICS. Department of Health and Rehabilita-
       tion Services, Public Health Statistics Section, P.O. Box 210, Jack-
       sonville, Fla. 32201. Annual. Map. Graphs. Tables. (1974)

> The vital statistics report of Florida includes the following
> information on divorce: (1) the number of divorces and
> rates for the past ten years, (2) a chart of the crude di-
> vorce rates since 1925, and (3) divorces and annulments
> by month and county. There is a one-year time lag prior
> to publication of the data.

GEORGIA

6-69   GEORGIA VITAL AND HEALTH STATISTICS. Health Services Re-
       search and Statistics, Division of Physical Health--DHR, Room 356-S,
       47 Trinity Avenue., S.W., Atlanta, Ga. 30334. Annual. Charts.
       Graphs. Maps. Tables. (1974)

> This state report contains the following information: (1)
> a chart on the divorce rates for the past twenty years,
> (2) the number and rate of divorces and annulments for
> the past twenty years, (3) divorces by month of occur-
> rence, (4) divorces by grounds for which divorces were
> granted, (5) divorces by duration of the marriage for the
> past five years, (6) divorces by the age of the husband
> and wife, and (7) divorces and annulments by county of
> occurrence. There is a fifteen-month time lag prior to

publication of the data.

HAWAII

6-70   STATISTICAL SUPPLEMENT. Health Education Office, Department
        of Health, P.O. Box 3378, Honolulu, Hawaii 96801. Annual.
        Graphs. Tables. (1974)

        The Hawaii annual report provides the following divorce
        statistics: (1) previous marital status of the bride and
        groom by age groups, (2) previous marital status of the
        groom by the previous marital status of the bride, (3)
        divorces and annulments by place and month of occur-
        rence, (4) divorces and annulments by the number of
        children under age eighteen, (5) divorces and annul-
        ments by race and age of the husband, (6) divorces
        and annulments by the age of the wife, (7) divorces
        and annulments by race of the husband and wife,
        (8) divorces and annulments by legal grounds and dura-
        tion of the marriage, (9) divorces and annulments by
        education of husband and wife, (10) divorces and an-
        nulments by residence of husband and of the wife, and
        (11) divorces and annulments by age of husband and of
        wife. There is a nine-month time lag prior to publica-
        tion of the data.

IDAHO

6-71   ANNUAL SUMMARY OF VITAL STATISTICS. Bureau of Vital Sta-
        tistics, Department of Health and Welfare, Statehouse, Boise, Idaho
        83720. Annual. Graphs. Maps. Tables. Appendix. (1974)

        The tables in this report are: (1) decennial table of
        divorces granted by region and county of occurrence,
        (2) number of children affected by divorce, (3) bi-
        ennial table showing grounds for divorces and annul-
        ments, (4) divorces and annulments granted by dura-
        tion of marriage, and (5) crude divorce rates by region
        and county. There is a two-year time lag prior to pub-
        lication of the data.

ILLINOIS

6-72   VITAL STATISTICS OF ILLINOIS. State Center for Health Statistics,
        Illinois Department of Public Health, 525 West Jefferson Street,
        Springfield, Ill. 62761. Annual. Map. Tables. (1974)

        The divorce data included in this document are:
        (1) marital status of the bride and groom at the time
        of the marriage, (2) divorces and annulments by dura-
        tion of the marriage, (3) number of divorces and annul-
        ments and rates since 1958, (4) divorces by age of the

husband and wife, and (5) number of previous marriages
for the bride and groom. There is a one-year time lag
prior to publication of the data.

INDIANA

6-73   INDIANA VITAL STATISTICS. Public Health Statistics, Indiana State
Board of Health, 1330 West Michigan Street, Indianapolis, Ind.
46206. Annual. Tables. (1974)

No divorce data are contained in this report to date.
There is a two-year time lag prior to the publication
of the data.

IOWA

6-74   IOWA DETAILED REPORT OF VITAL STATISTICS. Division of Records
and Statistics, Iowa State Department of Health, Des Moines, Iowa.
50319. Annual. Tables. Appendix. (1974)

The tables pertaining to divorce in this report are:
(1) divorces by month of occurrence, (2) divorces by
year of occurrence since 1910, (3) divorce rates since
1910, (4) number of divorces and the crude divorce rate
by county of occurrence, (5) number of divorces and the
crude divorce rate for cities, (6) previous marital status
of brides and grooms, (7) divorces by age and by color
of husbands and wives, (8) divorces by age by primary
marriage and remainder by husband and wife, (9) divorces
by duration of marriage, by color, and (10) number of
children under eighteen years affected by divorce, by
color.

6-75   IOWA SUMMARY OF VITAL STATISTICS. Division of Records and
Statistics, Iowa State Department of Health, Des Moines, Iowa
50319. Annual. Charts. Tables. Appendix. (1974)

This publication contains decennial charts of divorce
rates, marriage and divorce rates over a thirty-year
period, the percentage distribution of previous marital
status of brides and grooms, quinquennial percentage
distribution of all divorces by husband and wife for
selected age groups, and a quinquennial chart of divorces with selected durations as percent of all divorces.
This report also contains the following tables: (1) decennial table of the number of divorces and the crude
divorce rate for the state, (2) the number of divorces
and the crude divorce rate by county of occurrence,
(3) quinquennial table of previous marital status of brides
and grooms, (4) percentage distribution of all divorces
by age of husband and wife for the past five years, and

(5) percentage distribution of all divorces by duration
of marriage, for the past five years. There is a one-
year time lag prior to publication of the data.

KANSAS

6-76   ANNUAL SUMMARY OF VITAL STATISTICS OF KANSAS. Bureau of
Registration and Health Statistics, Kansas State Department of Health
and Environment, Topeka, Kans. 66620. Annual. Charts. Graphs.
Map. Tables. (1974)

Graphs contained in this report are: (1) premarital status
of brides and grooms, (2) percentage distribution of annulments by age groups and sex, five-year average, (3) percentage distribution of divorces by age groups and sex,
five-year average, and (4) percentage distribution of divorces and annulments by number of children affected and
by duration of marriage in years. The following tables
are included in this report: (1) divorces and annulments
by the duration of the marriage in years, (2) legal grounds
for divorces and annulments by plaintiff and to whom
granted, and (3) divorces and annulments by number and
rate for each county and for the state. There is a one-
year time lag prior to publication of the data.

KENTUCKY

6-77   KENTUCKY VITAL STATISTICS REPORT. Research and Special Proj-
ects, 275 East Main Street, 2d Floor, Room 241, Health Services
Building, Frankfort, Ky. 40601. Annual. Charts. Map. Graphs.
Tables. (1973)

This publication contains the number and the rate of divorces by county and by race. There is an eighteen-
month time lag prior to publication of the data.

LOUISIANA

6-78   VITAL STATISTICS OF LOUISIANA. Office of Public Health Statistics, Louisiana Health and Human Resources Administration, Division
of Health, P.O. Box 60630, New Orleans, La. 70160. Annual.
Charts. Maps. Pictures. Tables. (1973)

The data included in this report are: (1) divorces and
annulments granted by parish of occurrence (data are incomplete for some parishes), and (2) previous marital status
of groom by race. There is an eighteen-month time lag
prior to publication of the data.

MAINE

6-79   MAINE VITAL STATISTICS. Division of Research and Vital Records,

Department of Human Services, State House, Augusta, Maine 04330.
Annual. Irregular. Tables. (1975)

> This report contains the following tables on divorce:
> (1) number of divorces every fifth year, 1900-1935,
> and annually since 1935, (2) divorces and annulments
> by county of occurrence, (3) divorces and annulments
> by legal grounds for decree and by plaintiff, (4) divorces
> and annulments by number of children reported under eigh-
> teen years of age, (5) divorces and annulments by dura-
> tion of marriage in years, (6) previous marital status of
> bride and groom by age, and (7) previous marital status
> of bride by previous marital status of the groom. There
> is a fifteen-month time lag prior to publication of the
> data.

MARYLAND

6-80   ANNUAL VITAL STATISTICS REPORT. Maryland Center for Health
Statistics, Department of Health and Mental Hygiene, 201 West Pres-
ton Street, Baltimore, Md. 21201. Annual. Graphs. Tables.
(1973)

> The tables presented in this annual report are: (1) pre-
> vious marital status of grooms by age, (2) previous marital
> status of brides by residence status of the bride and groom,
> (3) previous marital status of groom by residence of bride
> and groom, (4) previous marital status of bride and groom
> by type of marital ceremony, (5) divorces and annulments
> by legal grounds for decree, region and political sub-
> division of occurrence, (6) divorces and annulments by
> party to whom decree was granted, (7) divorces and an-
> nulments by place where marriage was performed, (8) di-
> vorces and annulments by the age of the husband and wife
> at the time of decree, (9) divorces and annulments by race
> of husband and wife, (10) divorces and annulments by num-
> ber of children under eighteen years of age, and by dura-
> tion of marriage in years, and (11) divorces and annul-
> ments by number of marriages of husbands and number of
> marriages of wives. In addition, there is a graph showing
> the Maryland and the U.S. divorce rate from 1940 to the
> present time. There is a two-year time lag prior to pub-
> lication of the data.

MASSACHUSETTS

6-81   ANNUAL REPORT OF VITAL STATISTICS OF MASSACHUSETTS.
Vital Events Program, Lemuel Shattuck Hospital, 11th Floor, 170 Mor-
ton Street, Jamaica Plain, Mass. 02130. Annual. Graphs. Tables.
(1974)

> The divorce data contained in this document are: (1) the

number of divorces and annulments granted by county and
the percent of change from the previous year, and
(2) the number of divorces since 1969 and the percent
of annual increase. The report states that plans are under
way to include more information on divorce in future issues
of the report. There is a one-year time lag prior to publication of the data.

MICHIGAN

6-82   MICHIGAN HEALTH STATISTICS. Office of Vital and Health Statistics, Michigan Department of Public Health, 3500 North Logan
Street, Lansing, Mich. 48914. Annual. Charts. Maps. Fac-
similes. Tables. Appendix. (1973)

Factual information on divorce reported in this bulletin
consists of: (1) number and rates of divorce for selected
years since 1920, (2) divorces and annulments by duration
of the marriage, current year and ten-years age, (3) number of divorces and annulments by number of children,
(4) divorces and annulments by legal grounds for decrees,
(5) divorces granted by county of residence, and (6) divorce rates by county. This report contains graphs of
changes in the divorce rate since 1900, and of divorces
and annulments by legal grounds. There is a two-year
time lag prior to publication of the data.

MINNESOTA

6-83   MINNESOTA HEALTH STATISTICS. Minnesota Department of Health,
Section of Health Statistics, 717 Delaware Street S.E., Minneapolis,
Minn. 55440. Annual. Map. Tables. (1973)

This vital statistics report contains the following tables on
divorce: (1) divorces and annulments by county of occurrence, and (2) divorces and annulments by age of the
husband and wife. There is a fifteen-month time lag
prior to publication of the data.

MISSISSIPPI

6-84   VITAL STATISTICS, MISSISSIPPI. Public Health Statistics, State
Board of Health, P.O. Box 1700, Jackson, Miss. 39205. (1970)

The last report was issued in 1970. It contained the
following divorce data: (1) number of divorces and rates
for the past ten years by race, (2) number of divorces
and percentage distribution by cause and race, (3) number
of divorces and percentage distribution by number of minor
children and race, (4) number of divorces and percentage
distribution by number of years married and race, (5) number of divorces and rates by county and race, (6) number

of divorces by year and by race since 1926, and (7) previous marital status of brides and grooms by race. There is a three-year time lag prior to publication of the data.

MISSOURI

6-85   MISSOURI VITAL STATISTICS. Missouri Center for Health Statistics, Missouri Division of Health, Broadway State Office Building, P.O. Box 570, Jefferson City, Mo. 65101. Annual. Graphs. Map. Tables. (1974)

Divorce statistics included in this report are: (1) marital status for selected age groups, for both bride and groom, (2) marital status of the bride by the marital status of the groom, (3) divorces and legal separations by the number of previous marriages for the husband and wife, (4) divorces and legal separations by the duration of the marriage, (5) divorces and legal separations by the number of children affected, (6) divorces and legal separations by maintenance and settlement, (7) divorces and legal separations by legal grounds for the decree, (8) divorces and legal separations by color for husband and wife, (9) divorces and legal separation by number of cases contested, and (10) number of divorces and divorce rate for counties. There is an eighteen-month time lag prior to publication of the data.

MONTANA

6-86   MONTANA VITAL STATISTICS. Bureau of Records and Statistics, Montana Department of Health and Environmental Sciences, Capitol Station, Helena, Mont. 59601. Annual. Graphs. Map. Tables. (1975)

The Montana report contains the following data on divorce: (1) the number of divorces and annulments by county, (2) number and rates of divorces and annulments since 1944, (3) marriages by age and previous marital status of the bride and groom, (4) divorces and annulments by legal grounds for the decree, (5) divorces and annulments by the age of the husband and the age of the wife, (6) divorces and annulments by the age of the mother and the number of children under eighteen years, and (7) number of previous abortions of divorced women. A list of additional unpublished tabulations on divorce and annulment is included in this report. There is a one-year time lag prior to publication of the data.

NEBRASKA

6-87   STATISTICAL REPORT. Bureau of Vital Statistics, Division of Health

Data and Statistical Research, Department of Health, Lincoln Building, 1003 O Street, Lincoln, Nebr. 68508. Annual. Graphs. Maps. Tables. (1974)

The demographic data on divorce in this publication are: (1) the number of divorces and divorce rates since 1925, (2) the number of divorces and annulments by month for the current year, (3) a graph of marriage and divorce rates since 1925, (4) previous marital status of the bride and groom, (5) number and rates of divorce by county, (6) divorces by the age of the husband and the wife, (7) divorces by the race of the husband and the wife, (8) number of children affected by divorce, (9) divorces by the duration of the marriage in years, and (10) annulments by cause and county. There is a nine-month time lag prior to publication of the data.

NEVADA

6-88   VITAL STATISTICS OF NEVADA. Nevada State Division of Health, Section of Vital Statistics, 505 East King Street, Carson City, Nev. 89710. Annual. Graphs. Tables. (1974)

This report contains a graph on the Nevada divorce rates since 1945. This vital statistics report, which began in 1974, will be published annually.

NEW HAMPSHIRE

6-89   NEW HAMPSHIRE VITAL STATISTICS. Bureau of Vital Statistics, New Hampshire State Department of Health, 60 South Spring Street, Concord, N.H. 03301. Annual. Graphs. Maps. Tables. (1973)

The following statistics are reported in this work: (1) the number of divorces each year since 1884, (2) the crude divorce rate and the ratio of marriages to divorces annually since 1884, (3) previous marital status of the bride by the previous marital status of the groom, (4) divorces, legal separations, annulments, and separate maintenance by county, cause, and sex of plaintiff, (5) divorces, legal separations, annulments, and separate maintenances by county of occurrence and the number of minor children affected, and (6) divorces, legal separations, and annulments by duration of the marriage in years. There is a two-year time lag prior to publication of the data.

NEW JERSEY

6-90   NEW JERSEY HEALTH STATISTICS. Public Health Statistics Program, State Department of Health, P.O. Box 1540, Trenton, N.J. 08625. Annual. Tables. Appendix. (1974)

There are no statistics on divorce in this report. One
table contains references to the previous marital status of
husband and wife. There is a one-year time lag prior to
publication of the data.

NEW MEXICO

6-91   NEW MEXICO SELECTED HEALTH STATISTICS. State Health Agency,
Health and Social Services Department, P.O. Box 2348, Santa Fe,
N.Mex. 87503. Map. Tables. Graphs. (1975)

The 1975 edition contained nonagency collected data on
divorce for each county for 1974 and 1975. These data
did not agree with the data reported in the U.S. vital
statistics for 1974. There is about a one-year time lag
for publication of this data.

NEW YORK

6-92   VITAL STATISTICS OF NEW YORK STATE. New York State Depart-
ment of Health, Office of Biostatistics, Tower Building, Empire State
Plaza, Albany, N.Y. 12237. Annual. Charts. Graphs. Maps.
Tables. (1974)

The tables contained in this report are: (1) divorces by
duration of the marriage and type of dissolution, and
(2) divorces by county of occurrence and type of decree
for the past three years. There is a fifteen-month time
lag prior to publication of the data.

NORTH CAROLINA

6-93   NORTH CAROLINA VITAL STATISTICS, POPULATION, BIRTHS,
DEATHS, MARRIAGES, DIVORCES. Public Health Statistics Branch,
North Carolina Division of Health Services, P.O. Box 2091, Raleigh,
N.C. 27602.

This report contains statistics on the number of divorces as
well as the rates and five-year average rates for current
years, by counties, regions, and for the state. There is
a six-month time lag prior to publication of the data.

NORTH DAKOTA

6-94   REPORT. North Dakota State Department of Health. Division of
Vital Statistics, State Capitol, Bismarck, N.Dak. 58501. Annual.
Charts. Maps. Tables. (1972-73)

The North Dakota report includes the following data:
(1) the number of divorces and annulments by the duration
of marriage and the number of children present, (2) the
number of divorces by county, and (3) the number of di-

vorces and the number of children affected by divorce, 1950-72. There is a two-year time lag prior to publication of the data.

OHIO

6-95   VITAL STATISTICS. State of Ohio, Department of Health, P.O. Box 118, Columbus, Ohio 43216. Attention: Statistical Analysis Unit. Annual. Charts. Tables. (1974)

Divorce tables included in this state report are: (1) divorces and annulments by legal grounds for the decree, (2) divorces and annulments by the number of children under eighteen years of age, (3) divorces and annulments by duration of the marriage, (4) number and rates of divorces and annulments since 1950, and (5) divorces and annulments by county and by month. There is a fifteen-month time lag prior to publication of the data.

OKLAHOMA

6-96   OKLAHOMA HEALTH STATISTICS. Oklahoma State Department of Health, Public Health Statistics Division, N.E. 10th and Stonewall, P.O. Box 53551, Oklahoma City, Okla. 73105. Annual. Graphs. Maps. Tables. Appendix. (1974)

This report contains only the number and rate of divorces and annulments by county.

OREGON

6-97   ANNUAL VITAL STATISTICS REPORT. Oregon State Health Division, Vital Statistics Section, P.O. Box 231, Portland, Oreg. 97207. Annual. Graphs. Tables. (1974). Fee charged.

This summary of vital events contains the following data: (1) the ratio of divorces to marriages performed in state and out of state for selected years, (2) the percentage of marriages by previous marital status for selected years, (3) percentage of divorces during the first five years of marriage, by order of marriage, (4) number and rate of divorces annually since 1935, (5) number and rate of divorces by county, (6) ratio of divorces to marriages by county, (7) previous marital status of the groom by age, (8) previous marital status of the bride by age, (9) number and rates of divorces by month, (10) divorces and annulments by duration of marriage and by order of marriage for husbands and wives, (11) divorces and annulments by age of husband and wife and by order of marriage, (12) number of minor children affected by divorce, (13) divorces and annulments by age of husband and wife, and duration of the marriage, and (14) divorces and annulments by state or region where marriage occurred, by duration of the marriage. There are also graphs on the marriage and divorce rates since 1930, and the number of divorces and children affected since 1950. There is a one-year time lag prior to publication of the data.

PENNSYLVANIA

6-98   MARRIAGE AND DIVORCE STATISTICS. Pennsylvania Department of Health, P.O. Box 90, Harrisburg, Pa. 17120. Annual. Graphs. Tables. (1973)

The divorce data included in this report are: (1) number and rate of divorces by county, (2) previous marital status of the bride by race and type of ceremony, (3) previous marital status of groom by race and type of ceremony, (4) previous marital status by race of bride, (5) previous marital status by race and age of groom, (6) number and rate of divorces and annulments since 1944, (7) divorces and annulments by legal grounds for the decree, (8) divorces and annulments by party granted the decree, (9) divorces and annulments by plaintiff, (10) legal grounds for divorce or annulment by duration of marriage in years, (11) divorces and annulments by age of wife and number of times married, (12) divorces and annulments by age of husband and number of times married, (13) age of wife at time of divorce or annulment by duration of first marriage or remarriage, (14) age of husband at time of divorce or annulment, by duration of first marriage or remarriage, and (15) divorces or annulments distributed according to state where marriage was performed. There are also charts on divorce rates and grounds for divorce. There is a fifteen-month time lag prior to publication of the data.

RHODE ISLAND

6-99   VITAL STATISTICS. Division of Vital Statistics, Rhode Island Department of Health, Davis Street, Room 101, Providence, R.I. 02908. Annual. Charts. Graphs. Map. Tables. (1973)

Information on divorce includes the following tables: (1) number and rates of divorce since 1945, (2) age at marriage and previous marital status of the bride and groom, (3) divorces by age of the wife and by age of the husband, (4) number of previous marriages prior to divorce for husband and wife, (5) divorces by previous marital status and age of husband and wife, (6) divorces of remarried persons by termination of previous marriage for husbands and wives, (7) number of divorces by county and by number of children under eighteen years affected

by divorce, and (8) divorces according to last grade in
school completed, for husbands and wives. The introduction contains information about the legal grounds used for
divorce. There is a fifteen-month time lag prior to publication of the data.

SOUTH CAROLINA

6-100   SOUTH CAROLINA VITAL AND MORBIDITY STATISTICS. Division
of Biostatistics, South Carolina Bureau of Health and Environmental
Control, 2600 Bull Street, Columbia, S.C. 29201. Annual.
Graphs. Map. Tables. Appendix. (1974)

This statistical report contains the following divorce data:
(1) number and rates of divorces and annulments since
1960, (2) divorces and annulments, by number of children
involved by race, for each county, (3) divorces by race
and age, (4) annulments by race and age, (5) divorces
by plaintiff, by legal grounds for the decree for each
county, and (6) divorces and annulments by duration of
the marriage, and by race. The appendix contains a
sample of the divorce or annulment report. There is a
fifteen-month time lag prior to publication of the data.

SOUTH DAKOTA

6-101   SOUTH DAKOTA VITAL STATISTICS. Division of Public Health
Statistics, State Department of Health, Office Building #2, Pierre,
S.Dak. 57501. Annual. Charts. Graphs. Map. Tables. (1974)

This state document has data on divorce as follows:
(1) the number of divorces and the divorce rate since
1906, (2) the number of divorces and the divorce rate
by counties, (3) the number of divorces by month,
(4) previous marital status by age of the bride, and
order of marriage, (5) previous marital status by age of
the groom, and order of marriage, (6) previous marital
status of brides and grooms, (7) previous marital status
of brides and grooms residing in the state, (8) divorces
and annulments by county and to whom granted, (9) divorces and annulments by age of wife and number of
minor children, (10) divorces and annulments by number
of children under eighteen years, (11) divorces and annulments by cause of action and party to whom granted,
(12) divorces and annulments by age of husband and by
age of wife, (13) legal grounds for divorce by duration
of the marriage, (14) legal grounds for annulment by
duration of the marriage, and (15) divorces and annulments by state where marriage occurred and duration of
the marriage. There is an eighteen-month time lag prior
to publication of the data.

TENNESSEE

6-102   TENNESSEE VITAL STATISTICS. Center for Health Statistics, Tennessee Department of Public Health, Cordell Hull Building, Nashville, Tenn. 37219. Annual. Graphs. Map. Tables. (1972)

The Tennessee vital statistics report contains the following divorce data: (1) the number and rates of divorce for the past ten years, and (2) the number and rates of divorce by counties. The introduction contains summary data on the most frequently used grounds for divorce, the duration of the marriage prior to divorce, and the proportion of divorces involving minor children. There is a three-year time lag prior to publication of the data.

TEXAS

6-103   TEXAS VITAL STATISTICS. Texas Department of Health Resources, Texas Department of Health, Austin, Tex. 78756. Annual. Tables. (1973)

One table on divorce is included in this report: divorces by county, sex, and age groups. There is a two-year time lag prior to publication of the data.

UTAH

6-104   VITAL STATISTICS, MARRIAGE AND DIVORCE. Bureau of Health Statistics, Division of Health, 554 South 3d East, Salt Lake City, Utah   84113. Annual. Charts. Tables. (1972)

This very detailed analysis of divorce statistics includes: (1) divorce rates by county, (2) divorces by order of marriage and by median age of wife and husband, 1956–72, (3) number of children involved in divorce, children per divorce, and involved children per 1,000 population under eighteen years, (4) marriages by age and previous marital status of brides and grooms, (5) marriages by education, previous marital status, and race of bride and groom, (6) first marriages and remarriages by previous marital status of the bride and groom, and by type of officiant at the ceremony, (7) divorces and annulments by month and county of occurrence, (8) divorces and annulments occurring in Utah according to state where marriage was performed, (9) divorces by race of wife, and by race of husband, (10) divorces and annulments by duration of the marriage in years, (11) divorces and annulments, by the number of this marriage for the husband and the wife, (12) divorces and annulments by age of the husband and the wife, and the number of times married, (13) divorces by the age of the wife, and by the age of the husband, (14) divorces and annulments by the

order of this marriage, and by the years of education of
the husband and wife, (15) divorce and annulments by the
number of dependent children under eighteen years of age,
and by the number of years of education and marriage
order of the wife, (16) divorces and annulments by the
number of dependent children under eighteen years of age,
and by the number of years of education and the marriage
order for the husband, (17) divorces and annulments by
the religion of the husband and wife by the type of marriage ceremony performed, (18) divorces and annulments
by the legal grounds for the decree, (19) divorces and
annulments by the party to whom the divorce was granted,
and (20) divorces and annulments by the number of dependent children under eighteen years of age. There is
a two-and-one-half-year time lag prior to publication of
the data.

VERMONT

6-105   ANNUAL BULLETIN OF VITAL STATISTICS. Department of Health,
Public Health Statistics, 115 Colchester Avenue, Burlington, Vt.
05401. Annual. Graphs. Tables. (1972-73). Fee charged.

This state publication presents the following information
on divorce: (1) the number and rates of divorce for the
biennia, 1930-31 to 1944-45, (2) the number and rates
of divorce since 1946, (3) the number and rates of divorce by county, (4) plaintiff by county in which the
divorce was granted, (5) number of children under eighteen affected by divorce, by county, (6) duration of the
marriage by plaintiff, (7) duration of the marriage by
number of children under age eighteen years, (8) divorces
and annulments by duration of the marriage and county of
occurrence of the divorce, (9) ground for divorce by county
of occurrence, and (10) divorces by age of the husband
and wife. There is a time lag of over two years prior
to publication of the data.

VIRGINIA

6-106   STATISTICAL ANNUAL REPORT. Virginia State Department of Health,
Bureau of Vital Records and Health Statistics, James Madison Building,
P.O. Box 1000, Richmond, Va. 23208. Annual. Graphs. Maps.
Tables. (1973)

The divorce information in this document is as follows:
(1) divorces and annulments by race and sex, (2) the
number of divorces and annulments by race and number
of children under eighteen years of age, (3) number of
divorces and annulments by grounds for divorce and by
person to whom the divorce was granted, (4) daily average

number of divorces and annulments, (5) number of years of education completed by divorced wives and husbands, (6) number of divorces by county, (7) annual number and rates of divorce since 1954, (8) previous marital status of the groom, by previous marital status of the bride, by the race of the groom, (9) divorces and annulments by month of the decree and by race, (10) divorces and annulments by place of marriage and by race, (11) divorces and annulments by the number of minor children in the family and by race, (12) divorces and annulments by race and by grounds for divorce and by county of occurrence, (13) grounds for divorce by plaintiff, and duration of the marriage, and (14) divorces and annulments by the age of the husband and wife. There is a time lag of over two years prior to publication of the data.

WASHINGTON

6-107   VITAL STATISTICS SUMMARY. Bureau of Vital Statistics, Health Services Division, Department of Social and Health Services, P.O. Box 709, Olympia Airport, Olympia, Wash. 98504. Annual. Graphs. Map. Tables. (1973)

This document contains data on divorce in the following areas: (1) deaths by marital status and sex, (2) divorces by number of children affected and by county, (3) divorces by type of decree and by county of occurrence, (4) divorces and annulments by grounds and to whom granted, and (5) divorces by plaintiff and to whom granted. There is a fifteen-month time lag prior to publication of the data.

WEST VIRGINIA

6-108   PUBLIC HEALTH STATISTICS OF WEST VIRGINIA. Division of Vital Statistics, State Department of Health, 1800 Washington Street, East, Charleston, W. Va. 25305. Annual. Charts. Map. Tables. (1974)

This vital statistics report contains the following information on divorce: (1) marriage by previous marital status of the bride and groom, (2) divorces and annulments by region and county of occurrence, (3) divorces and annulments by age of husband and wife, (4) divorces and annulments by plaintiff and years duration of the marriage, (5) divorces and annulments by the number of children under eighteen years, and (6) divorces and annulments by plaintiff and by age groups. There is a one-year time lag prior to publication of the data.

WISCONSIN

6-109   PUBLIC HEALTH STATISTICS OF WISCONSIN. PART ONE: BIRTHS,
         MARRIAGES, DIVORCES. Bureau of Health Statistics, Section of
         Statistical Services, P.O. Box 309, Madison, Wis. 53701. Annual.
         Graphs. Tables. (1972)

> The following tables contain information on divorce:
> (1) previous marital status by race and age for the bride
> and groom, (2) divorces and annulments, both number and
> rate since 1910, (3) divorces and annulments by county
> for the past five years, (4) divorces, annulments, and
> legal separations granted by county of occurrence, (5) di-
> vorces and annulments by legal ground for the decree,
> (6) divorces by duration of the marriage, (7) percentage
> distribution of divorces by duration of the marriage for
> the past five years, and (8) the number of children under
> eighteen years of age affected by divorce, for the past
> ten years. There is a two-and-one-half-year time lag
> prior to publication of the data.

WYOMING

6-110   WYOMING VITAL STATISTICS. Vital Records Services, Department
         of Health and Social Services, Hathaway Building, Cheyenne, Wyo.
         82001. (1967-70)

> The last vital statistics report published by the state of
> Wyoming contained these data: (1) the number of divorces
> and annulments by the month of occurrence for 1967-70,
> (2) the number of divorces and annulments by county for
> 1967-70, and (3) the number of divorces and annulments
> by month and by county for 1967-70. No future reports
> are planned.

PUERTO RICO

6-111   ANNUAL VITAL STATISTICS REPORT. Division of Demographic
         Registry and Vital Statistics, Department of Health, San Juan, Puerto
         Rico. Annual. Tables. (1967)

> This report contains the number of divorces and the divorce
> rate for the years 1942-67.

VIRGIN ISLANDS

6-112   VITAL STATISTICS. Virgin Islands Department of Health, Charlotte
         Amalie, V.I. Annual. Charts. Tables. (1972). Fee charged.

> The divorce data from this territory includes: (1) the
> previous marital status of the bride and groom, (2) the
> number of divorces by place of the husband and wife,

(3) the number of divorces by the citizenship of the husband and wife, (4) the number of divorces by the ages of
the husband and wife, (5) the number of divorces by the
duration of the marriage, and the number of children under
eighteen years of age, and (6) the number of divorces and
the divorce rates since 1953. There is a two-and-one-
half year time lag prior to publication of the data.

D. ADDITIONAL GOVERNMENT STATISTICS ON DIVORCE

In addition to the census and vital statistics data on divorce, described in parts B
and C of this chapter, other data are available from published reports of other studies by the U.S. government or directly from the associated computer data bases.
In this section, the two main groups of sample survey data described are from the
Current Population Survey and from the surveys being conducted by the National
Center for Health Statistics. Further data are provided by the National Institute
of Mental Health which publishes general institutional survey data, by the Bureau
of Labor Statistics, and by the Internal Revenue Service. The Superintendent of
Documents number accompanies many of the publications cited in this section for
easier location in libraries that use this system of shelving documents.

1. Current Population Survey

The Current Population Survey, which was initiated in 1947, publishes each
month the results of its continuing study of a representative sample of 50,000
households in the United States. In addition to the published reports, since
1959 it has placed the results of this carefully drawn sample on computer tapes
to facilitate additional study. These two sources of information are described
below.

6-113   U.S. Bureau of the Census. CURRENT POPULATION REPORTS:
         POPULATION CHARACTERISTICS. Series P-20. Washington, D.C.:
         Government Printing Office, 1947-- . Monthly. C56.218:P-20/no.

On the basis of a systematically selected sample of American households, the Current Population Survey makes estimates of the number of separated and divorced persons by
age, sex, race, rural-urban residence, marital status of
parents with children under eighteen years of age, marital
status by family status, and marital status of subfamilies.
This report is published each spring under the title MARI-
TAL STATUS AND LIVING ARRANGEMENTS; prior to
1970 it was entitled MARITAL STATUS AND FAMILY
STATUS. The introduction contains an interpretation of
the findings, and makes comparisons with previous years.
The appendix explains the definitions used in the survey,
the reliability of these estimates, and the sample design.
The titles of other reports in this series that contain some

divorce data are: HOUSEHOLDS AND FAMILIES, BY
TYPES, HOUSEHOLDS AND FAMILY CHARACTERISTICS,
and PERSONS OF SPANISH ORIGIN IN THE UNITED
STATES. This ongoing survey is an extremely important
source of divorce information which in a sense updates
the national census on a sample basis.

6-114   The survey data gathered by the Current Population Survey, item 6-
113 above, since 1959 has been stored on computer tapes for additional research. Two ongoing tape series which provide information
on divorce are tapes P:D6 and P:D38.

Tape P:D6 contains data on mobility, fall school enroll-
ments, educational attainment, households by type and
characteristics, marital status and family status, and
Negro population. Since 1969, it has included data
on persons of ethnic origins and persons of Spanish origin.
Other topics such as metropolitan growth, fertility, and
voter participation, are included at various times.

Tape P:D38, which stores data from the March supplement
of the Annual Demographic File, was begun in 1968.
These data are the result of interviews conducted annually
in March for the entire United States and its regions.
The file contains approximately 200,000 records for each
year, including data on various family and household
characteristics, age, race, sex, ethnic origin, educational attainment, income amounts by types, and work
experience during the previous calendar year, hours and
weeks worked, or reasons for unemployment.

Tape purchases or special tabulations can be made. For further
details, refer to the latest CATALOG OF UNITED STATES CENSUS
PUBLICATIONS, described in item 6-180.

6-115   U.S. Bureau of Labor Statistics. MONTHLY LABOR REVIEW.
Washington, D.C.: Government Printing Office. 1915-- .
Monthly. Annual Index.

Since 1960 an annual article on "Marital and Family
Characteristics of Workers" has been published, usually
in the spring, which contains data from the Current
Population Survey on the number and percentage of
divorced persons in the labor force, by race and sex.
These articles are then issued as SPECIAL LABOR
FORCE REPORTS with additional statistical tabulations
in an appendix.

2. National Health and Mental Health Surveys

The National Center for Health Statistics and the National Institute of Mental

Health provide publications which are of substantial value as sources of data on divorce. The Vital and Health Statistics Series are an especially important source of data on social variables not reported elsewhere. Particular reports in these series that contain information on divorce are described in detail below. Computer data bases from the health surveys are described as well.

6-116   U.S. National Center for Health Statistics. VITAL AND HEALTH STATISTICS. Series 1-22. Washington, D.C.: Government Printing Office, 1963-- . Irregular. Graphs. Maps. Tables.

These very important series of reports contain the results of national health interviews and health examinations on a very large representative sample of the U.S. population. Special vital statistics are also included in these series. The series numbered 10, 11, 12, 13, 20, 21, and 22, which are described in this section, all contain divorce as a variable in some of their reports. The relevant reports are cited, along with the variables related to divorce information. Continuing issues of these series should be checked regularly for pertinent studies published since the last report described in each series. For each report cited below, the publication date of the report appears in parentheses, followed by the Superintendent of Documents number which may help the researcher in locating these reports in libraries that shelve them by this numbering system.

Series 10

6-117   U.S. National Center for Health Statistics. VITAL AND HEALTH STATISTICS. Series 10: DATA FROM THE HEALTH INTERVIEW SURVEY. Washington, D.C.: Government Printing Office, 1963--.

This series contains information on divorced persons relating to illness, accidental injuries, disability, use of the hospital, as well as medical, dental, and other health related topics. The information is based on data collected in a continuing nationwide household interview survey. The relevant reports in this series to date are described below in the manner indicated in item 6-116 above and are arranged by the number of each report.

6-118   30.--HOSPITAL DISCHARGES AND LENGTH OF STAY: SHORT-STAY HOSPITALS--UNITED STATES, JULY 1963-JUNE 1964. (1966). FS2.85/2:10/30.

This report provides statistics on divorced persons as patients discharged from short-stay hospitals, and rate of discharge by age and sex. Also included are data on hospital days and average length of stay by age and sex.

6-119 50.--PERSONS HOSPITALIZED BY NUMBER OF HOSPITAL EPISODES AND DAYS IN A YEAR--UNITED STATES, JULY 1965-JUNE 1966. (1969). FS2.85/2:10/50.

> This report provides data on marital status and percentage of short-stay hospital episodes. Additional information on the number and percentage of hospital days during short-stay hospital episodes is also given.

6-120 64.--PERSONS HOSPITALIZED BY NUMBER OF HOSPITAL EPISODES AND DAYS IN A YEAR--UNITED STATES. 1968. (1971). HE20.2210:10/64.

> Information is presented on the percentage of married, divorced, and single persons hospitalized per year, the number and percentage of hospital episodes, the number and percentage of hospital days, and the pattern of hospital stays.

6-121 66.--HOSPITAL AND SURGICAL INSURANCE COVERAGE--UNITED STATES, 1968. (1972). HE20.2210:10/66.

> This report provides data on marital status and the number and percentage of persons with hospital and surgical insurance coverage, by the age of the person.

6-122 104.--DIFFERENTIALS IN HEALTH CHARACTERISTICS BY MARITAL STATUS--UNITED STATES, 1971-72. (1976). HE20.6209:10/104.

> This report contains statistics on restricted activity days, chronic limitations of activity, acute conditions, physician visits, and hospital episodes by marital status, age, sex, color, family income, and family size.

6-123 107.--HOSPITAL DISCHARGES AND LENGTH OF STAY: SHORT STAY HOSPITALS--UNITED STATES. 1972. HE20.6209:10/107.

> The discharge rate and average length of stay by marital status is contained in this report.

> See also addendum 6-123A, 6-123B.

Computer tapes with the data from the Health Interview Survey are available. Refer to the National Center for Health Statistics publication, STANDARDIZED MICRO-DATA TAPE TRANSCRIPTS (6-55).

Series 11

6-124 U.S. National Center for Health Statistics. VITAL AND HEALTH STATISTICS. DATA FROM THE HEALTH EXAMINATION SURVEY. Series 11. Washington, D.C.: Government Printing Office, 1964--.

Series 11 differs from the preceding series in that direct medical examinations and tests were made instead of simply interviewing persons about health conditions. On the basis of these nationwide population samples, estimates were made as to the prevalence of a variety of diseases, physical and physiological conditions. Significant reports with relevant information regarding divorced persons are described below. See also thé addendum 6-124A.

6-125   9.--FINDINGS ON THE SEROLOGIC TEST FOR SYPHILIS IN ADULTS--UNITED STATES, 1960-62. (1965). FS2.85/2:11/9.

Data are reported on positive reactions to the serological test for syphilis for persons by race, sex, and marital status.

6-126   10.--CORONARY HEART DISEASE IN ADULTS--UNITED STATES, 1960-62. (1965). FS2.85/2:11/10.

This study reports the actual and expected prevalence rates of coronary heart disease by sex, marital status, and type of manifestation.

6-127   13.--HYPERTENSION AND HYPERTENSIVE HEART DISEASES IN ADULTS--UNITED STATES, 1960-62. (1966). FS2.85/2:11/13.

Data on heart disease are analyzed by race, sex, and marital status. Both actual and expected rates are reported.

6-128   17.--RHEUMATOID ARTHRITIS IN ADULTS--UNITED STATES, 1960-62. (1966). FS2.85/2:11/17.

The actual and expected prevalence rates of rheumatoid arthritis in adults are analyzed by sex and marital status.

6-129   18.--BLOOD GLUCOSE LEVELS IN ADULTS--UNITED STATES, 1960-62. (1966). FS.85/2.11/18.

Data on the actual and expected mean glucose levels in men and women are analyzed by marital status.

6-130   20.--OSTEOARTHRITIS IN ADULTS, BY SELECTED DEMOGRAPHIC CHARACTERISTICS--UNITED STATES, 1960-62. (1966). FS2.85/2:11/20.

This is a report on the actual and expected prevalence rates of osteoarthritis of the hands and/or feet by sex, marital status, and severity.

6-131   24.--MEAN BLOOD HEMATOCRIT OF ADULTS--UNITED STATES,
         1960-62. (1967). FS2.85/2:11/24.

         Actual and expected rates of anemia by sex, race, and
         marital status is the subject of this study.

6-132   36.--NEED FOR DENTAL CARE AMONG ADULTS--UNITED STATES,
         1960-62. (1970). HE20.2210:11/36.

         A study of dentulous adults who need dental care, by
         race, sex, and marital status.

6-133   37.--SELECTED SYMPTOMS OF PSYCHOLOGICAL DISTRESS--
         UNITED STATES. (1970). HE20.2210:11/37.

         This investigation reports the presence or absence of
         twelve stress indicators by race and sex for single,
         married, and divorced persons.

Computer tapes with the data from the two cycles, 1959-62 and 1963-65, of
the Health Examination Survey are available. Refer to the National Center
for Health Statistics publication, STANDARIZED MICRO-DATA TAPE TRAN-
SCRIPTS (6-55).

Series 12

6-134   U.S. National Center for Health Statistics. VITAL AND HEALTH
         STATISTICS. DATA FROM THE INSTITUTIONAL POPULATION
         SURVEYS. Series 12. Washington, D.C.: Government Printing
         Office, 1965--.

         This series presents data on the health characteristics
         of persons in institutions, and the type of medical,
         nursing, and personal care they receive. The data
         are based on national samples of establishments pro-
         viding these services, and on samples of the residents
         or patients. Significant reports with relevant informa-
         tion regarding divorced persons are described below.

6-135   12.--MARITAL STATUS AND LIVING ARRANGEMENTS BEFORE
         ADMISSION TO NURSING AND PERSONAL CARE HOMES--UNITED
         STATES, MAY-JUNE 1964. (1969). FS2.85/2:12/12.

         Statistics are provided on the marital status of persons
         before admission to nursing and personal care homes, the
         type of care received, the primary type of service, the
         number of chronic conditions and impairments, the length
         of stay, and the frequency of visitors, according to the
         age and sex of the resident.

6-136   24.--MEASURES OF CHRONIC ILLNESS AMONG RESIDENTS OF

NURSING AND PERSONAL CARE HOMES--UNITED STATES, JUNE-AUGUST, 1969. (1974). HE20.6209:12/24.

This study contains the number and percentage distribution of residents in nursing and personal care homes by the number of chronic conditions and impairments, according to age, color, sex, and marital status. Also included are the number and percentage distribution of residents in nursing and personal care homes by mobility status, age, color, sex, and marital status. See also addendum 6-136A.

Series 13

6-137   U.S. National Center for Health Statistics. VITAL AND HEALTH STATISTICS. DATA FROM THE HOSPITAL DISCHARGE SURVEY. Series 13. Washington, D.C.: Government Printing Office, 1966--.

The main subject of this research initiated in 1962 relates to discharged patients in short-stay hospitals. The data was gathered from a sample of patient records in a national sample of hospitals. Significant reports relevant to divorce are described below.

6-138   1.--PATIENTS DISCHARGED FROM SHORT-STAY HOSPITALS--UNITED STATES, OCTOBER-DECEMBER 1964. (1966). FS2.85/2:13/1.

This survey cites statistics on the number and percentage of married, divorced, and single patients discharged.

Computer tapes with data from the Hospital Discharge Survey from 1966-68 are available. Data include age, sex, color, marital status (including divorce), discharge status, and length of stay per discharged patient. Refer to the National Center for Health Statistics publication, STANDARDIZED MICRO-DATA TAPE TRANSCRIPTS (6-55).

Series 20

6-139   U.S. National Center for Health Statistics. VITAL AND HEALTH STATISTICS. DATA ON MORTALITY. Series 20. Washington, D.C.: Government Printing Office, 1965-- .

Series 20 contains special analyses of mortality statistics that are not included in the annual vital statistics reports, discussed in part C of this chapter. Significant reports relevant to divorce are described below.

6-140   5.--SUICIDE IN THE UNITED STATES, 1950-1964. (1967). FS2.85/2:20/5.

Suicide statistics are analyzed by age, color, sex, and marital status.

6-141   6.--HOMICIDE IN THE UNITED STATES, 1950-64. (1967). FS2. 85/2:20/6.

Murder rates are presented by age, color, sex, and marital status.

6-142   8.--MORTALITY FROM SELECTED CAUSES BY MARITAL STATUS-- UNITED STATES. Pts. A and B. (1970). HE20.2210:20/8a & 8b.

This is a very important study of the death rates from tuberculosis, cancers, leukemia, diabetes, strokes, arteriosclerotic heart disease including coronary heart disease, cirrhosis of the liver, motor vehicle accidents, all other accidents, suicide, and homicide by age, race, sex, and marital status.

6-143   9.--MOTOR VEHICLE ACCIDENTS IN THE UNITED STATES, 1950- 67. (1970). HE20.2210:20/9.

Motor vehicle accidents are analyzed by age, color, sex, and marital status.

6-144   10.--DIABETES MELLITUS MORTALITY IN THE UNITED STATES-- 1950-67. (1971). HE20.2210:20/10.

The death rates for diabetics are studied by age, color, sex, and marital status.

6-145   The National Mortality Followback Survey in 1966-68 collected data on smoking habits of decedents aged 35-84. It also asked questions on marital status, household composition, family income, and matched these data with the death certificates. These data are available on computer tapes. Refer to the National Center for Health Statistics publication, STANDARDIZED MICRO-DATA TAPE TRANSCRIPTS (item 6-55).

Series 21

6-146   U.S. National Center for Health Statistics. VITAL AND HEALTH STATISTICS. DATA ON NATALITY, MARRIAGE, AND DIVORCE. Series 21. Washington, D.C.: Government Printing Office, 1964-- .

This series contains special analyses of divorce data from the National Vital Statistics System by demographic vari- ables not usually included in the annual vital statistics report discussed in part C of this chapter. Significant reports relevant to divorce are described below.

6-147   7.--DIVORCE STATISTICS ANALYSIS--UNITED STATES, 1962.
         (1965). FS2.85/2:21/7.

         The national divorce statistics are analyzed for the year
         1962. The personal characteristics of husbands and wives
         who were divorced in Hawaii, Iowa, Tennessee, and
         Wisconsin are examined for the years 1960-61. Other
         variables studied are age, race, interracial divorces,
         marriage order, state of residence, marriages of divorced
         couples, children of divorced couples, and legal aspects
         of divorce.

6-148   13.--DIVORCE STATISTICS ANALYSIS--UNITED STATES, 1963.
         (1967). FS2.85/2:21/13.

         This study analyzes the national divorce data for 1963
         and considers the probabilities of divorce by age, age
         at marriage, marriage order, duration of the marriage,
         and race. It also contains discussion of interracial di-
         vorce, migratory divorces, and the legal grounds used
         in obtaining divorces.

6-149   17.--DIVORCE STATISTICS ANALYSIS--UNITED STATES, 1964 AND
         1965. (1969). FS2.85/2:21/17.

         The national divorce data for 1964-65 are studied in this
         report. Special topics included are the divorce rates for
         Standard Metropolitan Statistical Areas, estimates of di-
         vorce rates by the age of the husband and the wife, race,
         marriage order, duration of the marriage, number of chil-
         dren, and the legal grounds used in obtaining a divorce.

6-150   18.--CHILDREN OF DIVORCED COUPLES: UNITED STATES
         SELECTED YEARS. (1970). HE20.2210:21/18.

         The number of children under the age of eighteen that
         are involved in divorce are given by state, race, age of
         parents, marriage order, and duration of the marriage in
         years.

6-151   20.--INCREASES IN DIVORCES: UNITED STATES--1967. (1970).
         HE20.2210:21/20.

         The main topics analyzed in this study are divorce rates
         in the United States compared with foreign countries,
         changes in the divorced and separated population, and
         the remarriage and death of divorced persons.

6-152   22.--DIVORCES: ANALYSIS OF CHANGES--UNITED STATES,
         1969. (1973). HE20.2210:21/22.

133

This special report analyzes the U.S. divorce statistics for 1968–69 and the increasing divorce rates for 1963–69 by the characteristics of divorcing couples, age at marriage, age at the time of the decree, race, marriage order, education, children under eighteen, and the duration of marriage and separation.

6-153   23.--TEENAGERS: MARRIAGES, DIVORCES, PARENTHOOD, AND MORTALITY. (1973). HE20.6209:21/23.

A short discussion of teen-age divorce is included in this report.

6-154   24. --100 YEARS OF MARRIAGE AND DIVORCE STATISTICS--UNITED STATES, 1867-1967. (1973). Bibliography. HE20.6209.21/24.

This report contains an important overview of divorce in the United States for the past century, including information on: divorce data collection procedures for the period; time trends in national and regional totals and rates; a century of comparisons in U.S. divorce rates by regions and states for selected years; rates for selected major cities; the duration cf marriage for the United States and for the states for selected years; the percentage of divorced couples married in the state where the divorce was granted; the mean number of children per divorce was granted; the mean number of children per divorce for the United States and states for selected years; and the legal grounds used for divorce for selected years. An important bibliography of marriage and divorce statistical studies published by the U.S. government is included in this report.

6-155   25.--REMARRIAGES: UNITED STATES. (1973). HE20.6209:21/25.

The national trend in remarriages is analyzed by previous marital status, race, variations by state, remarriage rates by age and sex, period of time between divorce or widowhood, remarriage, and the type of marriage ceremony.

See also addendum 6-155A.

Series 22

6-156   U.S. National Center for Health Statistics. VITAL AND HEALTH STATISTICS. DATA FROM THE NATIONAL NATALITY AND MORTALITY SURVEYS. Series 22. Washington, D.C.: Government Printing Office, 1965--.

These statistics were taken from sample surveys of birth and death records and were analyzed on a variety of social

variables not usually analyzed in the vital statistics reports
discussed in part C of this chapter. The reports relevant to
divorce are described below.

6-157   10.--HEALTH INSURANCE COVERAGE OF ADULTS WHO DIED IN
1964 OR 1965. (1969). FS2.85/2:22/10.

This report presents the number and percentage of decedents
covered by hospital and surgical insurance, by sex, age, income, and marital status.

6-158   11.--EXPENSES FOR HOSPITAL AND INSTITUTIONAL CARE DURING
THE LAST YEAR OF LIFE FOR ADULTS WHO DIED IN 1964 OR 1965:
UNITED STATES. (1971). HE20.2210:22/11.

The number and percentage of decedents with expenses for
care in hospitals during the last year of life, and the percentage of decedents with expenses by the amount of the bill,
by age, and marital status, comprise the subject of this investigation.

U.S. NIMH Reports

6-159   U.S. National Institute of Mental Health. Biometry Branch. Survey
and Reports Section. STATISTICAL NOTE. No. 1-- . Washing-
ton, D.C.: Government Printing Office, 1967-- . Irregular.
Charts. Graphs. Tables.

This series is comprised of short, four- to thirty-page,
statistical and interpretive reports on various topics
concerning psychiatric units, mental health centers, and
mental health research. Unlike the report series described earlier in part D, this series reports research
based on surveys and analyses of general institutional
data, instead of being based on data gathered by sampling
procedures. All of the reports cited below contain information on divorced, married, and single persons. The
report number, its title, and publication date are cited
for each report. The number assigned by the Superintendent of Documents for each report is also included in
order to facilitate location of the report in libraries that
shelve documents by this system. Continuing issues of
this series since the summer of 1978 should be checked
regularly for recently published relevant reports.

6-160   32.--ADMISSION RATES BY AGE, SEX, AND MARITAL STATUS:
STATE AND COUNTY MENTAL HOSPITALS, 1969. (1970). HE20.
2424:32.

Separated and divorced persons are reported together.

6-161 35.--ADMISSIONS RATES BY MARITAL STATUS: OUTPATIENT PSY-
CHIATRIC SERVICES, 1969. (1970). HE20.2424:35.

 Separated and divorced persons are reported together.

6-162 79--.ADMISSIONS TO OUTPATIENT PSYCHIATRIC SERVICES BY AGE,
SEX, COLOR, AND MARITAL STATUS, JUNE 1970-MAY 1971. (1973).
HE20.2424:79.

6-163 82.--MARITAL STATUS OF DISCHARGES FROM PSYCHIATRIC INPA-
TIENT UNITS OF GENERAL HOSPITALS: UNITED STATES, 1970-71.
PART I: ANALYSIS BY AGE, COLOR AND SEX. (1973). HE20.8116:82.

6-164 83--.MARITAL STATUS OF DISCHARGES FROM PSYCHIATRIC INPA-
TIENT UNITS OF GENERAL HOSPITALS: UNITED STATES, 1970-71.
PART II: ANALYSIS BY REFERRAL SOURCE, LENGTH OF STAY AND
PRIMARY DIAGNOSIS. (1973). HE20.8116:83.

6-165 84.--MARITAL STATUS OF DISCHARGES FROM PSYCHIATRIC INPA-
TIENT UNITS OF GENERAL HOSPITALS: UNITED STATES, 1970-71.
PART III: ANALYSIS BY HOSPITAL CONTROL. (1973). HE20.8116:84.

6-166 100.--MARITAL STATUS, LIVING ARRANGEMENTS, AND FAMILY
CHARACTERISTICS OF ADMISSIONS TO STATE AND COUNTY MEN-
TAL HOSPITALS AND OUTPATIENT PSYCHIATRIC CLINICS: UNITED
STATES, 1970. (1974). HE20.8116:100.

 This report includes data on children of divorced or separated
 parents.

6-167 116.--UTILIZATION OF STATE AND COUNTY MENTAL HOSPITALS
BY SPANISH AMERICANS IN 1972. (1975). HE20.8116.116.

6-168 120.--MARITAL STATUS AND AGE OF MALE ADMISSIONS WITH DI-
AGNOSED ALCOHOL DISORDERS TO STATE AND COUNTY MENTAL
HOSPITALS IN 1972. (1975). HE20.8116:120.

6-169 124.--CHARACTERISTICS OF DIAGNOSED AND MISSED ALCOHOLIC
MALE ADMISSIONS TO STATE AND COUNTY MENTAL HOSPITALS,
1972. (1976). HE20.8116:124.

 This report includes data on separated or divorced males.

 See also the addendum 6-169A.

6-170 U.S. National Institute of Mental Health. Biometry Branch. Survey and
Reports Section. MARITAL STATUS AND MENTAL DISORDER: AN ANA-
LYTIC REVIEW. By Leona L. Bachrach. Report Series D on Mental
Health Statistics, no.3. Washington, D.C.: Government Printing

Office, 1975.   HE20.8110:D/3.

> This report is an excellent summary of the relationship
> between marital status and mental health.   An extensive
> bibliography is included.

3. Economic Opportunity Survey

6-171   Bowles, Gladys K.; Bacon, A. Lloyd; and Ritchey, P. Neal.
POVERTY DIMENSIONS OF RURAL-TO-URBAN MIGRATION: A
STATISTICAL REPORT. Vol. 1, pt. 1. U.S. Department of Agri-
culture, Statistical Bulletin, no. 511. Economic Research Service,
U.S. Department of Agriculture, in Cooperation with the Institute
of Behavioral Research, University of Georgia, and the Office of
Planning, Research, and Evaluation, Office of Economic Opportuni-
ty. Washington, D.C.: Government Printing Office, 1973.   335 p.
A1.34:511.

> This report contains data from the 1967 Survey of Eco-
> nomic Opportunity on rural-to-urban migration. Data on
> marital status of the poverty population, poor rural-to-
> urban migrants, poor urban population of urban origin,
> poor urban-to-rural migrants, and rural poor of rural
> origin are included.

4. Internal Revenue Service Reports

6-172   U.S. Internal Revenue Service. STATISTICS OF INCOME:
INDIVIDUAL INCOME TAX RETURNS. Washington, D.C.: Government Printing Office, 1954-- . Annual. T22.35/2:In2/year.

> This report provides statistics each year on the number
> of persons paying and receiving alimony, as well as the
> amount of alimony provided and received, by income
> categories. This is the only source for information of
> this type.

E. IDENTIFYING NEW SOURCES OF DIVORCE STATISTICS

Since the researcher very often is interested in the most up-to-date statistics
possible, as well as the most relevant statistics for his needs, it is of vital
importance that he find systematic ways of locating these data as they become
available. In earlier sections of this chapter and in chapters 2, 3, 4, and 5,
continuing works and series have been described which can be checked regularly for new sources of data. These can be identified in the above chapters
as those cited with the dates left "open," that is, with a dash following the
date in the citation.

At the same time, the researcher may keep abreast of new specific sources available
to him in the libraries that he uses by checking periodically in the subject card
catalog under such headings as "Divorce--U.S.--Statistics," and other subject

headings, such as those listed in item 2-5, which may be similarly subdivided.

The sources which are described below are also good for identifying divorce statistics as they appear, either in printed form or as part of computerized data bases.
Since significantly more statistical data are being stored in computers, and only
a portion of these data is tabulated and printed for general use, knowledge of the
locations and types of data in this form is becoming increasingly important.

6-173   AMERICAN STATISTICS INDEX: A COMPREHENSIVE GUIDE AND
         INDEX TO THE STATISTICAL PUBLICATIONS OF THE UNITED
         STATES GOVERNMENT. Washington, D.C.: Congressional Informa-
         tion Service, 1973-- . Annual, with monthly supplements.

         This very excellent index to specific statistical publica-
         tions of the U.S. government, which even cites specific
         tables within publications, is basic for identifying new
         data and data sources. It also indexes and describes
         statistical publications that have research significance
         from the 1960s, and intends to index and describe all
         statistical publications of the United States issued since
         1970. The indexing consists of a good subject index,
         a name index, a title index, and a category index
         containing demographic breakdowns. Each citation in-
         cludes the name of the issuing agency, the title of the
         publication, the assigned Superintendent of Documents
         number, the source of publication, price, date of issue,
         an abstract, and the title and page locations of tables
         in the work. It is somewhat difficult for the novice to
         use, however. Explanations for its use are found in the
         flyleaf. Microfiche copies of most of the printed pub-
         lications are available for purchase from the publisher
         of this index. The data file is now computerized, with
         a computer search service available.

         Consult: Families and   Marriage and divorce
                    households   Vital statistics

6-174   DIRECTORY OF COMPUTERIZED DATA FILES AND RELATED SOFT-
         WARE AVAILABLE FROM FEDERAL AGENCIES. Edited by Robert Jaxel.
         Springfield, Va.: National Technical Information Service, 1974--.
         Annual. C51.11/2/year.

         The volume for 1976 describes more than one thousand com-
         puterized data files from sixty federal agencies. Although
         there are not many files on divorce per se, it can be expected
         that there are many files that have "divorce" as one of their
         demographic variables. The editor of this important and much
         needed work states that this will be an annual survey.

6-175   Gerham, David, and Walker, Loretta. "A Subject Approach to Social
         Science Data Archives." RQ(REFERENCE QUARTERLY) 15 (1975):
         132-49.

This article gives the name, address, telephone number, and person to be contacted in regard to forty ongoing government and private computerized data archives in the United States. It also provides information on the subject scope of the holdings, fee structure, restrictions on the data and users, available lists of holdings, output format, and hardware for these data bases. Divorce data are included in some of these computerized data archives. It may be beneficial to follow the development of these archives.

6-176   Kruzas, Anthony T. ENCYCLOPEDIA OF INFORMATION SYSTEMS AND SERVICES. 2d international ed. Ann Arbor, Mich.: A.T. Kruzas Associates, 1974. xii, 1,271 p.

Refer to item 13-4.

6-177   REVIEW OF PUBLIC DATA USE. Arlington, Va.: Data Use and Access Laboratories (DUALabs), 1972-- . Quarterly.

This periodical contains information on the data bases that DUALabs sells, articles about unpublished data, and news items about new data sources, mostly from the U.S. government.

6-178   Sessions, Vivian S., ed. DIRECTORY OF DATA BASES IN THE SOCIAL AND BEHAVIORAL SCIENCES. New York: Science Associates/International, 1974. xv, 300 p.

This directory provides a description of data bases in some 550 data centers in the United States and over 130 centers in thirty-nine foreign countries. Each center has reported the following information: name, address, and telephone number of the center, the senior staff member, major subject field, file title, time frame, and geographic scope of the data, data sources and collecting agency, storage media, hardware, software, output media, data products, documentation, publications, and access. The contents are organized by the name of the center, and indexed by keywords and categories. Basically a source of nongovernmental data bases, this directory also includes some federal, state, and municipal bases as well as academic ones.

Consult: Family   Vital statistics
           Marriage

6-179   STATISTICS SOURCES: A SUBJECT GUIDE TO DATA ON INDUSTRIAL, BUSINESS, SOCIAL, EDUCATIONAL, FINANCIAL, AND OTHER TOPICS FOR THE UNITED STATES AND SELECTED FOREIGN COUNTRIES. Edited by Paul Wasserman and Joanne Paskar. 5th ed. Detroit: Gale Research Co., 1977. 892 p.

The present edition of the guide refers to no sources
other than those that have been described in this chapter. Forthcoming, editions, however, should be checked
for possible new sources.

6-180   U.S. Bureau of the Census. CATALOG OF UNITED STATES
         CENSUS PUBLICATIONS, 1946-- . Washington, D.C.: Govern-
         ment Printing Office, 1947-- . Title varies. Quarterly and annual
         cumulations, with monthly supplements. C3.163/3/year.

         This important listing of the printed publications of the
         Bureau of the Census as they are issued includes, since
         1964, the unpublished materials on computer tapes,
         punched cards, and so forth. An earlier cumulative
         publication for the years 1790 through 1972 is described
         in item 6-48.

6-181   _____. DATA ACCESS DESCRIPTIONS: MISCELLANEOUS SERIES.
         Washington, D.C.: Government Printing Office, 1973-- . Irregu-
         lar. C56.212/nos.

         These reports introduce means of access to the unpublished
         data of the Bureau of the Census for researchers with data
         requirements not fully met by the published census reports.
         They include descriptions of tapes available and new tabu-
         lations.

6-182   U.S. Library of Congress. Division of Documents. MONTHLY
         CHECKLIST OF STATE PUBLICATIONS, 1910-- . Washington,
         D.C.: Government Printing Office, 1912-- . Monthly, with an-
         nual index. LC30.9/v./no.

         By means of this source, it is possible to identify any
         state government publications likely to contain divorce
         statistics which are received by the Library of Congress.

         Consult: Divorce--statistics   Settlements (Law)
                   Divorce--statistics   Vital Statistics
                   (by states)
                   Domestic Relations

6-183   U.S. Superintendent of Documents. MONTHLY CATALOG OF
         UNITED STATES GOVERNMENT PUBLICATIONS. Washington,
         D.C.: Government Printing Office, 1895-- . Monthly, with an-
         nual cumulative index. GP3.8:year/no.

         By using each month the subject index to this basic list-
         ing of the publications issued by all branches of the
         U.S. government, the researcher is able to identify
         new publications which are likely to contain divorce
         statistics. For documents issued between 1900 and
         1970, refer to item 8-6.

Consult: Census   Marriage
          Census bureau   Vital statistics
          Divorce

Chapter 7

DIVORCE STATISTICS: CANADA AND GREAT BRITAIN

Basic sources for locating Canadian and British divorce statistics are described
and evaluated in this chapter. In part A, the general sources of divorce statistics are described for the user who does not require great detail. In part
B, the statistics on divorced persons as found in the Canadian and British censuses are described. In part C, the vital statistics on divorce are noted, and
in part D, methods of keeping up with new divorce statistics as they are issued
are discussed.

A. DIVORCE STATISTICS IN BRIEF

When reliable and up-to-date data are needed, the following basic annuals
are useful. Although there is very little analysis of the data in these volumes,
they are sufficient for the general user who needs quick, brief information.

7-1   CANADA YEAR BOOK, 1905-- . Ottawa: Statistics Canada,
        1971-- . Annual. Charts. Graphs. Maps. Tables. Bibliography.

        This annual review of current social, economic, and
        political developments in Canada contains a good sum-
        mary of Canadian divorce trends, as well as several
        tables on divorce by provinces, grounds for divorce,
        children involved, duration of the marriage, and pre-
        vious marital status. All the data are for the previous
        four years. Sources of the data reported are cited.
        There is a time lag of two years in the publication of
        the data. Volumes for 1905-71 were issued under the
        agency's former name, Bureau of Statistics.

        Consult: Divorce
                  Vital statistics--divorce

7-2   DEMOGRAPHIC YEARBOOK. New York: United Nations, 1948-- .
        Annual.

        This basic source for Canadian and British, as well as

worldwide, divorce statistics is further described in
item 6-2.

7-3   Great Britain. Central Statistics Office. ANNUAL ABSTRACT OF
       STATISTICS. London: H.M. Stationery Office, 1935/36-- . An-
       nual since 1948.

       This abstract of British statistics contains data for the
       past ten years on social, economic, and health condi-
       tions of the United Kingdom and Northern Ireland. It
       provides information on the number of divorces, the rate,
       the grounds, the number of annulments and separations,
       the duration of the marriage in years, the number of
       children involved, and the petitioner. There is a one-
       year time lag prior to publication of the data.

7-4   Mitchell, Brian R., and Jones, H.G. SECOND ABSTRACT OF
       BRITISH HISTORICAL STATISTICS. Cambridge: At the University
       Press. 1971. Tables. vii, 227 p.

       Providing data on the number of divorces by age and
       sex for 1921, 1931, 1951, and 1961, for England, Wales,
       and Scotland, this retrospective source also reports data
       on the number of divorces for these three countries from
       1855 to 1965.

       Consult: Age groups by marital condition
                 Divorces

7-5   U.S. Bureau of the Census. MARRIAGE AND DIVORCE, 1867-
       1906. 2 vols. Washington, D.C.: Government Printing Office,
       1908-9. Maps. Charts. Tables.

       Statistics on divorce and divorce laws in Canada and
       Great Britain are presented for the period 1867-1906.
       For further information, refer to item 6-51.

7-6   Urquhart, M.C., and Buckley, K.A.H., eds. HISTORICAL STA-
       TISTICS OF CANADA. Toronto: Macmillan; London: Cambridge
       University Press, 1965. xv, 672 p.

       Arranged like the HISTORICAL ABSTRACTS OF THE
       UNITED STATES, COLONIAL TIMES TO 1970 (item
       6-5), this guide to Canadian historical statistics contains
       information on the number of divorced men and women
       from 1901 to 1956. Other data included are the number
       of divorces and the divorce rates for Canada from 1921
       to 1960. The sources of the data are given.

       Consult: Marital status
                 Vital statistics--divorce

7-7   WORLD ALMANAC AND BOOK OF FACTS. New York: Newspaper Enterprise Associates, 1868-- . Annual.

> Statistics on the number of divorces and the divorce
> rates for Canada for selected years from 1936 to the
> present, as well as the number of divorces and divorce
> rates by province since 1961, are supplied by this source.
> There is a three-year time lag in the publication of the
> data. Refer further to item 3-18.

> Consult: Divorce

B. CENSUS STATISTICS: PUBLISHED AND COMPUTER STORED

In this section the kinds of divorce information found in the censuses of Canada
and Great Britain are described. The Canadian government first reported data
on divorced persons in the census of 1901, while British census statistics on
divorce were first collected in the census of 1921. In each case the most recent censuses, those of 1971, are described in detail for both countries in sections 1 and 3. This is followed by descriptions of the earlier census data on
divorce in the retrospective sections, 2 and 4.

1. Current Canadian Census Statistics

Since 1956 Canada has collected census statistics at mid-decade, in addition
to the regular decennial censuses. The 1971 Canadian census, the most current completed census available, is described below.

7-8   Canada. Statistics Canada. CENSUS OF CANADA, 1971. Vol.
1, pt. 2. Ottawa: 1973.

> TABLES:

> 17-22. This section reports data on divorced persons
> by sex, in provinces, in urban groups of various sizes,
> rural areas, census divisions, municipal divisions, and
> metropolitan areas.

7-9   _____. CENSUS OF CANADA, 1971. Vol. 1, pt. 4. Ottawa:
1973.

> TABLES:

> 1-3. Information on divorced persons is tabulated by
> sex and age groups, in provinces, urban and rural areas,
> and metropolitan areas.

> 14-17. Data on divorced men and women by age for
> ethnic groups in provinces and in urban, rural, and metropoli-
> tan areas are provided in these tables.

7-10   ____. CENSUS OF CANADA, 1971. Vol. 1, pt. 5. Ottawa: 1973.

          TABLE:

          8. This table reports statistics on vocational training for married, single, and divorced persons.

7-11   ____. CENSUS OF CANADA, 1971. Vol. 2, pt. 1. Ottawa: 1973.

          TABLES:

          54-55. These tables provide information on divorced heads of household by sex and number of persons in the household, both for provinces and metropolitan areas.

          58-65. The number of divorced men and women are tabulated by educational attainment for provinces and metropolitan areas. Statistics on divorced foreign-born persons, the year of immigration for both the provinces and metropolitan areas are reported. Information concerning divorce among ethnic groups in the metropolitan areas has also been tabulated. The occupation of the divorced heads of households is given for provinces and metropolitan areas.

7-12   ____. CENSUS OF CANADA, 1971. Vol. 2, pt. 2. Ottawa: 1973.

          TABLES:

          50-54. Comparative data on sex and marital status of heads of households for 1961, 1966, and 1971 are supplied in these tables. Statistics are also provided on divorced heads of households by family type, number and age of children, for both provinces and metropolitan areas.

7-13   ____. CENSUS OF CANADA, 1971. Vol. 3, pt. 2. Ottawa: 1973.

          TABLE:

          8. Information on the occupations of divorced persons for the provinces is found in this table.

7-14   ____. CENSUS OF CANADA, 1971. Vol. 3, pt. 6. Ottawa: 1973.

          TABLES:

          1,2,4. Statistics are reported on divorced persons and the source and amount of income for both provinces and metropolitan areas.

7-15   _____. STATISTICS CANADA CATALOGUE. Ottawa: 1954-- .
Annual.

This publication describes the source and availability of
the summary computer tapes of tabulated data from the
1971 census of population and some special tabulations
not included in the printed census reports. In addition,
for the first time, Information Canada is planning to
make available data from a 1 percent public use sample
of the 1971 census.

2. Retrospective Canadian Census Statistics

Questions concerning divorce were first included in the Canadian census of
1901. The following is a description of the types of divorce data reported in
the various Canadian censuses since that time. The censuses are listed in chronological order. The most recent census is described in part B, section 1,
above.

7-16   Canada. Census Office. FOURTH CENSUS OF CANADA, 1901.
4 vols. Ottawa: Printed by S.E. Dawson, 1902-6.

Volume 1 on population, in table 3, provides divorce
statistics on the number of divorced males and females
in each census district and province. Table 7 records
the number of divorced males and females in the towns
of the nation.

7-17   Canada. Census and Statistics Office. FIFTH CENSUS OF CANADA,
1911. 6 vols. Ottawa: Printed by C.H. Parmelee, 1912-15.
French and English.

In volume 1, tables 2, 3, and 4, the number of divorced
men and women by provinces, districts, and subdistricts
are reported.

7-18   Canada. Bureau of Statistics. SIXTH CENSUS OF CANADA, 1921.
21 vols. Ottawa: F.A. Acland, printer, 1924. Tables. Maps.
Diagrams. Forms. English and French.

Divorce data are more extensively analyzed in this census. In volume 2, tables 18-33, data is supplied on the
number and often the percentage of men and women by
age groups, nativity, rural-urban residence, residence in
cities, residence in cities and towns of over 5,000 inhabitants, and residence in provinces. In a number of
tables, there are comparisons with the 1901 and 1911
censuses. In volume 3, tables 25 and 26 have informa-

tion on the number of families having a divorced parent, with and without children, rural-urban residence, nativity, and residence in cities of more than 10,000 inhabitants.

7-19   _____. SEVENTH CENSUS OF CANADA, 1931. 13 vols. Ottawa: J.O. Patenaude, 1933. English and French.

Approximately forty tables in this census have divorce as a variable. Divorce is tabulated with reference to age, sex, birthplace, rural-urban, literacy, family composition, number of children, racial origin, blindness, deaf mutes, employment, and inmates of mental institutions, jails, and correctional institutions. Divorce is also tabulated with reference to cities, towns, provinces, and the nation.

7-20   _____. EIGHTH CENSUS OF CANADA, 1941. . . . published by the authority of the Hon.James A. Mac Kinnon, M.P., minister of trade and commerce. 11 vols. Ottawa: E. Cloutier, printer to the King, 1944-50. Maps. Tables. English and French.

This eighth census has questions and tabulations similar to the preceding census. Tabulations on permanent separation were also made. Volume 1 contains a good discussion of divorce and death rates.

7-21   _____. NINTH CENSUS OF CANADA, 1951. 11 vols. Ottawa: E. Cloutier, Queen's Printer and Controller of Stationery, 1953-56. Maps. Tables.

This census tabulated divorce with reference to age, sex, rural-urban residence, origin, family size, age of children, median earnings of the head of the family, divorced persons in the labor force, and occupation. Cities, towns, provinces, and the nation are the geographical variables tabulated. Death and.divorce statistics are discussed in volume 10.

7-22   _____. CENSUS OF CANADA, 1956. 4 vols. Ottawa: E. Cloutier, Queen's Printer, 1957-59. Maps. Diagrams. Forms. Tables.

Volume 1, in tables 23-31, of this census provides data on the number of divorced persons by sex and age groups for various political areas. Volume 3, in sections 3 and 4, contains a good analysis of marital status and the Canadian family.

7-23   _____. CENSUS OF CANADA, 1961. 7 vols. Ottawa: R.

Duhamel, Queen's Printer, 1963–69.   Maps.   Diagrams.   Forms.
Tables.   English and French.

The number of divorces by provinces for the years 1901,
1911, 1921, 1931, 1941, 1951, 1956, and 1961 are
reported.   Other variables are divorced persons by age,
sex, rural-urban residence, ethnic group, education,
number of children at home, earnings (median), occupations, and industry.   The geographical areas tabulated
are for cities, towns, metropolitan areas, and the nation.

7-24   _____.   1966 CENSUS OF CANADA, 1966.   5 vols.   Ottawa:
Dominion Bureau of Statistics, 1967-69.   Maps.   Diagrams.   Tables.
English and French.

This somewhat less extensive mid-decade census has about
twenty-five tables on divorce, with tabulations for other
variables such as age, sex, rural-urban residence, number of persons in the household, type of household, type
of dwelling, number of persons in the family, and number
of children.   Various geographical areas are cross-tabu-
lated with these variables.

7-25   U.S. Bureau of the Census.   MARRIAGE AND DIVORCE, 1867-
1906.   2 vols.   Washington, D.C.: Government Printing Office,
1908-9.   Maps.   Charts.   Tables.

Statistics on divorce in Canada for the period 1867-1906
are included in this very comprehensive statistical study
of divorce.   For further information, refer to item 6-51.

3. Current British Census Statistics

British censuses have been conducted in the second year of the decade except
during World War II when the 1941 census was not taken.   Questions on divorce have appeared in the British census since 1921.   In the analysis which
follows only the tables that have a separate category for divorce will be indicated; it is not useful to discuss the tables in which divorced and widowed
persons are tabulated together.   The term "marital condition" is equivalent to
the American term "marital status."

The British census volumes are often cataloged as separate volumes and thus
all may not be shelved in the same numerical sequence in libraries.   Library
of Congress entries have been used in the bibliographic citations below.

The latest and most current census published at the time that this information
guide is being written is the 1971 census.   Relevant portions of this census
are described in this section.   The 1976 census was canceled.

7-26   Great Britain. Office of Population Censuses and Surveys. CEN-
SUS 1971, ENGLAND AND WALES: COUNTY REPORT. Pt. 1.
London: H.M. Stationery Office, 1972-- . Maps.

These tables for each county and subdivision contain the
following information on divorce:

TABLES:

8. Divorced persons are reported by age and sex for
county, local authority areas, and conurbation centers.

13. Data are given for divorced persons by sex and
birthplace for county, county boroughs, urban areas of
over 50,000 persons, and county remainder.

14. Divorced persons are tabulated by country of birth
or visitor status for counties and county boroughs.

7-27   _____. CENSUS 1971, ENGLAND AND WALES: HOUSEHOLD
COMPOSITION TABLES. Pt. 2. (10 percent sample). London:
H.M. Stationery Office, 1975. xxxi, 219 p.

TABLES:

19. Divorced heads of households are reported by sex
and age groups for England and Wales, regions, and
conurbations.

31. Statistics on divorced housewives are given by sex
and age groups for England and Wales, regions, and
conurbations.

7-28   _____. CENSUS 1971, ENGLAND AND WALES: HOUSEHOLD
COMPOSITION TABLES. Pt. 3. (10 percent. sample). London:
H.M. Stationery Office, 1975. xxx, 247 p.

TABLE:

53. The number of divorced persons is tabulated by
economic activity, hours worked, the number and age
of dependent children for both England and Wales.

7-29   _____. CENSUS 1971, ENGLAND AND WALES: MIGRATION
REGIONAL REPORT. (10 percent sample). London: H.M. Stationery Office, 1975-- . 9 regions, 2 pts. each.

TABLES:

5A. Data are supplied on the sex and number of
divorced migrants who moved within one year preceding the census, by type of move, for regions,
conurbations, and subdivisions by regions.

5B. This table reports the sex and number of divorced

migrants who moved within five years preceding the census, by type of move and for regions, conurbations, and subdivisions of regions.

7A. The number of divorced persons moving within one year preceding the census is listed by type of move, sex, and single years of age fifteen to forty-four, for regions and conurbations.

7B. An analysis of the divorced persons who moved within five years preceding the census, by type of move, sex, and single years of age fifteen to forty-four, for regions and conurbations.

7-30   _____. CENSUS 1971, ENGLAND AND WALES: USUAL RESI-
DENCE TABLES. London: H.M. Stationery Office, 1974. xxvii, 59 p.

TABLE:

5. The number of divorced visitors to England and Wales are analyzed by sex, and country of usual residence.

7-31   _____. CENSUS 1971, GREAT BRITAIN: AGE, MARITAL CONDI-
TION, AND GENERAL TABLES. London: H.M. Stationery Office; Edinburgh: General Register Office, 1974. xxvi, 67 p.

TABLES:

5. This table gives the number of divorced persons by sex and age groups for Great Britain.

6. The proportions of divorced persons are listed by sex and age groups for the years 1921, 1931, 1951, 1961, and 1971 for Great Britain, England and Wales, Scotland, and Wales.

9. The number of divorced persons are tabulated by sex and age (single years), for Great Britain, England and Wales, and Scotland.

10. The number of divorced persons are analyzed by sex and age groups for regions, conurbations, subdivisions of England and Wales, and planning subregions of Scotland.

7-32   _____. CENSUS 1971, GREAT BRITAIN: COUNTRY OF BIRTH
TABLES. London: H.M. Stationery Office; Edinburgh: General Register Office, 1974. xxxiii, 194 p.

TABLES:

1. The number of divorced persons are listed by country

of birth, parents' country of birth, and sex, for Great
Britain.

3. This table gives the number of divorced persons by
area of enumeration, country of birth, and visitors to
the United Kingdom.

7-33   _____. CENSUS 1971. GREAT BRITAIN: ECONOMIC ACTIVITY.
Pt. 4. (10 percent sample). London: H.M. Stationery Office;
Edinburgh: General Register Office, 1975. xlvii, 261 p.

TABLES:

27. Statistics on the number of divorced retired persons
are listed by sex, age groups, and former occupations,
for Great Britain.

28. The number of divorced retired persons is enumerated
by sex, and age groups over fifty years, for Great Britain.

29. The number of divorced persons is analyzed by
social class, and socioeconomic class, by sex and
age groups, for Great Britain, England and Wales,
and Scotland.

7-34   _____. CENSUS 1971. GREAT BRITAIN: MIGRATION TABLES.
Pt. 1. (10 percent sample). London: H.M. Stationery Office;
Edinburgh: General Register Office, 1974. xxiii, 172 p. Map.

TABLES:

3A. The number of divorced persons moving within one
year preceding the census is presented by type of move
and sex, for Great Britain, England and Wales, Scotland,
regions, and conurbations.

3B. The number of divorced persons who moved within
five years preceding the census is analyzed by type of
move and sex, for Great Britain, England and Wales,
Scotland, regions, and conurbations.

5A. This table enumerates the number of divorced persons
moving within one year preceding the census, by type of
move, sex, and single years of age fifteen to forty-four,
for Great Britain.

5B. The number of divorced persons who moved within
five years preceding the census are listed by type of
move, sex, and single years of age fifteen to forty-four,
for Great Britain.

7-35   _____. CENSUS 1971. GREAT BRITAIN: NON-PRIVATE HOUSE-
HOLDS. London: H.M. Stationery Office; Edinburgh: General

Register Office, 1974. xxvii, 190 p.

TABLES:

6. The number of divorced persons in private households, nonprivate establishments and elsewhere, by sex and age groups, for Great Britain, England and Wales, Scotland, regions, and subregions are listed.

7. The number of divorced persons in hospitals, homes for the aged and disabled, and detention homes are tabulated by age groups and sex, for Great Britain, England and Wales, Scotland, regions, and conurbations.

8. Divorced persons are enumerated in defense establishments by sex and age groups, for Great Britain, England and Wales, and Scotland.

10. Divorced persons are enumerated in hotels and boarding houses by age groups and sex, for Great Britain, England and Wales, Scotland, regions, and conurbations.

7-36 _____. CENSUS 1971. GREAT BRITAIN: SUMMARY TABLES. (1 percent sample). London: H.M. Stationery Office; Edinburgh: General Register Office, 1973. lii, 176 p. Forms.

TABLES:

1. The number of divorced persons are given by sex and age (single years) for England and Wales, and Scotland.

2. This table lists the number of divorced persons by age groups, and sex, for England and Wales, by region.

3. The number of divorced persons is tabulated by sex, country of birth, and parents' country of birth, for Great Britain.

5. The number of divorced persons is reported by sex, country of birth, and visitor status for Great Britain and regions.

29. The divorced heads of household are listed by age and sex.

4. Retrospective British Census Statistics

The first British census to report statistics on divorce was the census of 1921. This and the succeeding British censuses are described below, indicating the type of divorce data provided by each one. The most recent British census is described in section 3 above.

7-37 Great Britain. Census Office. CENSUS OF ENGLAND AND WALES, 1921. . . . 61 vols. London: H.M. Stationery Office, 1922-25.

TABLES:

14 (County Reports). This table reports the number of divorced persons by age groups and sex, for rural and urban areas.

32, 33, 42 (General Tables). These tables indicate the number of divorced persons by age and sex, for geographical areas, and the number of divorced persons in institutions.

7-38   _____. CENSUS OF ENGLAND AND WALES, 1931. 51 vols. London: H.M. Stationery Office, 1932-40. Maps.

TABLES:

14, 15 (County Reports). These tables give the number of divorced persons by age groups and sex for counties, urban areas, and rural districts.

18, 19 (General Tables). These tables show the number of divorced persons by age and sex for urban and rural areas.

There was no census taken in 1941.

7-39   Great Britain. General Register Office. CENSUS 1951, ENGLAND AND WALES. COUNTY REPORT(S). 44 vols. London: H.M. Stationery Office, 1953-55. Maps.

TABLE:

21. The number of divorced persons is tabulated by sex and age groups for administrative counties.

7-40   _____. CENSUS 1951, ENGLAND AND WALES. GENERAL TABLES COMPRISING POPULATION, AGES AND MARITAL CONDITION, NON-PRIVATE HOUSEHOLDS, BIRTHPLACE, NATIONALITY, AND EDUCATION. London: H.M. Stationery Office, 1956. xiii, 224 p. Map. Form.

TABLES:

17. The number of divorced persons is recorded by age and sex for England and Wales.

26. This table presents the number of divorced persons by age groups and sex for regions.

7-41   _____. CENSUS 1951, ENGLAND AND WALES. AGE, MARITAL CONDITION AND GENERAL TABLES. London: H.M. Stationery

Office, 1956. xiii, 224 p.

TABLES:

8, 12, 13, 16, 18, 19, 24, 26. These tables contain the number and proportions of divorced persons by age, age groups, and sex for England and Wales, rural and urban areas, and regions. They also contain the number of divorced persons in institutions, hotels, and boarding houses by age and sex.

7-42 _____. CENSUS 1951, ENGLAND AND WALES. REPORT ON GREATER LONDON AND FIVE OTHER CONURBATIONS. London: H.M. Stationery Office, 1956. 486 p. Maps. Diagrams.

TABLE:

21. The number of divorced persons is presented by age groups and sex for each area.

7-43 _____. CENSUS 1961, ENGLAND AND WALES; AGE, MARITAL CONDITION AND GENERAL TABLES. London: H.M. Stationery Office, 1964. xv, 108 p. Map.

TABLES:

8, 12, 13, 14, 16, 18, 19, 24, 26. The number of divorced persons is tabulated by age and sex for counties, local authority areas, conurbations, new towns, regions, and the entire country. Also tabulated are the divorced persons in institutions of various types and in hotels and boarding houses.

7-44 _____. CENSUS 1961, ENGLAND AND WALES; BIRTHPLACE AND NATIONALITY TABLES. London: H.M. Stationery Office, 1964. xi, 70 p. Maps.

TABLE:

6. Divorced alien residents are reported by county of usual residence, and by sex.

7-45 _____. CENSUS 1961, ENGLAND AND WALES; COMMON-WEALTH IMMIGRANTS IN THE CONURBATIONS. London: H.M. Stationery Office, 1965. xviii, 116 p. Maps. Forms.

TABLES:

1, 2, 10. These tables describe divorced persons born in specified Commonwealth countries and territories, duration of residence, and socioeconomic groups, by age and sex.

7-46   _____. CENSUS 1961, ENGLAND AND WALES; COUNTY RE-
PORT(S). 60 vols. London: H.M. Stationery Office, 1963–64.
Maps.

TABLE:

6. The number of divorced persons is presented by
county.

7-47   _____. CENSUS 1961, ENGLAND AND WALES; GREATER
LONDON TABLES. London: H.M. Stationery Office, 1966. xvi,
68 p. Map.

TABLE:

6. Divorced persons by sex and age groups are given
for London, greater London, and London boroughs.

7-48   _____. CENSUS 1961, ENGLAND AND WALES; OCCUPATION
TABLES. London: H.M. Stationery Office, 1966. xiv, 267 p.
Map. Forms.

TABLES:

2, 3, 7–15, 17, 19–21, 25. These tables describe
divorced persons by occupations, socioeconomic groups,
social class, males in part-time employment and by hours
worked, by age groups and sex. Also data on divorced
retired persons are reported by former occupations.

7-49   _____. CENSUS 1961, ENGLAND AND WALES; USUAL RESI-
DENCE TABLES. London: H.M. Stationery Office, 1964. xiii,
47 p. Map.

TABLES:

4, 5. Divorced visitors to England and Wales are reported by age, sex, and home country.

7-50   _____. CENSUS 1961, GREAT BRITAIN; SUMMARY TABLES.
London: H.M. Stationery Office, 1966. iii, 158 p. Forms.

TABLES:

4, 6, 32, 33, 35. Data on divorced persons by age
groups, sex, occupation, part-time employment, and
hours worked in Great Britain are shown in these tables.

7-51   _____. SAMPLE CENSUS 1966. HOUSEHOLD COMPOSITION
TABLES. London: H.M. Stationery Office, 1968. xxii, 316 p.
Forms. Maps.

TABLES:

31. The number of divorced persons are tabulated by age groups and by sex of the chief economic supporter of households, for England and Wales, regions and conurbations.

35. The number of divorced housewives is given for England and Wales, regions and conurbations.

7-52   _____. SAMPLE CENSUS 1966. ECONOMIC ACTIVITY TABLES. Pt. 3. London: H.M. Stationery Office, 1968-69.

TABLES:

26. Information on retired divorced persons is presented by sex and former occupation.

28. Data on divorced persons by socioeconomic groups, age, and sex are given.

29. Divorced persons are reported by occupational group, age group, and sex.

C. PUBLISHED VITAL STATISTICS

Vital statistics, unlike census statistics, are reports of events as they occur rather than data collected at certain points in time. Vital statistics on divorce contain information about persons at the time when the divorce decree became final. Governments collect and report these data regularly.

1. Canadian Vital Statistics

7-53   Canada. Statistics Canada. Vital Statistics Section. VITAL STATISTICS. Vol. 2. MARRIAGES AND DIVORCES. Ottawa: 1921-- . Annual. Tables. Graphs. Glossary.

The number and rates of divorce for Canada since 1921 are reported by this annual. The statistics are not analyzed. There is a three-year time lag in the publication of the data. Quarterly vital statistics are available but these do not contain data on divorce. Certain additional divorce data are available upon request from:

> Vital Statistics Section
> Health Division
> Statistics Canada
> Ottawa, KIA 025

2. British Vital Statistics

7-54   Great Britain. General Register Office. THE REGISTRAR-

GENERAL'S STATISTICAL REVIEW OF ENGLAND AND WALES.
Pt. 2. POPULATION. London: H.M. Stationery Office, 1921-- .
3 pts. Annual.

> This vital statistics report for England and Wales pre-
> sents divorce statistics on dissolutions and annulments,
> 1876-1973, grounds used for divorce, the petitioner,
> the age of the spouses, the duration of the marriage
> in years and the age of the spouses, rates, age at
> marriage, marital status at the time of marriage, and
> the number of children involved. There is about a one-
> and-one-half year time lag prior to publication of the
> data.

D. IDENTIFYING NEW SOURCES OF DIVORCE STATISTICS

It often is of utmost importance for the researcher to locate the most up-to-
date and relevant statistics available for his research. By keeping up with
some of the ongoing publications mentioned earlier in this chapter, as well as
the national and trade bibliographies and catalogs described in chapter 2, parts
A and B, along with the sources for reference books described in chapter 3,
part E, the researcher may remain alert for new publications on divorce statistics as they appear. At the same time, this can be accomplished by checking
periodically in the subject card catalog of large research libraries under such
headings as "Divorce--Great Britain--Statistics," or "Divorce--Canada--
Statistics."

The sources which are described below may also be used for identifying compilations of divorce statistics as they appear, either in printed form or as parts
of computerized data bases. The knowledge of the locations and types of this
latter form of the data is becoming increasingly important.

7-55   Canada. Statistics Canada. STATISTICS CANADA CATALOGUE.
        Ottawa: 1954-- . Annual.

> The statistical publications of the Canadian government
> are described in this work as they are issued. It also
> describes the sources and availability of the summary
> tapes of tabulated data for the 1971 census. Refer to
> item 7-15. Since more special tabulations and tabula-
> tions from sample data are likely to become more avail-
> able, in printed or in computer data base form, this
> source is the appropriate place to find out about them.

7-56   Great Britain. Stationery Office. GOVERNMENT PUBLICATIONS.
        London: 1936-- . Monthly, with annual cumulations.

> This index to the official documents published by the
> British government includes new census and vital sta-

tistics publications. There is a subject index and a quinquennial cumulation of the index; Former titles were: GOVERNMENT PUBLICATIONS: CONSOLIDATED LIST 1922-53; GOVERNMENT PUBLICATIONS CATALOGUE 1954-55; and CATALOGUE OF GOVERNMENT PUBLICATIONS 1956-57.

Consult: Divorce
Office of Population Censuses and Surveys

7-57   Kruzas, Anthony T. ENCYCLOPEDIA OF INFORMATION SYSTEMS AND SERVICES. 2d international ed. Ann Arbor, Mich.: A.T. Kruzas Associates, 1974. xii, 1,271 p.

           Refer to item 13-4.

7-58   Sessions, Vivian S., ed. DIRECTORY OF DATA BASES IN THE SOCIAL AND BEHAVIORAL SCIENCES. New York: Science Associates/International, 1974. xv, 300 p.

           Refer to item 6-178.

7-59   STATISTICS SOURCES: A SUBJECT GUIDE TO DATA ON INDUSTRIAL, BUSINESS, SOCIAL, EDUCATIONAL, FINANCIAL, AND OTHER TOPICS FOR THE UNITED STATES AND SELECTED FOREIGN COUNTRIES. Edited by Paul Wasserman and Joanne Paskar. 5th ed. Detroit: Gale Research Co., 1977. 892 p.

           Refer to item 6-179.

Chapter 8

DIVORCE INFORMATION IN LEGAL LITERATURE

Since the legal literature is very complex, no attempt is made here to explain in depth the general approaches and procedures for legal research. The most generally useful sources for information on divorce from the legal perspective are simply described. There are various good handbooks which provide basic nontechnical introductions to the legal literature among which are the following:

8-1   Cohen, Morris L. LEGAL RESEARCH IN A NUTSHELL. 2d ed. St. Paul, Minn: West Publishing Co., 1971. 259 p.

   A good explanation of the organization of U.S. statute law, case law, legislative history, and administrative law is presented here as an aid to research in these areas. Important secondary sources are also discussed. Some English legal works are included.

8-2   Lloyd, David. FINDING THE LAW: A GUIDE TO LEGAL RE-SEARCH. Legal Almanac Series, no. 74. Dobbs Ferry, N.Y.: Oceana Publications, 1974. v, 119 p.

   This basic introduction to searching the law explains the use of basic legal tools. It contains also a list of commonly used legal abbreviations.

8-3   Pollack, Ervin H. ERVIN H. POLLACK'S FUNDAMENTALS OF LEGAL RESEARCH. 4th ed., edited by J. Myron Jacobstein and Roy M. Mersky. Mineola, N.Y.: Foundation Press, 1973. xxix, 565 p.

   Intended as an aid to students beginning the study of law, this work is somewhat more detailed than the above two sources.

See especially addendum 8-3A.

The U.S. government does not have the power to make laws directly concerning marriage and divorce. This authority is relegated to the states. However, since the federal government is at times indirectly involved with divorce-related matters, federal along with state sources of legal information on divorce are described in this chapter. It should be kept in mind, however, that information on divorce from federal sources is sparse. In the cases of Canada and Great Britain, the national governments are directly concerned with divorce law, and thus this chapter treats sources of information for these countries at the national level.

It is recommended that the researcher with little or no legal training confer as closely as possible with librarians, especially law librarians, or with lawyers, when using the legal literature. A great deal of skill and practice in the literature is necessary for effective research in this area.

The sources of legal information described in this chapter are those considered most useful for locating divorce information. There may be others not listed here that might provide more limited or more specialized information. These can be identified from handbooks or trained personnel as indicated above.

After locating information on divorce from one or more of the sources described in this chapter, the investigator may consider it necessary to verify the current status of a particular decision, regulation, or law. To do this he may have to trace its legislative or judicial history to see if and how it has been changed by later interpretations, decisions, or enactments. This often requires the use of works known as citators, some of which are described in this chapter. Information on these and their use can also be acquired from the above basic handbooks, but very often professional assistance is necessary.

A. LEGISLATIVE PUBLICATIONS: LAWS, STATUTES

1. United States

Since the federal government is only indirectly involved in divorce legislation, only a limited amount of information in areas such as alimony, nonpayment of child support, and social security and federal pensions for divorced spouses is likely to be found in the sources that follow.

8-4   Congressional Information Service. CIS U.S. SERIAL SET INDEX. 12 pts. Washington, D.C.: 1975-- . Scheduled for completion in 1979.

> When completed this index will provide access to the 14,000 volumes of the U.S. Serial Set which is comprised of the House and Senate documents, the House and Senate reports, and all other papers ordered printed by either house of the Congress. There are subject indexes and finding lists for each part. The parts cover specific chronological periods. As divorce information in this set relates primarily to the District of Columbia and to federal services to divorced persons, it is of some-

what limited value.

Consult: Desertion   Family abandonment
          Divorce   Family law
          Domestic relations   Nonsupport
          Families

8-5   _____ . INDEX TO PUBLICATIONS OF THE UNITED STATES CONGRESS. Washington, D.C.: 1970-- . Monthly, with quarterly cumulative indexes, along with annual and quinquennial cumulations.

Known as the CIS INDEX, this work indexes and also provides abstracts of committee hearings, House and Senate documents, reports, miscellaneous publications, and Senate executive reports and documents on pending bills. There is a good subject index and a personal name index, as well as an index by number of bills, reports, and documents. The cumulative annual volumes are known as the CIS/ANNUALS. Computer searching is available for this data base from the publisher.

Consult: Aid to families with   Family abandonment
             dependent children   Family law
          Children   Marriages
          Divorce   Social Security
          Domestic relations   State governments
          Families   Women

8-6   CUMULATIVE SUBJECT INDEX TO THE MONTHLY CATALOG OF UNITED STATES GOVERNMENT PUBLICATIONS, 1900-1971. 14 vols. Compiled by William W. Buchanan and Edna M. Kanely. Washington, D.C.: Carrollton Press, 1973-75.

This cumulative subject index provides indexing in one alphabet, of over eight hundred thousand documents for the period. It cites the year and page or item number in the MONTHLY CATALOG (item 8-11) where the document description can be found. No assigned Superintendent of Documents numbers are provided.

Consult: Divorce
          Marriage

8-7   UNITED STATES CODE. 15 vols. Washington, D.C.: Government Printing Office, 1971. Annual cumulative supplements. Subject index.

This official subject compilation of public, general, and permanent federal laws is arranged under fifty titles subdivided into chapters. A good subject index is included.

Annotated editions of the code, such as the UNITED STATES CODE ANNOTATED, 1927-- , by the West Publishing Company, as well as the FEDERAL CODE ANNOTATED and the UNITED STATES CODE SERVICE (item 8-8) by the Lawyers Co-operative Publishing Company, provide much more information with references also to other legal works.

Consult:
Alimony	Income tax--divorce
Desertion	Marriage--annulment
Divorce	Separate maintenance
Guardian and ward	Social Security--divorce
Income tax--alimony	Stepparents and step-
Income tax--children	children

8-8   UNITED STATES CODE SERVICE. Lawyers Edition. Rochester, N.Y.: Lawyers Co-operative Publishing Co., 1972-- . Continual revision. General index.

This work fully annotates all federal laws of general and permanent nature, arranged under fifty titles in accordance with the section numbering of the UNITED STATES CODE (item 8-7). Its annotations refer to further information in the UNITED STATES SUPREME COURT REPORTS, Lawyers Edition (item 8-94), the AMERICAN LAW REPORTS FEDERAL (item 8-87), the AMERICAN LAW REPORTS (item 8-88), and AMERICAN JURISPRUDENCE, second edition (item 8-120). This service supersedes the FEDERAL CODE ANNOTATED. It is a good source with which to start a search for legislative information on divorce.

Consult: Divorce (Note: this one heading will lead to other headings)

8-9   UNITED STATES CODE CONGRESSIONAL AND ADMINISTRATIVE NEWS. St. Paul, Minn.: West Publishing Co., n.d. Semimonthly when Congress is in session and monthly when not in session, with annual cumulative volumes. Cumulative monthly indexes and annual indexes.

During the sessions of Congress, this work contains the full text of all of the public laws. It also provides legislative history, administrative regulations, proclamations, and executive messages and orders throughout the year.

Consult:
Children and minors	Support
Social Security	Women

8-10   U.S. Library of Congress. Legislative Reference Service. DIGEST

OF PUBLIC GENERAL BILLS AND SELECTED RESOLUTIONS WITH INDEX. Washington, D.C.: Government Printing Office, 1936-- Five cumulative issues per session, with supplements.

> This excellent work presents a digest of public general bills and selected resolutions and traces the changes that occur to them as they pass through the legislative process.

> Consult: Domestic relations

8-11   U.S. Superintendent of Documents. MONTHLY CATALOG OF UNITED STATES GOVERNMENT PUBLICATIONS. Washington, D.C.: Government Printing Office, 1895-- . Monthly, with monthly and annual cumulative indexes. GP 3.8:year/no.

> By using the subject index to this basic monthly listing of publications issued by all branches of the U.S. government, the researcher is able to identify bills, resolutions, and laws. For documents issued between 1900 and 1970, refer to item 8-6.

> Consult: Alimony   Domestic-relations courts
>   Children   Families
>   Divorce

> After July 1976, use the Library of Congress subject headings listed in item 2-5.

8-12   UNITED STATES LAW WEEK; A NATIONAL SURVEY OF CURRENT LAW. Washington, D.C.: Bureau of National Affairs, 1933-- . Weekly, in two sections. Loose-leaf service.

> Refer to item 8-95.

2. Uniform Divorce Laws in the United States

Since the late nineteenth century, there has been interest in uniform laws regulating divorce in the United States. Social reform organizations lobbied for change, national conferences were held, bills were introduced in the Congress, and the popular press debated the issue. For bibliographies on this subject, refer to items 1-13, 1-14, and 1-15 in chapter 1. Several more recent works useful on this topic are listed below.

8-13   DESK GUIDE TO THE UNIFORM MARRIAGE AND DIVORCE ACT. Editors of the Family Law Reporter. Washington, D.C.: Bureau of National Affairs, 1974. 102 p.

> The text of the Uniform Marriage and Divorce Act, and comments on the same, make up the main portion of this work. A good brief introduction to the Uniform Act is included. Also included are the complementary uniform acts proposed on support, child custody, adoption, and

parentage. The names and addresses of the commissioners in each state are also provided.

8-14   Levy, Robert J. UNIFORM MARRIAGE AND DIVORCE LEGISLA-
        TION: A PRELIMINARY ANALYSIS. Chicago[?]: 1968[?]. Var.
        pag.

        This work was prepared for the Special Committee on
        Divorce of the National Conference of Commissioners
        on Uniform State Laws.

Additional information can be obtained by writing to the following special group:

8-15   National Conference of Commissioners on Uniform State Laws, 645
        N. Michigan Avenue, Suite 510, Chicago, Illinois 60637

        Publications of this conference may also be located in
        libraries by looking in the author section of the card
        catalog under the heading "National Conference of Com-
        missioners on Uniform State Laws."

3. Individual States of the United States

Since divorce laws and regulations in the United States are the responsibility
of the state governments, the information on divorce found in state legislative
publications is much more specific and extensive than that found in the federal
publications. However, divorce legislation in process or enacted by the individual states is difficult to locate and keep up with. The legislative journals
available are not very complete. Bills, committee reports, and hearings are
hard to locate and often are not published officially. Commercial services
such as those of the West Publishing Company, the Commerce Clearing House,
and the Michie Company, may be helpful for the text of session laws for some
states. Their catalogs should be consulted. Various other useful sources of
information on divorce legislation in the individual states, both current and
retrospective, are described below. Chief among the current sources is the
FAMILY LAW REPORTER (item 8-16), which since 1974 has greatly alleviated
the aforementioned difficulties.

8-16   FAMILY LAW REPORTER. Washington, D.C.: Bureau of National
        Affairs, 1974-- . Weekly, with index. Loose-leaf service.

        This weekly news service is an indispensable tool for
        keeping abreast of the changing legal situation on divorce
        and other family-related matters in the United States. It
        reports on the legislative activities and court decisions of
        the fifty states, plus federal court decisions and regula-
        tions of federal agencies, relating to the family. These
        reports are somewhat difficult to use because of the ar-

rangement of the contents. The materials are arranged
in three parts: (1) articles on proposed or accepted
state and federal court cases concerning the family,
(2) court opinions, reports, and legislative proposals,
and (3) occasional monographs. Currently, the full
text of state divorce statutes is included in the appendix, and is updated when significant changes are made.
The texts of uniform and model acts pertaining to the
family are also included in the appendix. The information usually has only a one- or two-week time lag until
publication.

8-17   MARTINDALE-HUBBELL LAW DIRECTORY. Vol. 6. Summit, N.J.:
        Martindale-Hubbell, 1931-- . Annual, with mid-year supplements.

        The main value of this huge reference set for legal in-
        formation on divorce lies in volume 6 which contains a
        nearly 5,000-page digest of the laws of the fifty states,
        Canada and its provinces, and fifty-two other countries,
        including most of the English-speaking world, Europe, and
        Latin America. The laws are summarized under almost
        one hundred topics by qualified lawyers who update this
        work annually, with midyear supplements that include
        new legislation. The contents are arranged alphabetically
        by states and by countries. Within these geographical
        areas, the summaries are arranged by topics. This work
        is a merger of MARTINDALE'S AMERICAN LAW DIREC-
        TORY, 1868-1930, and HUBBELL'S LEGAL DIRECTORY,
        1870-1930.

        Consult: Divorce   Marriage
                  Dissolution of marriage

For the person who is interested in very specific and up-to-the-minute information on divorce legislation for any particular state, the state legislative reference service or library may be contacted. In many states these are indepen-
dent or branch agencies of the state government. An excellent current source
for aid in locating legislative reference libraries, bureaus, or other such service
is the Council of State Governments. Several of its helpful publications are
described below.

8-18   Council of State Governments. BOOK OF THE STATES. Lexington,
        Ky.: 1935-- . Biennial, with supplements in the odd-numbered
        years.

        Although the information provided by this source may
        not be as current as that of the two sources described
        below, this work may be sufficient to identify the ap-
        propriate person or agency in any given state which

provides information services dealing with divorce legislation.

8-19 _____. "Legislative Session Sheet." Lexington, Ky.: 1946-- .
Monthly. Mimeographed.

This fact sheet is very useful as a means of ascertaining
the schedules of meetings and adjournments for regular
and special sessions of the state legislatures.

8-20 _____. PRINCIPAL LEGISLATIVE STAFF OFFICERS. P.O. Box
11910, Lexington, Ky.: 1976. 95 p. Published at least annually.

This booklet lists rosters of legislative offices and staff
members for each state legislature, with addresses and
telephone numbers. At the same time it lists the
agencies responsible for bill drafting, for statute, code
and law revision, and for research and policy analysis,
as well as the legislative reference bureaus and legislative libraries.

It may be necessary for the researcher to refer directly to the volumes of the
session laws, statutes, or codes of the individual state. These, if available,
may be found in libraries by searching in the author section of the card catalog, under headings as illustrated for the state of Illinois:

Illinois. Laws, statutes, etc.

In some libraries, even in some law libraries, these extensive sets may not be
cataloged as illustrated above, but simply shelved in an orderly manner, usually alphabetically by state. The several sets within each state grouping are
generally shelved in some orderly manner. In this case, the sets within the
state groupings are best identified by the titles on the spines of the volumes.
These titles are often referred to as the "running" titles, or "common" titles,
as distinguished from the correct bibliographic titles which are derived from
the title page of the works and which appear on library catalog cards. For
situations where these sets are not cataloged, therefore, but simply shelved as
indicated above, the state-by-state checklist below is provided as an aid for
identification and location of several basic sets for each state.

For each state and territory listed below, the ongoing official set of session
laws published during or at the end of each session of the legislature is presented first. The format, organization, and official title for each set may
vary at any time. For the dates of initial publication, and more specific bibliographic information when citing, refer to the work by Pimsleur (item 8-74).

The second set cited for each state, in the checklist below, is a codified,
often annotated, set of laws in effect. These "codes" are usually prepared
commercially, and may be much easier and faster to use and also more helpful

because of special features, including cross-references and other legal citations. Within the sets, the laws in effect are grouped in as many as 100
broad subjects, often referred to as "Titles." For example, family law may
be under the "Title" of Marriage and Divorce, Domestic Relations, or Husband
and Wife. These "Title" numbers generally appear on the spine of the volumes.
The "Titles" may be further divided into chapters, articles, and sections. In
the checklist which follows, these are noted for each set to help the user find
the precise location of the appropriate section on divorce legislation.

The state-by-state checklist is as follows:

ALABAMA

8-21a   ACTS OF ALABAMA. Montgomery, Alabama.

        Consult: Divorce
                  Marriage and divorce

8-21b   CODE OF ALABAMA ANNOTATED. 15 vols. in 17. Charlottesville, Va.: Michie Co., 1940-- . Recompiled 1958.

        Consult: Title 34, Chapter 2, Sections 20-39

ALASKA

8-22a   ALASKA SESSION LAWS. Juneau, Alaska.

        Consult: Dissolution of marriage

8-22b   ALASKA STATUTES. 7 vols. Charlottesville, Va.: Michie Co.,
1962-- . Loose-leaf.

        Consult: Title 9, Chapter 55, Article 3, Sections 70-231

ARIZONA

8-23a   SESSION LAWS OF ARIZONA. Phoenix, Arizona.

        Consult: Title 25, Marriage and domestic relations

8-23b   ARIZONA REVISED STATUTES ANNOTATED. 20 vols. in 22. St.
Paul, Minn.: West Publishing Co., 1956-- .

        Consult: Title 25, Chapter 3, Sections 311-39

ARKANSAS

8-24a   GENERAL ACTS OF ARKANSAS. Little Rock, Arkansas.

        Consult: Divorce

8-24b   ARKANSAS STATUTES ANNOTATED. 10 vols. in 23. Indianapolis: Bobbs-Merrill, 1947-- .

        Consult: Title 34, Chapter 12, Sections 1201-18

CALIFORNIA

8-25a   STATUTES AND AMENDMENTS TO THE CODES: CALIFORNIA. Sacramento: California.

        Consult: Dissolution of marriage

8-25b   WEST'S ANNOTATED CALIFORNIA CODES. 129 vols. St. Paul, Minn.: West Publishing Co., 1974-- .

        Consult: Civil Code, Part 5, Title 3, Sections 4350-4540

COLORADO

8-26a   SESSION LAWS OF COLORADO. Denver, Colorado.

        Consult: Dissolution of marriage

8-26b   COLORADO REVISED STATUTES. 20 vols. Denver: Bradford-Robinson, 1973-- .

        Consult: Title 14, Article 10, Sections 101-33

CONNECTICUT

8-27a   CONNECTICUT PUBLIC AND SPECIAL ACTS. Hartford, Connecticut.

        Consult: Dissolution of marriage

8-27b   GENERAL STATUTES OF CONNECTICUT. 11 vols. Hartford, Connecticut. Revised to 1975.

        Consult: Title 46, Chapter 811, Sections 32-64b

DELAWARE

8-28a   LAWS OF DELAWARE. Wilmington, Delaware.

        Consult: Divorce

8-28b   DELAWARE CODE ANNOTATED. 20 vols. Charlottesville, Va.: Michie Co., 1974-- .

        Consult: Title 13, Chapter 15, Sections 1501-22

DISTRICT OF COLUMBIA

8-29a   DISTRICT OF COLUMBIA CODE. 3 vols. Washington, D.C.: Government Printing Office, 1973-- .

    Consult: Title 16, Chapter 9, Sections 901-22

FLORIDA

8-30a   LAWS OF FLORIDA. Tallahassee, Florida.

    Consult: Dissolution of marriage

8-30b   FLORIDA STATUTES ANNOTATED. 35 vols. in 62. Atlanta: Harrison Co., 1943-- .

    Consult: Sections 61.001 to 61.20

GEORGIA

8-31a   GEORGIA LAWS. Atlanta, Georgia.

    Consult: Divorce

8-31b   GEORGIA CODE ANNOTATED. 34 vols. in 60. Atlanta: Harrison Co., 1935-- .

    Consult: Title 30, Chapter 30, Sections 101-301

HAWAII

8-32a   SESSION LAWS OF HAWAII. Honolulu, Hawaii.

    Consult: Divorce

8-32b   HAWAII REVISED STATUTES. 8 vols. Honolulu, Hawaii: 1968-- .

    Consult: Title 31, Chapter 580, Sections 1-76

IDAHO

8-33a   SESSION LAWS--IDAHO. Boise, Idaho.

    Consult: Title 32, Chapter 5

8-33b   IDAHO CODE ANNOTATED. 12 vols. in 19. Indianapolis: Bobbs-Merrill, 1947-- .

    Consult: Title 32, Chapter 5, Sections 501-805

ILLINOIS

8-34a   LAWS OF ILLINOIS. Springfield, Illinois.

       Consult: Divorce

8-34b   SMITH-HURD ILLINOIS ANNOTATED STATUTES. 92 vols. St. Paul, Minn.: West Publishing Co., 1953-- .

       Consult: Chapter 40, Sections 1-32

INDIANA

8-35a   ACTS--INDIANA. Indianapolis, Indiana.

       Consult: Divorce

8-35b   BURNS INDIANA STATUTES ANNOTATED. Code edition. 27 vols. Indianapolis: Bobbs-Merrill, 1975-- .

       Consult: Title 31, Article 1, Chapter 12-1 to 22-5

IOWA

8-36a   ACTS--IOWA. Des Moines, Iowa.

       Consult: Dissolution of marriage

8-36b   IOWA CODE ANNOTATED. 60 vols. in 70. St. Paul, Minn.: West Publishing Co., 1949-- .

       Consult: Chapter 598, Sections 1-35

KANSAS

8-37a   SESSION LAWS OF KANSAS. Topeka, Kansas.

       Consult: Divorce

8-37b   KANSAS STATUTES ANNOTATED. 7 vols. in 13. Topeka, Kansas: 1963-- .

       Consult: Sections 60-1601 to 60-1611

KENTUCKY

8-38a   KENTUCKY ACTS. Frankfort, Kentucky.

       Consult: Divorce
               Domestic relations

8-38b   KENTUCKY REVISED STATUTES ANNOTATED. 20 vols. Indianapolis: Bobbs-Merrill, 1971-- .

Consult: Chapter 403, Sections 010-350

LOUISIANA

8-39a   ACTS--STATE OF LOUISIANA. Baton Rouge, Louisiana.

Consult: Marriage and divorce

8-39b   WEST'S LOUISIANA STATUTES ANNOTATED. Civil Code. 76 vols.
St. Paul, Minn.: West Publishing Co., 1951-- .

Consult: Title 4, Chapter 6, Articles 136-60

MAINE

8-40a   LAWS OF MAINE. Augusta, Maine.

Consult: Divorce

8-40b   MAINE REVISED STATUTES ANNOTATED. 18 vols. in 20. St.
Paul, Minn.: West Publishing Co., 1964-- .

Consult: Title 19, Chapter 13, Sections 631-752

MARYLAND

8-41a   LAWS OF MARYLAND. Annapolis, Maryland.

Consult: Divorce

8-41b   ANNOTATED CODE OF MARYLAND. 12 vols. in 18. Charlottesville, Va.: Michie Co., 1957-- .

Consult: Article 16, Sections 24-32

MASSACHUSETTS

8-42a   ACTS AND RESOLVES OF MASSACHUSETTS. Boston, Massachusetts.

Consult: Probate courts--divorce

8-42b   MASSACHUSETTS GENERAL LAWS ANNOTATED. 59 vols. in 48.
Charlottesville, Va.: Michie Co., 1958-- .

Consult: Chapter 208, Sections 1-47

MICHIGAN

8-43a   PUBLIC AND LOCAL ACTS--MICHIGAN. Lansing, Michigan.

Consult: Domestic relations

8-43b   MICHIGAN COMPILED LAWS ANNOTATED. 45 vols. in 50. St.
         Paul, Minn.: West Publishing Co., 1967-- .

         Consult: Section 552.1 to 552.459

MINNESOTA

8-44a   LAWS OF MINNESOTA. St. Paul, Minnesota.

         Consult: Divorce

8-44b   MINNESOTA STATUTES ANNOTATED. 47 vols. in 69. St. Paul,
         Minn.: West Publishing Co., 1975-- .

         Consult: Chapter 518, Sections 001-67

MISSISSIPPI

8-45a   GENERAL LAWS OF MISSISSIPPI. Jackson, Mississippi.

         Consult: Divorce

8-45b   MISSISSIPPI CODE ANNOTATED. 21 vols. in 23. Atlanta: Har-
         rison Co., 1972-- .

         Consult: Title 93, Chapter 5, Section 1 to Chapter 7,
                   Section 13

MISSOURI

8-46a   LAWS--MISSOURI. Jefferson, Missouri.

         Consult: Dissolution of marriage

8-46b   VERNON'S ANNOTATED MISSOURI STATUTES. Kansas City, Mo.:
         Vernon Law Book Co., 1951-- .

         Consult: Chapter 452, Sections 300-415

MONTANA

8-47a   LAWS OF MONTANA. Helena, Montana.

         Consult: Divorce

8-47b   REVISED CODES OF MONTANA ANNOTATED. 9 vols. in 15.
         Indianapolis: Allen Smith Co., 1947-- .

         Consult: Title 48, Sections 316-41

NEBRASKA

8-48a   LAWS OF NEBRASKA. Lincoln, Nebraska.

Consult: Divorce

8-48b REVISED STATUTES OF NEBRASKA. 10 vols. Lincoln, Neb.: 1943-- .

Consult: Chapter 42, Articles 341-79

NEVADA

8-49a STATUTES OF NEVADA. Carson City, Nevada.

Consult: Divorce

8-49b NEVADA REVISED STATUTES. 33 vols. Carson City, Nev.: 1973-- . Loose-leaf.

Consult: Chapter 125, Sections 010-440

NEW HAMPSHIRE

8-50a N.H., LAWS. Concord, New Hampshire.

Consult: Divorce

8-50b NEW HAMPSHIRE REVISED STATUTES ANNOTATED. 6 vols. in 12. Rochester, N.Y.: Lawyers Co-operative Publishing Co., 1955-- .

Consult: Title 43, Chapter 458, Sections 1-35

NEW JERSEY

8-51a LAWS OF NEW JERSEY. Trenton, New Jersey.

Consult: Title 2A, Chapter 34

8-51b NEW JERSEY STATUTES ANNOTATED. 81 vols. St. Paul, Minn.: West Publishing Co., 1939-- .

Consult: Title 2A, Chapter 34, Sections 1-27

NEW MEXICO

8-52a LAWS OF NEW MEXICO. Santa Fe, New Mexico.

Consult: Marriage
                Probate code--divorce

8-52b NEW MEXICO STATUTES ANNOTATED. 12 vols. in 19. Indianapolis: Allen Smith Co., 1953-- .

Consult: Chapter 22, Article 7, Sections 1-22

NEW YORK

8-53a   LAWS OF NEW YORK. Albany, New York.

        Consult: Domestic relations law

8-53b   MCKINNEY'S SESSION LAWS OF NEW YORK. St. Paul, Minn.: West Publishing Co.

        Consult: Divorce

8-53c   MCKINNEY'S CONSOLIDATED LAWS OF NEW YORK ANNOTATED. 149 vols. St. Paul, Minn.: West Publishing Co., 1976-- .

        Consult: Chapter 14, Article 9, Sections 140–46
                  Chapter 14, Article 10, Sections 170–75
                  Chapter 14, Article 11A, Sections 200–251

NORTH CAROLINA

8-54a   SESSION LAWS OF NORTH CAROLINA. Raleigh, North Carolina.

        Consult: Divorce

8-54b   GENERAL STATUTES OF NORTH CAROLINA. 4 vols. in 16. Charlottesville, Va.: Michie Co., 1975-- .

        Consult: Section 50-2 to Section 50-18

NORTH DAKOTA

8-55a   LAWS OF NORTH DAKOTA. Bismarck, North Dakota.

        Consult: Divorce

8-55b   NORTH DAKOTA CENTURY CODE. 15 vols. Indianapolis: Allen Smith Co., 1959-- .

        Consult: Title 14, Chapter 4, Sections 1-5
                  Title 14, Chapter 5, Sections 1-26
                  Title 14, Chapter 6, Sections 1-6

OHIO

8-56a   LAWS OF OHIO. Columbus, Ohio.

        Consult: Divorce

8-56b   PAGE'S REVISED CODE ANNOTATED. 20 vols. Cincinnati: H.W. Anderson Co., 1953-- .

        Consult: Title 31, Chapter 3105.01 to Chapter 3105.99

OKLAHOMA

8-57a OKLAHOMA SESSION LAWS. St. Paul, Minn.: West Publishing Co.

Consult: Divorce

8-57b OKLAHOMA STATUTES ANNOTATED. 63 vols. St. Paul, Minn.: West Publishing Co., 1971-- .

Consult: Title 12, Chapter 22, Sections 1271-90

OREGON

8-58a OREGON LAWS. Salem, Oregon.

Consult: Dissolution of marriage

8-58b OREGON REVISED STATUTES. 6 vols. Salem, Ore.: 1953-- . Loose-leaf.

Consult: Chapter 107, Sections 005-610

PENNSYLVANIA

8-59a LAWS OF PENNSYLVANIA. Harrisburg, Pennsylvania.

Consult: Divorce

8-59b PURDON'S PENNSYLVANIA STATUTES ANNOTATED. 77 vols. St. Paul, Minn.: West Publishing Co.; and Philadelphia: George T. Bisel, 1938-- .

Consult: Title 23, Sections 10-98

PUERTO RICO

8-60a LAWS OF PUERTO RICO. Orford, N.H.: Equity Publishing Co.

Consult: Divorce

8-60b LAWS OF PUERTO RICO ANNOTATED. 11 vols. in 25. Orford, N.H.: Equity Publishing Co., 1975-- . Spanish and English editions.

Consult: Title 31, Sections 321-85

RHODE ISLAND

8-61a PUBLIC LAWS OF R.I. Also ACTS AND RESOLUTIONS. Providence, Rhode Island.

Consult: Title 15, Chapter 5

8-61b   GENERAL LAWS OF RHODE ISLAND. 8 vols. in 14. Indianapolis: Bobbs-Merrill, 1956-- .

         Consult: Title 15, Chapter 5, Sections 1-23

SOUTH CAROLINA

8-62a   ACTS AND JOINT RESOLUTIONS OF SOUTH CAROLINA. Columbia, South Carolina.

         Consult: Divorce

8-62b   CODE OF LAWS OF SOUTH CAROLINA ANNOTATED. 26 vols. Rochester, N.Y.: Lawyers Co-operative Publishing Co., 1976-- .

         Consult: Title 20, Chapter 3, Section 10-440

SOUTH DAKOTA

8-63a   LAWS OF SOUTH DAKOTA. Pierre, South Dakota.

         Consult: Divorce

8-63b   SOUTH DAKOTA COMPILED LAWS ANNOTATED. 17 vols. Indianapolis: Allen Smith Co., 1976-- .

         Consult: Title 25, Chapter 4, Sections 1-49

TENNESSEE

8-64a   TENNESSEE PUBLIC ACTS. Nashville, Tennessee.

         Consult: Divorce

8-64b   TENNESSEE CODE ANNOTATED. 15 vols. in 20. Indianapolis: Bobbs-Merrill, 1956-- .

         Consult: Title 36, Chapter 8, Sections 801-36

TEXAS

8-65a   GENERAL AND SPECIAL LAWS--TEXAS. Austin, Texas.

         Consult: Divorce

8-65b   VERNON'S TEXAS CODES ANNOTATED. 93 vols. St. Paul, Minn.: West Publishing Co., 1968-- .

         Consult: Family Code, Title 1, Chapter 3, Sections 01-66

UTAH

8-66a   LAWS OF UTAH. Salt Lake City, Utah.

    Consult: Husband and wife

8-66b   UTAH CODE ANNOTATED. 10 vols. in 16. Indianapolis: Allen Smith Co., 1953-- .

    Consult: Title 30, Chapter 3, Sections 1-18

VERMONT

8-67a   LAWS OF VERMONT. Montpelier, Vermont.

8-67b   VERMONT STATUTES ANNOTATED. 9 vols. in 17. Montpelier, Vt.: 1959-- .

    Consult: Title 15, Chapter 11, Sections 511-761

VIRGINIA

8-68a   ACTS OF ASSEMBLY. Richmond, Virginia.

    Consult: Domestic relations

8-68b   CODE OF VIRGINIA ANNOTATED. 12 vols. in 20. Charlottesville, Va.: Michie Co., 1950-- .

    Consult: Title 20, Chapter 6, Sections 89.1-122

VIRGIN ISLANDS

8-69a   VIRGIN ISLAND SESSION LAWS. Charlotte Amalie, Virgin Islands.

    Consult: Divorce

8-69b   VIRGIN ISLANDS CODE ANNOTATED. 5 vols. in 10. Washington, D.C.: Government Printing Office, 1957-- .

    Consult: Title 16, Chapter 3, Sections 101-11

WASHINGTON

8-70a   LAWS OF WASHINGTON. Olympia, Washington.

    Consult: Dissolution of marriage

8-70b   REVISED CODE OF WASHINGTON ANNOTATED. 61 vols. San Francisco: Bancroft-Whitney Co., 1962-- .

    Consult: Title 26, Chapter 9, Sections 010-902

WEST VIRGINIA

8-71a   ACTS OF THE LEGISLATURE OF WEST VIRGINIA. Charleston, West Virginia.

Consult: Divorce

8-71b   WEST VIRGINIA CODE ANNOTATED. 21 vols. Charlottesville, Va.: Michie Co., 1966-- .

Consult: Chapter 48, Article 2, Sections 1-31

WISCONSIN

8-72a   LAWS OF WISCONSIN. Madison, Wisconsin.

Consult: Divorce

8-72b   WEST'S WISCONSIN STATUTES ANNOTATED. 46 vols. in 60. St. Paul, Minn.: West Publishing Co., 1957-- .

Consult: Section 247.01 to 247.39

WYOMING

8-73a   SESSION LAWS--WYOMING. Cheyenne, Wyoming.

Consult: Domestic relations

8-73b   WYOMING STATUTES ANNOTATED. 10 vols. in 11. Charlottesville, Va.: Michie Co., 1957-- .

Consult: Title 20, Chapter 2, Sections 101-17

Various printed checklists of the session laws, statutes, and codes may be referred to by the researcher, both for current compilations and for searching through earlier compilations and sets.

The remainder of this section describes these checklists, noting also, where possible, how the researcher can purchase or borrow microform copies of the documents listed. The checklist by Pimsleur (item 8-78) is retrospective and current; the others are retrospective.

8-74   National Association of State Libraries. Public Documents Clearing House Committee. CHECK-LIST OF LEGISLATIVE JOURNALS OF STATES OF THE UNITED STATES OF AMERICA. Compiled by Grace E. MacDonald. Providence, R.I.: Oxford Press, 1938. 274 p.

The published journals of the forty-eight state legislatures from colonial and territorial times through 1938 are listed in this volume, which provides the dates for the sessions, the type of session, and the number of volumes and pages.

8-75 _____. CHECK-LIST OF SESSION LAWS. Compiled by Grace E. MacDonald. New York: H.W. Wilson Co., 1936. 266 p. Supplement.

This list of the published compilations of session laws of the forty-eight states includes the following information: date and type of session, and number of pages. It also includes session laws from territorial and colonial times through 1933. For the period from 1934 to 1954, a "Twenty-Year Supplement to MacDonald's Checklist of Session Laws," compiled by the American Association of Law Librarians' Committee on Cooperation with State Libraries appears in the LAW LIBRARY JOURNAL 49 (February 1956): 30ff.

8-76 _____. CHECK-LIST OF STATUTES OF THE STATES OF THE UNITED STATES OF AMERICA INCLUDING REVISIONS, COMPILATIONS, DIGESTS, CODES AND INDEXES, compiled by Grace E. MacDonald. Providence, R.I.: Oxford Press, 1937. 147 p.

This checklist provides the names, the dates, and names and dates of publishers of the codes of the forty-eight states and former territories. Included also is the number of pages.

8-77 _____. SUPPLEMENT CHECK-LIST OF LEGISLATIVE JOURNALS OF THE STATES OF THE UNITED STATES OF AMERICA. Compiled by William S. Jenkins. Boston: The Association[?], 1943. 87 p.

For the period from 1938 through 1941, many additional journals not included in MacDonald's earlier work (item 8-75) are included in this supplement. Many earlier journals are also added, especially for the states of Connecticut, Massachusetts, Rhode Island, and South Carolina.

8-78 Pimsleur, Meira G., ed. CHECKLISTS OF BASIC AMERICAN LEGAL PUBLICATIONS. 3 vols. to date. South Hackensack, N.J.: Fred B. Rothman, for the American Association of Law Libraries, 1962-- . Loose-leaf service.

The purpose of this loose-leaf service is to provide authoritative lists of the primary legal publications of all of the states in as complete a form as possible. Volume 2 has lists of the published session laws. This work was based on MacDonald's work (item 8-75) and that of her successors. The session laws of the colonies, states, and former territories are now available on microfiche from Xerox University Microfilms through 1969.

8-79   Pullen, William R. A CHECK LIST OF LEGISLATIVE JOURNALS
       ISSUED SINCE 1937 BY THE STATES OF THE UNITED STATES OF
       AMERICA. Chicago: American Library Association, 1955. 59 p.

       This work is a listing of the state legislative journals
       published from 1937 to 1954.

8-80   U.S. Library of Congress. GUIDE TO THE MICROFILM COLLEC-
       TION OF EARLY STATE RECORDS. Compiled by William S. Jen-
       kins; edited by Lillian A. Hamrick. Washington, D.C.: Photo-
       duplication Service of the Library of Congress, 1950. 800 p.

       Based on the work of MacDonald (items 8-74, 8-75, 8-76)
       and the supplementary additions, this massive volume is
       a guide to 1,600 reels of microfilmed documents of the
       forty-eight states and former territories. The documents
       contain legislative records, journals, minutes, debates
       and proceedings, statutory and special laws, constitu-
       tional, administrative, executive, and court records.
       The cut-off date varies, but most of the material is pre-
       twentieth century. Locations of the original documents
       are given. The microfilm is available on interlibrary
       loan from the Center for Research Libraries in Chicago
       through its cooperating libraries.

8-81   _____. GUIDE TO THE MICROFILM COLLECTION OF EARLY
       STATE RECORDS: SUPPLEMENT. Compiled and edited by William
       S. Jenkins. Washington, D.C.: Library of Congress, 1951. 171 p.

       One hundred seventy reels of microfilm added to the
       above collection (item 8-80) are described in this volume.
       The materials include local records, both city and county,
       records of native American Indian nations, fifty reels of
       early newspapers, rudimentary states, and miscellaneous
       materials. This microfilm is also available from the
       Center for Research Libraries.

4. Canada and Great Britain

English law is perhaps more similar to that of the United States than any other
country, because of the heritage that was shared during the colonial period of
U.S. history. Canada shared the same heritage. Because of this common
background, the family and divorce laws of these countries are of particular
mutual interest. At the present time, for both Canada and Great Britain,
divorce laws are enacted by the national legislative bodies, not as in the
United States by the states. Some of the more useful sources for information
on divorce legislation in England and Canada are described below. For sources
on early English law, consult chapter 20 of item 8-3.

8-82   CURRENT LAW YEAR BOOK. London: Sweet and Maxwell, 1947-- . Monthly. Annual volumes.

This extensive research service is useful as a citator of English statutory law. Separate editions are also published for Canada and Scotland. For further information, refer to item 8-122.

Consult: Divorce and matrimonial causes

8-83   HALSBURY'S LAWS OF ENGLAND. 4th ed. London: Butterworth, 1973-- . Annual cumulative supplements, with loose-leaf service. Annual indexes.

Volume 13 of this general legal encyclopedia includes extensive information on divorce. This is of particular value in that the volume was published in 1975. For Canada, its CANADIAN CONVERTER, 1954-1973, provides information on Canadian federal and provincial statutes, excluding the province of Quebec. For more information, refer to 8-123.

8-84   HALSBURY'S STATUTES OF ENGLAND. Edited by A.D. Yonge. 42 vols. 3d ed. London: Butterworth, 1968-72. Index.

This well-indexed subject arrangement of acts in force has volume indexes as well as a cumulative index.

Consult: Divorce
        Family provision

8-85   INDEX TO STATUTES IN FORCE. London: H.M. Stationery Office, 1948-- . Cumulated and revised annually. Subject index.

Covering the years 1235 through 1972, this is a companion volume to the CHRONOLOGICAL TABLE OF STATUTES. The excellent subject index also serves as an index to at least four other compilations of English law.

Consult: Divorce

8-86   MARTINDALE-HUBBELL LAW DIRECTORY. Vol. 6. Summit, N.J.: Martindale-Hubbell, 1931-- . Annual, with mid-year supplements.

This work provides legislative information on divorce for England and Canada. For more information, refer to item 8-17.

B. JUDICIAL PUBLICATIONS: COURT REPORTS, DIGESTS

1. United States

In this section, compilations of the written opinions and decisions of the Supreme Court of the United States, the courts of appeals, and the district courts are described as sources of information on divorce.

8-87   AMERICAN LAW REPORTS. ALR FEDERAL: CASES AND ANNOTA-
TIONS. Rochester, N.Y.: Lawyers Co-operative Publishing Co.,
1969-- . Several annual volumes. Pocket supplements. FEDERAL
QUICK INDEX. 2d ed., 1975. Pocketparts.

This work is a selective reporter of federal appellate
court decisions which are thought to become "leading"
cases. The annotations and further references are highly
valued. Prior to 1969 the type of information included
in this work was included in the AMERICAN LAW RE-
PORTS: CASES AND ANNOTATIONS (item 8-88), but
since 1969, as the federal litigation increased, the publishers decided to start this new series. The FEDERAL
QUICK INDEX, 2d ed., 1975, with pocketparts, is very
useful for important references on the judicial aspects of
divorce, and should be one of the first points of entry
into this area. It leads the investigator also to the
AMERICAN LAW REPORTS: CASES AND ANNOTA-
TIONS (item 8-88), the UNITED STATES SUPREME
COURT REPORTS, Lawyers Edition (item 8-94), the
UNITED STATES CODE SERVICE, AMERICAN JURIS-
PRUDENCE, 2d series (item 8-120), and several other
compilations.

Consult: Divorce and separation

8-88   AMERICAN LAW REPORTS. ALR 3d: CASES AND ANNOTATIONS.
Rochester, N.Y.: Lawyers Co-operative Publishing Co., 1965-- .
Several annual volumes. Pocket supplements. QUICK INDEX, 2d
ed., 1973-- . Pocketparts.

This work is a selective reporter of appellate court decisions which are considered significant. The annotations
and further references are highly valued. The first series
of this set started in 1919. The QUICK INDEX is very
useful in much the same way as described in item 8-87.
This is a very important first point of entry into the area
of the judicial aspects of divorce. There is a WORD
INDEX for the second series of this work which is also
helpful.

Consult: Alimony   Remarriage
          Divorce and separation

8-89   FEDERAL REPORTER. 2d series. St. Paul, Minn.: West Publishing
        Co., 1880-- . FEDERAL SUPPLEMENT. St. Paul, Minn.: West
        Publishing Co., 1931-- .

        These two works are part of West's National Reporter
        System which is described in 8-96 and which uses the
        American Digest System for locating opinions. They are
        unofficial publications of the decisions of the U.S. Courts
        of Appeals and the district courts. Information on divorce
        is difficult to locate in these sets.

8-90   GENERAL DIGEST. Fifth series: COVERING STATE AND FEDERAL
        COURTS. St. Paul, Minn.: West Publishing Co., 1976-- .
        Monthly. 2 to 4 cumulative volumes per year. Decennial indexes.
        DESCRIPTIVE WORD INDEX.

        As part of West's National Reporter System, this work
        has good subject access, as described in item 8-96.
        Since 1886, going back to 1650, the West Publishing
        Company has been receiving and dividing digests of all
        cases into seven main classes, and then into subclasses,
        and then further into topics. There are now 435 topics,
        each corresponding to a legal concept, and each assigned
        a key number. Each month, all digests received are
        arranged and issued in the GENERAL DIGEST. These
        issues are cumulated several times a year, and later into
        cumulative decennial volumes, referred to as the DECEN-
        NIAL DIGEST. From 1966, each decennial cumulation,
        as well as all the issues, are called the GENERAL DI-
        GEST. Since the coverage is so broad and the DESCRIP-
        TIVE WORD INDEX, because of the key numbers, is so
        specific, the GENERAL DIGEST quickly provides many
        references to divorce in various areas of the legal system.

        Consult: Divorce

8-91   MODERN FEDERAL PRACTICE DIGEST; ALL FEDERAL CASE LAW OF
        THE MODERN ERA. 58 vols. St. Paul, Minn.: West Publishing
        Co., 1960-62. Replacement volumes and pocket supplements.
        DESCRIPTIVE WORD INDEX.

        Covering, since 1939, U.S. Supreme Court decisions
        and the material in the FEDERAL REPORTER and the
        FEDERAL SUPPLEMENT (8-89) and the FEDERAL RULES
        DECISIONS, this work is arranged under West's National
        Reporter System (refer to items 8-96 and 8-90) with topics
        and key numbers. Because of this, it provides good
        access to any information on divorce included. For
        federal case laws of historical significance, its predeces-
        sor, the FEDERAL DIGEST, is still referred to.

        Consult: Divorce

8-92   SUPREME COURT REPORTER. St. Paul, Minn.: West Publishing
        Co., 1883-- .

> This work, which is part of West's National Reporter
> System and indexed by West's American Digest System
> (item 8-96), started with volume 106, 1882, of the
> UNITED STATES REPORTS (item 8-93). The full texts
> of the decisions are included, without summaries. Pagi-
> nation does not correspond with the official editions.
> This reporting service also includes the state court systems.
> Not much information directly related to divorce appears
> to be included to date.

8-93   U.S. Supreme Court. UNITED STATES REPORTS. Washington,
        D.C.: Government Printing Office, 1789-- . Annual volumes,
        with advance sheets of opinions as made. Title varies. Volume
        subject index.

> This official edition of the U.S. Supreme Court decisions
> actually started in 1790 under a variety of publishing
> arrangements, but was not known as the UNITED STATES
> REPORTS until 1875 with what is now volume 91. The
> first volumes are usually referred to by their authors:
> Dallas, Cranch, Wheaton, Peters, Howard, Black, and
> Wallace. A brief subject index is at the back of each
> volume.

> Consult: Divorce

8-94   _____. UNITED STATES SUPREME COURT REPORTS. Lawyers
        Edition. Books 1-100, 1790-1955; 2d series, vol. 1, 1956-- .
        Rochester, N.Y.: Lawyers Co-operative Publishing, 1901-- .
        Semimonthly, with index. Annual cumulative volumes and subject
        index. Title varies.

> This work reprints all of the decisions included in the
> official set (item 8-93), with the text given in full.
> Pagination does not correspond with the official edition.
> Summaries and annotations are highly valued. A very
> important subject index to the annotations of the Lawyers
> Edition and to the AMERICAN LAW REPORTS FEDERAL
> (item 8-87) is the companion set, the SUPREME COURT
> REPORTS INDEX TO ANNOTATIONS, which started in
> 1972. Prior to this INDEX TO ANNOTATIONS, the
> annotations were indexed in the UNITED STATES SUPREME
> COURT REPORTS DIGEST. The INDEX TO ANNOTA-
> TIONS should be perhaps one of the first works to be
> consulted when information is needed on Supreme Court
> decisions and opinions regarding divorce.

> Consult: Divorce and separation

8-95   UNITED STATES LAW WEEK; A NATIONAL SURVEY OF CURRENT
         LAW. Washington, D.C.: Bureau of National Affairs, 1933-- .
         Weekly, in two sections. Loose-leaf service.

         This service is in two parts: a periodical and a refer-
         ence service. Part 2 is in two sections: (1) Supreme
         Court section, and (2) general laws section. Section 1
         includes the complete text of opinions of the Supreme
         Court, along with a topical index. Section 2 includes
         the most important of current federal statutes, summaries
         and analyses of federal trends, and some agency rulings.
         There is a general topical index for the entire work.
         This is a speedy service.

For information in regard to loose-leaf reporting services on special topics, refer
to item 8-107.

2. Individual States of the United States

Since the powers of legislation and regulation of divorce laws have been
largely delegated to the states in the United States, it follows that state court
opinions and decisions on cases disputed or appealed, on the bases of these
laws and regulations, are also of great importance in the study of divorce.

Official state law reports or court reports are published as authorized by legislation. Not all states publish these themselves, but contract the work out to
private publishers. Private companies also publish judicial decisions with or
without legislative directive. Sometimes these unofficial reports are the only
ones available. Some of these are very accurate and may have added features.
One of the major publishers of these unofficial reports is the West Publishing
Company, with its National Reporter System.

One method of identifying or locating in libraries the digests or reporters for
any given state is to consult the subject section of the card catalog under the
following heading, which uses the state of Mississippi as an example:

         Law reports, Digests, etc.--Mississippi

8-96   National Reporter System, of the West Publishing Company, St. Paul,
         Minnesota.

         As noted in the previous section, the National Reporter
         System provides federal court reporting services and pub-
         lications. It also plays an important part in the reporting
         of opinions of the state appellate and trial courts, both
         for the individual states, and for seven regional groupings
         of states. These reporters use West's American Digest
         System for locating the decisions. This is a system of

classifying each decision by a key number and thus providing a Descriptive Word Index arranged topically under each key number. The state reporters or digests cover all state decisions and federal cases which began in the state in question. Refer also to item 8-90.

8-97   FAMILY LAW REPORTER. Washington, D.C.: Bureau of National Affairs, 1974-- . Weekly, with index. Loose-leaf service.

This publication is very useful for locating court opinions and reports on divorce case law for each of the states. For further information, refer to item 8-16.

8-98   GENERAL DIGEST. Fifth series: COVERING STATE AND FEDERAL COURTS. St. Paul, Minn.: West Publishing Co., 1976-- . Monthly. Two to four cumulative volumes per year. Decennial indexes. DESCRIPTIVE WORD INDEX.

Refer to item 8-90.

8-99   U.S. Library of Congress. Division of Documents. MONTHLY CHECKLIST OF STATE PUBLICATIONS, 1910-- . Washington, D.C.: Government Printing Office, 1912-- . Monthly, with annual indexes. LC30.9/vol./no.

By using this source, it is possible to identify state judicial publications, as they are received by the Library of Congress, which are likely to contain information on divorce.

Consult: Divorce
          Marriage

3. Canada and Great Britain

Although there were earlier English judicial reports, modern English law reporting began in 1865. The most useful of these reporters for information on divorce are listed below. For information on the earlier reports, consult Cohen (8-1) and Pollack (8-3). It should be noted that divorces were granted by the British Parliament prior to 1858.

8-100   REPORTS OF FAMILY LAW: A SERIES OF REPORTS OF SELECTED CASES FROM ALL CANADIAN COURTS OF FAMILY LAW, TOGETHER WITH ARTICLES AND CASE COMMENTS. Edited by David M. Steinberg. Toronto: Carswell Co., 1971-- . Annual, with subject index.

With each annual volume being largely concerned with the subject of divorce, this work is a very useful source of information on Canadian divorce case law.

Consult: Alimony   Nullity
           Custody   Property
           Divorce (with numer- Separation
              ous subtitles)   Taxation
           Maintenance

8-101   WEEKLY LAW REPORTS, CONTAINING DECISIONS IN THE HOUSE
        OF LORDS, THE PRIVY COUNCIL, THE SUPREME COURT OF
        JUDICATURE, ASSIZE COURTS, AND ECCLESIASTICAL COURTS.
        London: Council of Law Reporting for England and Wales, 1953-- .
        Weekly, with three annual volumes.

        This is the most complete of all the English reporting
        services. Earlier volumes, since 1867, are entitled
        LAW REPORTS. In volume 3, each year, there is a
        short Subject Matter Index at the front of the volume.

        Consult: Husband and wife--divorce
                   Husband and wife--financial provision
                   Husband and wife--maintenance
                   Husband and wife--nullity
                   Husband and wife--property

C. ADMINISTRATIVE PUBLICATIONS: RULES, REGULATIONS

Regulatory agencies have the power to formulate regulations to carry out legislation, and when these regulations are violated, they have the power to hold
quasi-legal hearings. This power came about as the problems of society became too complex to be handled entirely by legislative bodies at the various
levels of government. Some of the most useful sources of information on the
regulations and orders in regard to divorce are described in the following sections.

1. United States

Since the U.S. government, as stated earlier in this chapter, is not directly
involved in the area of divorce, information on divorce found in the following
sources is likely to be sparse and tangential in nature.

8-102   CODE OF FEDERAL REGULATIONS. 1949 ed. Published by the
        Division of the Federal Register, National Archives and Records
        Service. 76 vols. Washington, D.C.: Government Printing Office,
        1949-72. Fifty completed revised supplements annually. Separate
        general index volume.

        This set is a codification of federal administrative rules
        and regulations, general and permanent, such as presi-
        dential proclamations and executive orders, rules and

regulations of the U.S. government departments and bureaus, as well as decisions and statements from special investigatory bodies. The code is organized into fifty titles similar to the UNITED STATED CODE (item 8-7). Each of these titles is completely revised and published anew each year. The code must often be used in conjuction with the FEDERAL REGISTER, and it is also kept up-to-date by the individual issues of the FEDERAL REGISTER. An annual volume entitled FINDING AIDS should be consulted by the researcher unfamiliar with the use of this set. Consult the general index under headings such as "family."

8-103   FAMILY LAW REPORTER. Washington, D.C.: Bureau of National Affairs, 1974-- . Weekly, with index. Loose-leaf service.

This indispensable service for keeping up with the changing legal situation on divorce and other family-related matters In the United States includes information on regulations of federal agencies. For further information, refer to item 8-16.

8-104   UNITED STATES CODE CONGRESSIONAL AND ADMINISTRATIVE NEWS. St. Paul, Minn.: West Publishing Co., n.d. Semimonthly when Congress is in session and monthly when not in session, with annual cumulative volumes. Cumulative monthly indexes and annual indexes.

This service provides information on administrative regulations, proclamations, and executive messages and orders throughout the year.

Consult: Children and minors   Support
           Social Security   Women

8-105   UNITED STATES LAW WEEK; A NATIONAL SURVEY OF CURRENT LAW. Washington, D.C.: Bureau of National Affairs, 1933-- . Weekly, in two sections. Loose-leaf service.

This service provides only limited information on agency rulings. A general topical index for the entire work is helpful. For more information, refer to item 8-95.

8-106   WEEKLY COMPILATION OF PRESIDENTIAL DOCUMENTS. Published by the Office of the Federal Register, National Archives and Records Office. Washington, D.C.: Government Printing Office, 1965-- . Weekly, with weekly, quarterly, semiannual, and annual indexes.

Containing statements, remarks, messages to Congress, letters, transcripts of news conferences, public speeches,

pronouncements, and other materials released by the
White House Press Office each week, this compilation
is useful and very well indexed.

Consult headings such as: Family assistance
Women

8-107   Various topical or subject reporters, usually in the form of loose-
leaf services, are helpful for information in special areas of interest
as they relate to divorce. For example, Prentice-Hall has several
loose-leaf reporters in the areas of estate planning, Social Security,
and taxation. Commerce Clearing House has others in areas such
as taxation, and labor and personnel relations. The Bureau of National Affairs is another such publisher. These services can be identified in libraries by looking under the subject of interest in the subject section of the card catalog, by looking under the name of the
company in the author section of the card catalog, or by asking for
reference assistance.

2. Individual States of the United States

Since divorce law, as well as rules and regulations for the same, is the particular concern of the individual states, it is especially important for the researcher to be able to locate information on administrative regulations and
rules made at the state level. However, this is often very difficult to do.
Some of the most useful sources for this information are described below.

8-108   AMERICAN LAW REPORTS. ALR 3d: CASES AND ANNOTATIONS.
Rochester, N.Y.: Lawyers Co-operative Publishing, 1965-- .
Several annual volumes. Pocket supplements. QUICK INDEX, 2d
ed., 1973-- , with pocketparts.

Although largely for reporting of court decisions, this
work often provides information on court cases which
refer to state administrative law problems. For further
information on this work, refer to item 8-88. The
QUICK INDEX is especially useful.

8-109   U.S. Library of Congress. GUIDE TO THE MICROFILM COLLEC-
TION OF EARLY STATE RECORDS. Compiled by William S. Jenkins; edited by Lillian A. Hamrick. Washington, D.C.: Photo-
duplication Service of the Library of Congress, 1950. 800 p.

For identifying and locating state publications on administrative decisions and regulations, this is a good
retrospective source. For further information refer to
item 8-80, and to 8-81 which is its supplement. Some
publications referred to may still be continued.

8-110   U.S. Library of Congress. Division of Documents. MONTHLY
         CHECKLIST OF STATE PUBLICATIONS, 1910-- . Washington,
         D.C.: Government Printing Office, 1912-- . Monthly, with an-
         nual indexes. LC30.9/vol./no.

         By using this source, it is sometimes possible to identify
         state publications, as they are received by the Library
         of Congress, which are likely to contain information on
         administrative rules and regulations on divorce.

         Consult: Divorce
                   Marriage

3. Canada and Great Britain

Since divorce laws for both Canada and Great Britain are enacted directly by
the national legislative bodies, the regulation and administration of these laws
are likewise the responsibility of the national governments. Some of the more
useful sources of information on this are described below. For further information in this area, the researcher is advised to consult with law librarians or
lawyers, especially with regard to Canada.

8-111   Canada. Information Canada. CANADIAN GOVERNMENT PUB-
         LICATIONS. Ottawa, 1954-- . Annual.

         Refer to 8-130.

8-112   GUIDE TO GOVERNMENT ORDERS, INDEXING S. R. & O'S.
         AND S.I'S. IN FORCE. London: H.M. Stationery Office,
         1891-- . Annual volumes. Title varies.

         This work indexes the official English administrative
         code, STATUTORY RULES AND ORDERS, 1890-1947,
         and STATUTORY INSTRUMENTS, 1948-- . This offi-
         cial code includes general and permanent administra-
         tive regulations.

8-113   HALSBURY'S STATUTORY INSTRUMENTS. 24 vols. 3d reissue.
         London: Butterworth, 1972-74. Updated by replacement volumes
         and loose-leaf supplements. Updated index volume. General index.

         An unofficial compilation of administrative rules and
         regulations, this work is indexed by subject and is a
         companion set to HALSBURY'S STATUTES OF ENGLAND
         (item 8-84). The updating service is similar to that of
         the CODE OF FEDERAL REGULATIONS in the United
         States (item 8-102).

         Consult: Ancillary relief   Matrimonial causes
                   Divorce

D. SECONDARY SOURCES AND FINDING AIDS

The materials described here are scholarly, although legally unauthoritative, secondary materials. While not incorporating in any official way the text of laws, regulations, or decisions, they are useful for finding these primary documents, or for summarizing, organizing, or reflecting upon the same. They may also aid the researcher in identifying new primary or secondary publications as they appear. Thus they are important means for the researcher to keep abreast of the current literature related to divorce, as well as to identify trends or new aspects as they develop. Other materials described here, on the other hand, may lead to further sources of retrospective information.

1. Indexes to Legal Periodicals

8-114   INDEX TO CANADIAN LEGAL PERIODICAL LITERATURE. Montreal: Canadian Association of Law Libraries, 1961-- . Bimonthly, with annual and decennial cumulations.

> Sixty-one Canadian law journals are indexed by author and subject in this publication. A table of cases and a book review index are also included. There is a time lag of about one year from the time the articles appear until they are indexed.

> Consult: Alimony and main-   Domestic relations
>   tenance   Husband and wife
>   Annulment   Marriage property
>   Community property   Marriage (civil law)
>   Desertion   property
>   Divorce

8-115   INDEX TO LEGAL PERIODICAL LITERATURE, 1886-1937. Vols. 1 and 2, edited by Leonard A. Jones; vols. 3-6, edited by Frank E. Chipman. Boston: Boston Book Co., 1888-1919 (vols. 1-3); Chipman, 1924 (vol. 4); Indianapolis: Bobbs-Merrill, 1933 (vol. 5); Los Angeles: Parker and Baird, 1939 (vol. 6).

> Materials indexed in this set include articles in legal periodicals, annotated cases, biographical notices, and papers of bar associations from the United States, England, Ireland, Scotland, and the English colonies. Up to 160 legal and general periodicals were indexed in the various volumes. A few sets of eighteenth-century periodicals were also included. Each volume has subject and author indexing, and volumes 3-6 also have title indexing. This index is a rich source of information on divorce for the nineteenth century.

> Consult: Alimony   Marriage
>   Divorce

8-116   INDEX TO LEGAL PERIODICALS, 1908-- . New York: H.W.
         Wilson Co., in cooperation with the American Association of Law
         Libraries, 1908-- . Monthly, except September, with annual and
         triennial cumulations.

         A basic author and subject index to nearly four hundred
         legal and law-related periodicals published in the United
         States, Canada, Great Britain, Northern Ireland, Austra-
         lia, and New Zealand, this work is an essential source
         for legal periodical articles on divorce. Book reviews,
         case notes, yearbooks, annual institutes, and annual
         reviews are indexed in this work in addition to articles.
         A table of cases is also included. A list of subject
         headings used appears in each annual cumulation. Ap-
         proximately four times as many legal periodicals are in-
         dexed by this index than are indexed in the SOCIAL
         SCIENCES CITATION INDEX (item 4-33). There is a
         six- to eight month time lag from the time the articles
         appear until they are indexed.

         Consult: Alimony and main-   Domicile and residence
                      tenance   Domestic relations
                   Annulment   Husband and wife
                   Child custody   Marriage: property
                   Community property   Settlements
                   Desertion   Support of dependents
                   Divorce and separa-
                      tion

8-117   INDEX TO PERIODICAL ARTICLES RELATED TO LAW. Dobbs Ferry,
         N.Y.: Glanville Publications, 1958-- . Quarterly with annual
         cumulations. 10-year index for vols. 1-10, 1958-68.

         This publication is a selective worldwide index to
         English-language articles that are not indexed in the
         INDEX TO LEGAL PERIODICALS (item 8-116). Very
         few of the articles indexed appear in the SOCIAL
         SCIENCES CITATION INDEX (item 4-33). There is
         no standard listing of periodicals indexed, but each
         issue includes a list of periodicals indexed in that
         issue. Articles are arranged by author and subject.
         A list of subject headings appears in each volume.
         There is a six- to twelve-month time lag from the time
         the articles appear until they are indexed.

         Consult: Domestic relations   Marriage and divorce
                   Domestic relations--   Marriage and divorce--
                      (by countries)   (by countries)

8-118   INDEX TO U.S. GOVERNMENT PERIODICALS, 1972-- . Chicago:
         Infordata International, 1975-- . Quarterly, with annual cumulative
         indexing.

An index to over 140 U.S. government periodicals, many of which are not indexed elsewhere, this publication is specifically a subject index based on a thesaurus of terms. Back volumes are in preparation to 1970. This work is easy to use. Microfiche copies to the text of all periodical articles indexed are available as listed in CURRENT U.S. GOVERNMENT PERIODICALS ON MICROFICHE, published by Microfilming Corporation of America, Glen Rock, New Jersey.

Consult: Divorce   Family services
          Family   Marriage
          Family life

Although not strictly a periodical index, the following source is very helpful.

8-119   CONTENTS OF CURRENT LEGAL PERIODICALS. Los Angeles: Law Publications, 1972-- . Monthly.

The purpose of this publication is to provide rapid awareness of the contents of legal periodical issues as they are published by reproducing the title page or table of contents of each periodical issue. Broad topical groupings under some seventy subject headings is provided. There is still a time lag of several months from the time the articles appear until they are cited in the issues of this publication.

Consult: Family law

2. Legal Encyclopedias

Legal encyclopedias are used as aids to legal research. They lack legal authority and cannot be cited as such, but they are helpful for the generalist looking for a broad summary treatment on a topic of interest. In this respect, they should be one of the first types of publications to be consulted when approaching a search in the legal literature. The main legal encyclopedias for American, English, and Canadian law are described below, followed by a short discussion of specific state law encyclopedias for the United States.

8-120   AMERICAN JURISPRUDENCE: A MODERN COMPREHENSIVE TEXT STATEMENT OF AMERICAN LAW, STATE AND FEDERAL. 82 vols. 2d ed. Rochester, N.Y.: Lawyers Co-operative, 1962-76. Updated by replacement volumes and pocket supplements. Volume and general indexes.

Arranged alphabetically by broad legal topics, this work is essentially on judicial law, although in this second edition more emphasis is on federal statutory and regulatory law and state statutory laws broadly viewed. It

often refers the user to more detail in the AMERICAN
LAW REPORTS (items 8-87 and 8-88), as well as other
sources.

Consult: Divorce and separation (this volume was written
in 1966).

8-121   CORPUS JURIS SECUNDUM; A COMPLETE RESTATEMENT OF THE
ENTIRE AMERICAN LAW AS DEVELOPED BY ALL REPORTED CASES
. . . 101 vols. in 136. St. Paul, Minn.: West Publishing Co.,
1936-74. Updated by replacement volumes and annual cumulative
pocket supplements. Five-volume general index.

Essentially providing information on and citations to
federal and state case law, this work also includes
some information on federal and state statutory law.
It also cites treatises and law periodical articles.
Through its cross-references, it connects with West's
AMERICAN DIGEST SYSTEM (see items 8-90, 8-96)
for more specific information. This work supersedes
CORPUS JURIS, 1914-37, still often referred to.

Consult: Divorce as a heading in the general index;
this will lead to other headings. (This
volume was published in 1959.)

8-122   CURRENT LAW YEAR BOOK. London: Sweet and Maxwell,
1947-- . Monthly. Bound annually.

The preface of this work states, "This comprehensive research service includes a case digest and citator, statutory digest and citator, and a limited index to British
legal periodicals and books. It is the most effective
citator for English law." Separate editions are also
published for Canada and Scotland.

Consult: Divorce and matrimonial causes

8-123   HALSBURY'S LAWS OF ENGLAND. 4th ed. London: Butterworth,
1973-- . Annual cumulative supplements and loose-leaf service.
Annual indexes.

A general legal encyclopedia with references to case
laws, statutes, and administrative law, this is a good
source for English divorce information. Each annual
supplement is well indexed. For Canada, its CANA-
DIAN CONVERTER, 1954-1973, provides information
on Canadian federal and provincial statutes, excluding
the province of Quebec.

Consult: Divorce (in volume 13 which was written in
1975.)

In regard to encyclopedic restatements and treatments of specific state statutory and judicial laws for the United States, the researcher is referred to state law encyclopedias when available. These again are topically arranged, and often provide references to the AMERICAN LAW REPORTS (items 8-87 and 8-88) and AMERICAN JURISPRUDENCE (8-120). The following, for example, are published by Bancroft-Whitney, San Francisco:

8-124   CALIFORNIA JURISPRUDENCE, 1952-- .

8-125   FLORIDA JURISPRUDENCE, 1955-- .

8-126   NEW YORK JURISPRUDENCE, 1958-- .

8-127   OHIO JURISPRUDENCE, 1953-- .

8-128   TEXAS JURISPRUDENCE, 1959-- .

8-129   The West Publishing Company, St. Paul, Minnesota, has published state encyclopedias for Florida, Illinois, Indiana, Maryland, Michigan, and Pennsylvania. Consult the company's catalog of publications for further information.

3. Bibliographies of Legal Works

The following is a list of useful sources for identifying official and unofficial works on or related to the legal aspects of divorce. The unofficial works may include treatises, summaries or restatements, guides, surveys, research reports, "hornbooks," casebooks, commentaries, manuals, or monographs on more specific topics. Some of the sources are current and may be useful for keeping up with new publications. Others are retrospective and thus useful for background and historical research on the subject.

8-130   Canada. Information Canada. CANADIAN GOVERNMENT PUBLICATIONS. Ottawa, 1954-- . Annual. Published in two series. MONTHLY CATALOGUE, 1953-- . Subject indexes.

An English-French listing of all government documents, both parliamentary and departmental, this work includes legal publications as well as other official publications, such as census and vital statistics reports. In addition to a general subject index, a subject index to government periodicals is included. This latter has a two-year time lag from the time the articles appear until they are cited. This work succeeded the CATALOGUE OF OFFICIAL PUBLICATIONS OF THE PARLIAMENT AND GOVERNMENT OF CANADA, 1928-1954, which is similarly arranged.

Consult: Divorce
         Population--marital status

8-131   Great Britain. Stationery Office. GOVERNMENT PUBLICATIONS.
London: 1936-- . Annual, with annual and quinquennial indexes.
Title varies. GOVERNMENT PUBLICATIONS MONTHLY LIST.

An index of official documents published by the British
government, this work is arranged alphabetically by the
issuing body. Census and vital statistics documents are
included. The catalog succeeds the QUARTERLY LIST
. . . OF OFFICIAL PUBLICATIONS, 1898-1922, and
CATALOGUE OF GOVERNMENT PUBLICATIONS, 1923-
34.

Consult: Divorce
         Marital condition

8-132   Israel, Stanley, comp. and ed. A BIBLIOGRAPHY ON DIVORCE.
New York: Bloch Publishing Co., 1974. vix, 300 p.

This bibliography contains a section, "Legal Aspects of
Divorce," pp. 3-107. For further information, refer to
item 1-4.

8-133   Jacobstein, J. Myron, and Pimsleur, Meira G., eds. LAW BOOKS
IN PRINT; BOOKS IN ENGLISH PUBLISHED THROUGHOUT THE
WORLD AND IN PRINT THROUGH 1974. 4 vols. Dobbs Ferry,
N.Y.: Glanville Publishers, 1976.

This index to currently available legal works does not
include statutes, law reports, digests, government publications, or periodicals. It contains an author-title index,
a subject index, and a publishers' index. It is kept current by LAW BOOKS PUBLISHED (item 8-134).

8-134   Pimsleur, Meira G., comp. and ed. LAW BOOKS PUBLISHED.
Dobbs Ferry, N.Y.: Glanville Publishers, 1969-- . Quarterly
with annual cumulations.

This publication, which updates LAW BOOKS IN PRINT
(item 8-133), contains an author-title index and a subject index.

8-135   U.S. Library of Congress. Division of Bibliography. LIST OF
REFERENCES SUBMITTED TO THE COMMITTEE ON THE JUDICIARY,
U.S. SENATE, 63RD CONGRESS, 3RD SESSION, 1915, IN CON-
NECTION WITH S.J. RES. 109, RESOLUTION PROPOSING AN
AMENDMENT TO THE CONSTITUTION OF THE UNITED STATES RELAT-
ING TO DIVORCES. Compiled by Hermann H.B. Meyer. Washington,

D.C.: Government Printing Office, 1915. 110 p.

>Two sections of this work, one on Great Britain,
>pp. 34-39, and the other on the United States,
>pp. 51-84, have very good retrospective references
>to legal works on divorce. For further information,
>refer to item 1-15.

8-136 _____. "Marriage and Divorce, with Special References to Legal Aspects: A Selected Bibliography." Compiled by Helen F. Conover. Washington, D.C.: 1940. 55 p. Mimeographed.

>Refer to item 1-16.

8-137 _____. "A Selected List of References on Alimony." Compiled by Florence S. Hellman, Acting Chief Bibliographer. Washington, D.C.: 1935. 12 p. Mimeographed.

>Refer to item 1-18.

8-138 U.S. Library of Congress. Division of Documents. MONTHLY CHECKLIST OF STATE PUBLICATIONS. Washington, D.C.: Government Printing Office, 1912-- . Monthly, with annual index. LC30.9/v./no.

>This is an important source for identifying state publications, as they are received by the Library of Congress, which may contain information on legal aspects of divorce.

>Consult: Divorce
>Marriage

8-139 U.S. Superintendent of Documents. MONTHLY CATALOG OF UNITED STATES GOVERNMENT PUBLICATIONS. Washington, D.C.: Government Printing Office, 1895-- . Monthly, with monthly and annual cumulative indexes.

>Refer to item 8-11.

For bibliographies relating to uniform divorce legislation, the user is referred to items 1-13, 1-14, and 1-15.

To keep up with new bibliographies of legal works as they may appear, the researcher is referred to the BIBLIOGRAPHIC INDEX (item 1-2). Also, to keep up with any new bibliographies on legal works that may be added to library collections, the researcher should consult the following subject heading in the library card catalog:

Divorce--Bibliography

Chapter 9

DIVORCE AND THE NEWS MEDIA

This chapter presents various approaches to finding information or opinions on divorce as they are reported, transmitted, or otherwise treated in the news media. Published indexes to current, large daily newspapers are listed and described. Other indexing services to the news are also reported, as are checklists of newspapers, past and present. Finally, sources of opinion polls on divorce are considered.

A. PUBLISHED INDEXES TO CURRENT DAILY NEWSPAPERS: UNITED STATES

Since newspapers report facts and opinions on all facets of social life, news articles are a rich source of information in regard to current events and opinion on divorce.

1. Multiple Newspaper Indexes

The multiple newspaper indexes described here selectively index a number of newspapers in one consolidated index.

9-1   CALIFORNIA NEWS INDEX. Claremont, Calif.: Claremont College, Center for Public Affairs, July 1970-- . Quarterly. Loose-leaf.

> All significant state and regional news of research value is indexed from the LOS ANGELES TIMES, and the SACRAMENTO BEE. Four other newspapers are indexed more selectively: the SAN DIEGO UNION, the SAN FRANCISCO EXAMINER, the SAN FRANCISCO CHRON-ICLE, and the SAN JOSE MERCURY. The NEWSPAPER INDEX series (item 9-3) does more thorough indexing of the LOS ANGELES TIMES and the SAN FRANCISCO CHRONICLE. Sunday supplements, editorials, and seven California magazines are also included in the indexing. A thesaurus of subject headings is included in each volume. There is a fifteen-month delay in the indexing,

with no cumulations of the index.

Consult: Divorce/dissolution

Marriage

9-2   NEWSBANK. Greenwich, Conn.: NewsBank, 1970--. Monthly, with cumulated annual index. Loose-leaf index. Articles on microfiche.

Over 100,000 news articles from nearly 200 U.S. daily newspapers are indexed and reproduced on microfiche each year by this unique index. In addition to selectively indexing nearly all of the 150 largest newspapers, one newspaper from each state capital as well as minority newspapers are also indexed. About 250 articles on divorce are reproduced each year. The index is arranged in thirteen broad subject categories. This is an excellent source of nationwide information on divorce.

Consult: Social relations--divorce, marriage, and family relations

2. Newspaper Indexes in Series

In a newspaper index series a number of individual newspapers are comprehensively and separately indexed using the same standardized format.

9-3   NEWSPAPER INDEX (series). Wooster, Ohio: Bell and Howell, 1972-- . Monthly, with annual cumulations.

This important series of eight separate, computerized, standardized indexes provides access to eight large metropolitan daily newspapers. Comprehensive indexing is attempted for each paper. The newspapers, with the date when each index began, are indicated below:

CHICAGO TRIBUNE 1972--
DETROIT NEWS 1976--
HOUSTON POST 1976--
LOS ANGELES TIMES 1972--
MILWAUKEE JOURNAL 1976--
NEW ORLEANS TIMES-PICAYUNE 1972--
SAN FRANCISCO CHRONICLE 1976--
WASHINGTON (D.C.) POST 1971--

All local, state, regional, national, and international news is indexed by means of a subject index and a name index. The supplements of the papers are indexed as well. PARADE MAGAZINE is indexed in the WASHINGTON POST index. The indexes are published within two months after the news appears in the newspapers.

Consult: Alimony and child   Child custody
        support   Divorce

3. Individual Newspaper Indexes

In this section the published indexes to newspapers with a daily circulation in excess of 100,000 are reported. For the states that do not have newspapers of this size, the index to the largest newspaper in the state has been noted. A special survey of the 150 largest newspapers in the United States was made by the authors in 1976 in order to find which of these have published indexes, since no list of indexes could be located. No attempt was made to find or locate the unpublished indexes that many public and academic libraries make for their local newspapers. The Library of Congress is working on this project. Nor was any attempt made to locate indexes that were once published but have ceased publication.

The indexes are arranged by states, and cities within each state. Most of these indexes were examined by the authors. In cases where the indexes were not examined the descriptions by the publishers were used. All indexes are available from the publishers in the format indicated. The Library of Congress has some but not all of these indexes.

ARKANSAS

9-4   ARKANSAS GAZETTE INDEX: AN ARKANSAS INDEX. Russell-ville, Ark.: Arkansas Technical University, 1964-- . Annual.

   State news is emphasized in this index.

CALIFORNIA

9-5   FRESNO BEE INDEX. Palo Alto, Calif.: Library Microfilms, 1870-- .

   This index, which focuses on state and local news, is published irregularly at two- and three-year intervals, and is available only on cards, 35mm microfilm, or microfiche.

9-6   NEWSPAPER INDEX, LOS ANGELES TIMES. Wooster, Ohio: Bell and Howell, 1972-- . Monthly, with annual cumulations.

   See NEWSPAPER INDEX series, item 9-3. The LOS ANGELES TIMES is also selectively indexed in the CALIFORNIA NEWS INDEX, item 9-1.

9-7   SAN DIEGO UNION INDEX. Riverside, Calif.: Custom Microfilm Systems, 1930-- . Annual. Microfiche.

The newspaper is indexed completely by this work, and is selectively indexed in the CALIFORNIA NEWS INDEX, item 9-1.

9-8 SAN FRANCISCO CHRONICLE INDEX. Wooster, Ohio: Bell and Howell, 1976-- . Monthly, with annual cumulations.

See NEWSPAPER INDEX series, item 9-3. This paper is also selectively indexed in the CALIFORNIA NEWS INDEX, item 9-1.

DISTRICT OF COLUMBIA

9-9 WASHINGTON POST. NEWSPAPER INDEX. Wooster, Ohio: Bell and Howell, 1971-- . Monthly, with annual cumulations.

See NEWSPAPER INDEX series, item 9-3.

GEORGIA

9-10 ATLANTA CONSTITUTION. A GEORGIA INDEX. Glen Rock, N.J.: Microfilming Corporation of America, 1971-- . Annual.

Georgia news is emphasized in this selective index.

Consult: Laws and legislation
Marriage and divorce

HAWAII

9-11 INDEX TO THE HONOLULU ADVERTISER AND HONOLULU STAR-BULLETIN. Honolulu: Friends of the Library, 1929-- . Annual. Some cumulations.

This index to Hawaiian newspapers contains extensive coverage of Hawaiian news, with considerable information on divorce. There is a one-and-one-half-year time lag.

Consult: Desertion
Divorce

ILLINOIS

9-12 CHICAGO TRIBUNE. NEWSPAPER INDEX. Wooster, Ohio: Bell and Howell, 1972-- . Monthly, with annual cumulations.

See NEWSPAPER INDEX series, item 9-3.

IOWA

9-13 DES MOINES REGISTER INDEX. Ames: Iowa State University Library, June, 1975-- . Biweekly, with quarterly and annual cumulations.

State and local news is indexed in this work.

LOUISIANA

9-14   NEW ORLEANS TIMES-PICAYUNE. NEWSPAPER INDEX. Wooster, Ohio: Bell and Howell, 1972-- . Monthly, with annual cumulations.

See NEWSPAPER INDEX series, item 9-3.

MASSACHUSETTS

9-15   THE CHRISTIAN SCIENCE MONITOR. INDEX. Wooster, Ohio: Bell and Howell, 1951-- . Monthly, with annual cumulations.

Refer to item 9-35.

MICHIGAN

9-16   DETROIT NEWS INDEX. Wooster, Ohio: Bell and Howell, 1976-- . Monthly, with annual cumulations.

See NEWSPAPER INDEX Series, item 9-3.

9-17   INDEX TO THE FLINT JOURNAL NEWSPAPER. Flint, Mich.: Mid-Eastern Library Cooperative, 1963-- . Monthly, with annual cumulations.

Regional, state, and local news is indexed by this work.

MINNESOTA

9-18   MINNEAPOLIS TRIBUNE AND MINNEAPOLIS STAR INDEX. Minneapolis: Minneapolis Public Library, 1971-- . Monthly, with semiannual cumulations.

Regional, state, and local news is indexed here, as are public opinion polls. There is a one-month time lag.

Consult: Child custody   Divorce
          Child support

9-19   ST. PAUL DISPATCH, AND PIONEER PRESS INDEX. St. Paul, Minn.: St. Paul Public Library, 1967-- .

Regional, state, and local news is featured in this index.

MISSOURI

9-20   INDEX TO ST. LOUIS NEWSPAPERS. St. Louis: St. Louis Public
        Library, 1975-- . Monthly, with semiannual cumulations.

        Four newspapers are indexed in this work: the ST.
        LOUIS POST DISPATCH, the ST. LOUIS GLOBE
        DEMOCRAT, ST. LOUIS SENTINEL, and ST. LOUIS
        ARGUS. National news is not emphasized. There is
        a one-month time lag.

        Consult: Alimony   Divorce
                  Annulments   Separation
                  Child support

NEW JERSEY

9-21   THE RECORD INDEX. Hackensack, N.J.: Johnson Public Library,
        1969-- . Annual.

        State and local news is the main focus of this index.

NEW YORK

9-22   THE NEW YORK TIMES. INDEXES. Glen Rock, N.J.: Micro-
        filming Corporation of America, 1851-- . Bimonthly, with annual
        cumulations.

        This basic newspaper index presents a brief summary of
        news articles in addition to extensive indexing for the
        news from the local to the international levels. There
        is good coverage of divorce and divorce legislation for
        the states of New York and New Jersey, with some re-
        ports on the subject from other states and foreign coun-
        tries. Book reviews and the Sunday supplements are also
        indexed. There is about a six-week time lag until the
        articles are indexed. Computer searching is available
        from 1969, see item 4-56.

        Consult: Alimony   Divorce, separations, and
                  Child custody   annulments (by states
                  Desertion   and countries)

9-23   WALL STREET JOURNAL. INDEXES. Princeton, N.J.: Dow Jones
        Books, 1955-- . Monthly, with annual cumulations.

        Refer to item 9-40.

NORTH CAROLINA

9-24   NEWS AND OBSERVER INDEX. Raleigh, N.C.: North Carolina
        State Library, 1967-- . Annual, with some cumulations.

The index to this Raleigh, North Carolina, newspaper emphasizes state and local news. Prior to 1975 this index was issued by the J.Y. Joyner Library of East Carolina University.

Consult: Divorce, separations, and annulments
Marriages

OHIO

9-25 INDEX TO CLEVELAND NEWSPAPERS: CLEVELAND PRESS, CLEVE-LAND PLAIN DEALER. Cleveland, Ohio: Cleveland Public Library, 1976-- . Monthly, with annual cumulations.

The emphasis of this index is on local news, with some indexing of state and regional news. There is a personal name and a subject index. There is a time lag of several months.

Consult: Alimony and child   Child custody
support   Divorce and annulment

OREGON

9-26 OREGONIAN INDEX. Eugene: University of Oregon Library, 1850-- . Monthly cards, annual cumulations on microfilm.

State and local news is emphasized in this index of the Portland OREGONIAN.

TEXAS

9-27 DALLAS MORNING NEWS INDEX. Dallas: Dallas Morning News, 1916-- . Irregular, on microfilm.

This index treats local, state, regional, and national news.

9-28 HOUSTON POST INDEX. Wooster, Ohio: Bell and Howell, 1976-- . Monthly, with annual cumulations.

See NEWSPAPER INDEX series, item 9-3.

UTAH

9-29 SALT LAKE TRIBUNE NAME AND SUBJECT INDEX. Salt Lake City: Omniwest Corp., 1941-- . Annual, on microfilm.

State, regional, and local news is indexed in this work.

WEST VIRGINIA

9-30 CHARLESTON NEWSPAPER INDEX. Charleston: West Virginia Library Commission, 1973-- . Annual.

The CHARLESTON GAZETTE and the CHARLESTON
DAILY MAIL are indexed in this annual. State, local,
and regional news is covered.

WISCONSIN

9-31   MILWAUKEE JOURNAL INDEX. Wooster, Ohio: Bell and Howell,
1976-- . Monthly, with annual cumulations.

See NEWSPAPER INDEX series, item 9-3.

B. PUBLISHED INDEXES TO CURRENT DAILY NEWSPAPERS: GREAT BRITAIN

9-32   TIMES, London. INDEX TO THE TIMES. Reading, Engl: Newspaper Archives Developments Unlimited, 1906-- . Quarterly.

This index to one of the world's leading newspapers
has indexing by personal name and subject in one
alphabet. Book reviews and the various supplements
are also indexed. Former titles of this index were
INDEX TO THE TIMES 1906-13, and the OFFICIAL
INDEX TO THE TIMES 1914-57. There is about a
one-year time lag in publishing the index. PALMER'S
INDEX TO THE TIMES NEWSPAPER, 1790-1941, covers
the earlier years of the TIMES.

Consult: Divorce
          Marriage

C. OTHER NEWS MEDIA INDEXES

In this section special types of news indexes and services are described.

9-33   ALTERNATIVE PRESS INDEX. Baltimore, Md.: Alternative Press
Center, 1969-- . Quarterly.

Over 110 alternative and underground journals and newspapers are indexed in this work, which is the only access to publications of many social movements of this
type in the United States. A subject index is included
along with a list of alternative publications and their
addresses. There is an eighteen-month time lag between
appearance of the papers and the index.

Consult: Divorce   Marriage
          Family

9-34   CANADIAN NEWS FACTS: THE INDEXED DIGEST OF CANADIAN
       CURRENT EVENTS. Toronto, Ontario: Canadian News Facts,
       1967-- . Bimonthly. Monthly, quarterly, and annual cumulated
       indexes. Loose-leaf.

           This digest of current events is compiled from eighteen
           Canadian newspapers in nine provinces, with no direct
           references to news items in specific newspapers. It is
           a good source for divorce news, legislation, and cases
           in Canada.

           Consult: Divorce   Marriage
                     Domestic relations   Property

9-35   THE CHRISTIAN SCIENCE MONITOR. INDEX. Wooster, Ohio:
       Bell and Howell, 1951-- . Monthly, with annual cumulations.

           This newspaper index, with nationwide coverage, often
           contains interpretive articles on divorce. The index
           covers all four regional editions. It is somewhat more
           difficult to use than other indexes; cross-references must
           be closely followed. There is a one-month time lag in
           this indexing.

           Consult: Alimony   Family relations
                     Divorce

9-36   EDITORIALS ON FILE. New York: Facts on File, 1970-- .
       Bimonthly, with monthly and annual cumulated indexes. Loose-leaf.

           The most important editorials from 150 of the larger
           U.S. and Canadian newspapers are reprinted in this
           work. There are occasional editorials on divorce.
           A two-month time lag exists in reprinting and in-
           dexing the editorials.

           Consult: Divorce

9-37   FACTS ON FILE: WEEKLY NEWS DIGEST. New York: Facts on
       File, 1941-- . Weekly, with bimonthly and annual cumulated in-
       dexes. Loose-leaf.

           This pamphlet news service provides a weekly summary
           of U.S. and world news. Divorce information is lim-
           ited to news of the divorces of well-known personalities,
           and to changes in the divorce laws of foreign countries.
           News appears in this digest several weeks after its oc-
           currence.

           Consult: Divorce

9-38   THE NATIONAL OBSERVER INDEX. Princeton, N.J.: Dow Jones,
       1969-1977. Annual.

This subject index to a U.S. weekly national newspaper of general interest often contains good summary articles. Bell and Howell have produced retrospective indexes for the years 1962-68.

Consult: Divorce

9-39   TELEVISION NEWS INDEX AND ABSTRACTS. Nashville, Tenn.: Vanderbilt Television News Archive, Joint University Libraries, 1972-- . Monthly, with annual cumulations.

The evening news broadcasts of ABC, CBS, and NBC are completely indexed in this work. The index contains a time-ordered abstract of each day's broadcast, with the names of the commentators and reporters included. From the index one can ascertain how the topic of divorce has been interpreted in the evening television news. Videotapes of the news have been preserved at the archive since August 5, 1968, and may be viewed at the archive or rented in a variety of videotape formats. About an eight-month time lag exists in this indexing.

Consult: Alimony payments   Marriage
        Divorce

9-40   WALL STREET JOURNAL. INDEXES. Princeton, N.J.: Dow Jones Books, 1955-- . Monthly, with annual cumulations.

This daily financial paper carries articles on divorce that relate to alimony, taxes relating to divorce, and Internal Revenue Service decisions about divorced persons. The index is divided into two parts: (a) corporate news, and (b) general news. It is important that the user consult the second part. Book reviews are also indexed. There is a one-month time lag in this indexing.

Consult: Families
        Marriage

D. NEWSPAPER CHECKLISTS

In this section several standard listings of newspapers, past and present, are described for both the United States and other countries, regardless of whether these newspapers have published indexes or not. When a newspaper of interest has not been indexed, finding information in it on divorce is a very tedious undertaking.

9-41   AYER DIRECTORY OF PUBLICATIONS. Philadelphia: Ayer, 1880-- . Annual. Title varies.

This standard listing of U.S. and Canadian daily, weekly, monthly, and quarterly newspapers is arranged by cities within states or within provinces. The information on each is very complete as to editions, circulation, etc. However, it does not indicate whether or not published indexes exist for these newspapers. In addition to newspapers, various other types of publications are included.

9-42   U.S. Library of Congress. Catalog Publication Division. NEWSPAPERS IN MICROFORM: FOREIGN COUNTRIES, 1948-1972. Washington, D.C.: 1973. xix, 269 p.

This guide to foreign newspapers in microform is a good source for locating Canadian and British newspapers both past and present. The guide is organized in the same way as its companion volume described in item 9-43.

9-43   _____. NEWSPAPERS IN MICROFORM: UNITED STATES, 1948-1972. 7th ed. Washington, D.C.: 1973. xxiii, 1,056 p.

This valuable work cites the location of over 34,000 newspaper titles published in the United States, from the eighteenth century to the present time, that are available in microform. The newspaper titles are arranged alphabetically by state, then alphabetically by city within the state, with a title index.

E. OPINION POLLS

Surveys and polls of public attitudes and opinions on a vast number of subjects have been researched since the 1930s. The results of these are often summarized and reported by the news media, although they may be reported and published in various other ways. The large-scale opinion polls are taken usually by special organizations, although many are done on a smaller scale by other researchers or by the news media itself. The major sources for locating information on these polls are described below.

9-44   CURRENT OPINION. Williamstown, Mass.: Roper Public Opinion Research Center, Williams College, 1973-- . Monthly.

This bulletin presents the results of current surveys conducted by the leading national and international opinion research organizations. Data from approximately ten to twenty-five surveys are described each month. Several surveys on divorce are reported each year. The source and date of each survey are indicated. There is usually a time lag of three to six months before the poll results are reported here. This bulletin is a good nontechnical source for divorce information of this type.

9-45   Gallup, George H. THE GALLUP POLL; PUBLIC OPINION, 1935-
1971. 3 vols. New York: Random House, 1972.

This compendium of data from Gallup's poll contains
information on divorce gathered between 1936 and
1966. Dates when the surveys were conducted and
tables of data on the respondents' answers regarding
divorce laws, reasons for divorce, etc., are given.

9-46   GALLUP OPINION INDEX. Princeton, N.J.: American Institute
of Public Opinion, 1965-- . Monthly.

Mostly economic and political issues are the concern
of the surveys reported by the Gallup organization
during each preceding two months. There has been
very little on divorce in recent years.

9-47   THE HARRIS SURVEY YEARBOOK OF PUBLIC OPINION. New
York: Louis Harris and Associates, 1970-- . Annual.

To date, several polls with questions on divorce have
been reported in this work. Currently there is a time
lag of approximately four years in the reportage.

9-48   Horton, Pamela. CANADIAN SOCIAL SCIENCE DATA CATALOG.
Compiled and edited by Pamela Horton, Wendy Thompson, and
Maureen Woodward. Downsview, Ontario: Institute for Behavioral
Research, York University, 1974. 110 p.

This work describes 214 attitude-opinion studies in
Canada and studies done in other countries with which
the data from the Canadian surveys can be compared,
all conducted between 1945 and 1973. Information
is given as to sample size, universe, collector, archive, and data status. Some of the studies pertain
to divorce.

9-49   March, Roman R., comp. CANADIAN INSTITUTE OF PUBLIC
OPINION PERMUTED INDEX, 1945-1967. Ottawa: Carleton
University, Department of Political Science, 1967. xi, 302 p.

Several polls based on questions about divorce in
Canada are included in this work. No data are
given, simply the titles. The index is by keyword-
in-context.

9-50   PUBLIC OPINION, 1935-1946. Edited by Hadley Cantril. Prepared by Mildred Strunk. Princeton, N.J.: Princeton University
Press, 1951. lix, 1,191 p. Tables.

The results of early polls taken in the United States,
Canada, and Great Britain are printed in this volume.
Most of the divorce information concern opinions on
the strictness or leniency of divorce laws and the need
for change.

9-51   For further information on poll data, the researcher is advised to
write to the following:

>Editor, Current Opinion
>Roper Public Opinion Research Center
>Williams College
>Williamstown, Mass.   01267

Chapter 10

NONPRINT MEDIA AND DIVORCE

Most of the previous chapters in this information guide deal with sources of printed materials on divorce in formats such as books, journals, reports, newspapers, microfiche, and microfilm. This chapter deals with sources of materials on divorce in essentially nonprint formats such as motion pictures, filmstrips, slides, sound and videotapes. Also treated are sources for reviews of these materials.

A. MOTION PICTURES FOR ENTERTAINMENT

Since the early days of filmmaking, divorce has been used as a theme for motion pictures. Motion pictures have been produced in the United States and elsewhere since the early 1890s, and have been produced for commercial viewing since about 1913. From the beginning of filmmaking in the United States, the Copyright Office has been granting rights to filmmakers, with the result that lists of films, without subject access or descriptions of the contents, are available. However, some of these early films have been lost, discarded, or have deteriorated. Until recently no adequate description of the films produced has existed. In the past decade projects have been initiated in both Great Britain and the United States to remedy this situation, and these projects are described in this section. The sources of reviews for these films are included in section C of this chapter.

10-1 The American Film Institute. THE AMERICAN FILM INSTITUTE CATALOG OF MOTION PICTURES PRODUCED IN THE UNITED STATES. Kenneth W. Munden, executive editor. New York and London: R.R. Bowker, 1971-- . In progress.

> When completed, this nineteen-volume set will be the most comprehensive description of American film production in existence. It contains an excellent subject index, and short but adequate descriptions of the plots of each film. Additional details are included with regard to the date produced, physical description of the film, the producer, the cast, and the type of film. The films are

arranged in alphabetical order within each decade.
The institute plans to describe all American feature
films, short films, and newsreels up to 1970. Feature
films will be described and annotated for the period
1893-1910, with one volume per decade thereafter.
Volumes for the decades of the 1920s and 1960s have
already been published. Approximately 6,600 films are
described in each volume, with nearly 200 films having
some treatment of divorce in the plot.

Consult: Alimony   Separation
         Bigamy   Stepbrothers
         Divorce   Stepfathers
         Desertion   Stepmothers
         Marriage--annulment   Stepsisters

10-2   Gifford, Denis. THE BRITISH FILM CATALOGUE 1895-1970: A
        REFERENCE GUIDE. New York: McGraw-Hill Book Co., 1973.
        967 p.

        This volume has done, in a brief way, for British film
        production what the AMERICAN FILM INSTITUTE CATA-
        LOG (item 10-1) plans to do for American films. This
        work contains information on over 14,000 British films
        produced for public entertainment. There are one-
        sentence summaries of the plots. No subject index is
        included, which lessens the value of this work for finding
        British films on divorce. Film titles are arranged in
        chronological order together with a description of the
        physical features of the film, the cast, producer, direc-
        tor, and story source. The films are classified within
        twenty-three broad categories.

10-3   Niver, Kemp R. MOTION PICTURES FROM THE LIBRARY OF
        CONGRESS PAPER PRINT COLLECTION, 1894-1912. Edited by
        Bebe Bergsten. Berkeley and Los Angeles: University of California
        Press, 1967. xxii, 402 p.

        About three thousand silent, paper-positive print films
        held by the Library of Congress are described in this
        important work. Excellent but brief summaries of the
        plot of each film are included. There is no subject
        index but the films are arranged alphabetically under
        twelve subject categories. Additional data included
        are the copyright date, the producer, length, and
        condition of the film. Prints of these films may be
        ordered from the Library of Congress.

10-4   U.S. Copyright Office. CATALOG OF COPYRIGHT ENTRIES.
        3d series, pts. 12 and 13, MOTION PICTURES. Washington, D.C.:

Government Printing Office, 1947-- . Semiannual. LC3.6/5v./ pt/no.

> This government document is a continuation of the copyright list of films described in item 10-5 and has similar data and format. There is about a two-year lag from the time that the picture is completed until it appears in this list.

10-5 _____. MOTION PICTURES, 1912-39-- . Cumulative series, CATALOG OF COPYRIGHT ENTRIES. Washington, D.C.: Government Printing Office, 1951-- . LC3.8:M85/date.

> A continuation of item 10-6 by Walls, this document series, along with the Walls publication, has practically no value as a subject guide to films, although they both serve as checklists for feature films, TV films and series, instructional films, and cartoons copyrighted in the United States. There are no annotations or subject indexes. Data are given concerning the date, sponsor, producer, script, and physical description of the films. Film titles are arranged alphabetically. Four cumulations have been made for the periods: 1912-39; 1940-49; 1950-59; 1960-69. This series is continued with item 10-4.

10-6 Walls, Howard Lamarr. MOTION PICTURES, 1894-1912, IDENTIFIED FROM THE RECORDS OF THE UNITED STATES COPYRIGHT OFFICE. Washington, D.C.: Copyright Office, Library of Congress, 1953.

> Refer to item 10-5 above.

B. NONPRINT MEDIA FOR EDUCATIONAL PURPOSES

In this section the sources of educational films, filmstrips, slide series, audio and video tapes on divorce are described. The review media for these materials are cited in section C of this chapter.

10-7 CANADIANA: PUBLICATIONS OF INTEREST RECEIVED BY THE NATIONAL LIBRARY, 1950-- . Ottawa: National Library, 1951-- . Monthly, with annual cumulations.

> See item 2-3 for this source of Canadian nonprint media.

10-8 National Information Center for Educational Media. NICEM MEDIA INDEXES. Los Angeles: University of Southern California. Periodic revision of each index. Supplements.

> This series of indexes provides access to a wide range of

educational audiovisual materials. A short summary of
the contents of each item is provided in the description
of the material. Each volume contains a subject-heading
outline, an index to subject headings, a subject guide,
followed by an alphabetical listing of the materials.
The indexes are revised biennially, and supplements are
issued periodically. This index series is also available
on microfiche. Current index volumes relevant to divorce are listed below.

Consult: Divorce

10-9   _____. INDEX TO EDUCATIONAL AUDIO TAPES. 4th ed.
1977-78.

10-10   _____. INDEX TO EDUCATIONAL OVERHEAD TRANSPARENCIES.
5th ed. 1977-78.

10-11   _____. INDEX TO EDUCATIONAL VIDEOTAPES. 4th ed. 1977-
78.

10-12   _____. INDEX TO 8mm MOTION CARTRIDGES. 5th ed. 1977-
78.

10-13   _____. INDEX TO 16mm EDUCATIONAL FILMS. 6th ed. 1977-
78.

10-14   _____. INDEX TO 35mm EDUCATIONAL FILMSTRIPS. 6th ed.
1977-78.

10-15   U.S. Library of Congress. LIBRARY OF CONGRESS CATALOGS:
FILMS AND OTHER MATERIALS FOR PROJECTION. Washington,
D.C.: 1974-- . Three quarterly issues, with annual and quin-
quennial cumulations.

This useful index attempts to catalog all educational
films, filmstrips, and since 1973, slide sets produced in
the United States and Canada from over six hundred publishers. A useful subject index, a short summary of the
contents of the material, a physical description, an author-
title index, and a list of producers and distributors with
addresses are included. This work has appeared under
various titles since 1948, with subject access since 1953.
The time lag for materials in this index is from one to
three years.

Consult: Broken homes   Divorce
            Children of divorced Divorcées
                parents   Separation (law)
                                  Single-parent family

C. NONPRINT MEDIA REVIEWS

Sources of reviews for nonprint media of all types are described here. For a more extensive treatment of reviewing sources, refer to item 10-18.

For sources of current reviews on entertainment films, consult the following indexes, under the subject headings indicated. Refer to chapter 4 for further information on each index.

> CANADIAN PERIODICAL INDEX: Moving picture reviews
> HUMANITIES INDEX: Moving picture reviews
> NEW YORK TIMES INDEX: Motion pictures--reviews
> READERS' GUIDE: Moving picture plays--criticisms, plots, etc.
> SOCIAL SCIENCES INDEX: Moving pictures--criticism

10-16   Bowles, Stephen E. INDEX TO CRITICAL FILM REVIEWS IN BRITISH AND AMERICAN FILM PERIODICALS, TOGETHER WITH: INDEX TO CRITICAL REVIEWS OF BOOKS ABOUT FILM, 1930-1972. 3 vols. New York: B. Franklin, 1974-75.

> The location of reviews in thirty scholarly film periodicals from the 1940s to 1971 is given in this index. There is no subject index.

10-17   Educational Film Library Association. FILM EVALUATION GUIDE. New Haven, Conn.: 1965-- . Loose-leaf. Two five-year cumulations.

> This card service evaluates educational films, giving the following information on each film: a physical description, an evaluation, a synopsis, the uses, the intended audience, technical comments, ratings, and awards won. There is about a two-year time lag between production and evaluation. A cumulated subject index is available.

> Consult: Family relationships
> Marriage

10-18   Gallup, Jennifer. REFERENCE GUIDE TO REVIEWS: A CHECK-LIST OF SOURCES IN THE HUMANITIES, SOCIAL SCIENCES, AND FINE ARTS. Vancouver: University of British Columbia Library, 1970. 38 p.

> An extensive list of sources of book reviews, drama reviews, film reviews, and other special topics appear in this work.

10-19   LANDERS FILM REVIEWS: THE INFORMATION GUIDE TO 16mm
         FILMS AND MULTIMEDIA REVIEWS. Los Angeles: Landers Associ-
         ates, 1956-- . Bimonthly (except June, July, and August).

         This reviewing service for educational media describes
         each film, and gives the subject area of the film, the
         audience suitability, the purpose, a synopsis, and an
         extensive review. The time lag for this service is short.

         Consult: Family relationships
                  Marriage

10-20   MEDIA REVIEW DIGEST. 1970-- . Ann Arbor, Mich.: Pierian
         Press, 1971-- . Annual, with quarterly supplements.

         This work is an index to and digest of reviews, evalua-
         tions, and descriptions of educational films, videotapes,
         filmstrips, records and voice tapes, and other nonbook
         media found in a wide variety of periodicals. Prizes
         that have been awarded to materials are also reported.
         There is a separate subject index. This work was formerly
         entitled MULTI REVIEWS INDEX.

         Consult: Divorce

10-21   THE NEW YORK TIMES FILM REVIEWS, 1913-1968. 6 vols. New
         York: New York Times, 1970.

         The complete text of sixteen thousand motion picture
         reviews published in the NEW YORK TIMES are reprinted
         in this work. There are title, personal name, and corpo-
         rated name indexes, but no subject index. Volume 6
         contains the indexes.

10-22   Salem, James M. A GUIDE TO CRITICAL REVIEWS. Part IV:
         THE SCREEN PLAY FROM THE JAZZ SINGER TO DR. STRANGE-
         LOVE. Metuchen, N.J.: Scarecrow Press, 1971.

         Film reviews of twelve thousand American and foreign
         films that appeared in U.S. and Canadian periodicals
         from 1927 to 1963 are indexed in this work. Reviews
         that appeared in the NEW YORK TIMES are also included.
         Critical film reviews from scholarly journals are not in-
         dexed. The reviews are arranged alphabetically by title
         with no subject index.

D. MUSEUM MEDIA AND REALIA

10-23   Wasserman, Paul. MUSEUM MEDIA: A BIENNIAL DIRECTORY
         AND INDEX OF PUBLICATIONS AND AUDIOVISUALS AVAILABLE
         FROM U.S. AND CANADIAN INSTITUTIONS. Detroit: Gale

Research Co., 1973. vii, 445 p.

This directory and index of materials available from museums includes books, pamphlets, catalogs of exhibits and collections, films, and filmstrips produced or available through these institutions. It is a marginal source of materials on divorce at present, but should be consulted when further editions are published.

Consult: Divorce

Chapter 11

DIVORCE IN LITERATURE

Over the past century and a quarter, divorce has been the theme of many novels, short stories, plays, essays, and some poetry. In recent years, also, more literature for children related to divorce has become available. In parts A through F of this chapter, sources for locating literary works of the types mentioned above, on divorce, are described. Some sources have been included here because they are specific landmark works or research reports on divorce in literature. Others included are general bibliographic works that have indexing which readily leads the user to specific literary works on the subject of divorce. The appropriate headings are listed with the description of each source.

In addition to the sources described in this chapter, there are many other bibliographic sources that list or index literary works, but most of these list or index by author and title only, sometimes also by chronological period. In order to do fairly comprehensive research on divorce in literature, or on divorce in a specific form of literature, these other bibliographic sources must be laboriously searched, along with examination of numerous items cited to identify which have divorce as a theme. As aids for the person interested in doing literary research of this type on the theme of divorce, the following guides are recommended. These cite bibliographic sources to be checked and also suggest techniques for doing so.

11-1   Altick, Richard Daniel. THE ART OF LITERARY RESEARCH. Rev. ed. New York: Norton, 1975. xii, 304 p.

>   An interestingly written general introduction "meant for everyone interested in the whys, whats, and hows of literary investigation" (preface, p. ix), this work does not claim to be a systematic treatise on the materials and methods of literary research. It is excellent for transmitting the general principles and attitudes necessary for literary research to the beginning scholar.

11-2   Altick, Richard Daniel, and Wright, Andrew. SELECTIVE BIBLIOGRAPHY FOR THE STUDY OF ENGLISH AND AMERICAN LITERATURE. 5th ed. New York: Macmillan Publishing Co.;

London: Collier Macmillan Publishers, 1975. xii, 168 p.

This selective guide lists for the student and beginning researcher those bibliographies and reference works which are most used by modern scholars.

11-3   Bond, Donald F. A REFERENCE GUIDE TO ENGLISH STUDIES. 2d ed. Chicago and London: University of Chicago Press, 1971. x, 198 p.

This highly selective and useful guide, prepared primarily for graduate students, "points out the essential sources which will enable the user to find his way quickly and surely to particular books and articles which he will need" (preface, p. ix). The scope includes literature in English from the United States and the British Commonwealth.

11-4   Patterson, Margaret C. LITERARY RESEARCH GUIDE; AN EVALUA- TIVE ANNOTATED BIBLIOGRAPHY OF IMPORTANT REFERENCE BOOKS AND PERIODICALS ON AMERICAN AND ENGLISH LITERA- TURE, OF THE MOST USEFUL SOURCES FOR RESEARCH IN OTHER NATIONAL LITERATURES, AND OF MORE THAN 300 REFERENCE BOOKS IN LITERATURE-RELATED SUBJECT AREAS. Detroit: Gale Research Co., 1976. 428 p.

This extremely well organized and annotated guide not only refers students and scholars to the most important sources for literary research, but also guides the user in logical and systematic research techniques and procedures as it goes along. This work thus is a very valuable source for the novice as well as the experienced scholar.

New works similar to the general aids listed above may be identified as they are published in the future by periodically checking library card catalogs under subject headings such as:

American literature--Bibliography
American literature--Bibliography--catalogs
English literature--Bibliography
Canadian literature--Bibliography
Literature--Bibliography

To locate listings of literary works on divorce as they may be published in the future, the following subject heading should be checked in library card cata- logs:

Divorce in literature--Bibliography

In part G of this chapter, sources for locating information on divorce as it is treated in Biblical and philosophical literature are described.

A. DIVORCE NOVELS

As indicated earlier, it is difficult to identify fiction relating to a particular subject, including divorce, because not many literary bibliographies provide subject indexes. Even library card catalogs generally use special subject headings for novels only when they center on historical events and characters. The following bibliographical sources can be used to identify divorce novels because they offer subject indexing which includes the subject of divorce. A few special studies on divorce novels are included here, which provide special listings. For American novels from 1858 to 1945, the works of Barnett (items 11-7 and 11-8) are the quickest sources. For finding current novels on divorce, the subject index to the BOOK REVIEW DIGEST (item 11-9), within its stated limitations, is the most useful source.

11-5   Baker, Ernest A. A DESCRIPTIVE GUIDE TO THE BEST FICTION, BRITISH AND AMERICAN, INCLUDING TRANSLATIONS FROM FOREIGN LANGUAGES. London: S. Sonnenschein and Co.; New York: Macmillan, 1903. viii, 610 p.

> The annotations in this selective list of 4,500 works of fiction are arranged by country and time periods. Most of the selections are from the nineteenth century.

> Consult: Divorce

11-6   Baker, Ernest A., and Packman, James. A GUIDE TO THE BEST FICTION, ENGLISH AND AMERICAN, INCLUDING TRANSLATIONS FROM FOREIGN LANGUAGES. New and enl. ed. New York: Macmillan, 1932. viii, 634 p.

> This new edition is similar to the previous work (item 11-5), but emphasizes twentieth-century fiction. Good annotations are provided.

> Consult: Divorce

11-7   Barnett, James H. DIVORCE AND THE AMERICAN DIVORCE NOVEL, 1858-1937; A STUDY IN LITERARY REFLECTIONS OF SOCIAL INFLUENCES. 1939. Reprint. New York: Russell and Russell. Bibliography. 168 p.

> This work is a scholarly analysis of social change relating to divorce in American society and how these changes were reflected in fifty-one divorce novels written during the period.

11-8   Barnett, James H., and Gruen, Rhoda. "Recent American Divorce Novels, 1938-1945: A Study in the Sociology of Literature." SOCIAL FORCES 26 (1947-48): 322-27.

This article updates item 11-7 with a critical study of twenty-five divorce novels published from 1938 to 1945.

11-9   BOOK REVIEW DIGEST. New York: H.W. Wilson Co., 1905-- . Monthly (except February and July). Annual cumulations, with five-year cumulative indexes.

Refer to item 2-36.

Consult: Fiction--divorce
Novels--divorce

11-10   CUMULATIVE BOOK INDEX: A WORLD LIST OF BOOKS IN THE ENGLISH LANGUAGE. New York: H.W. Wilson Co., 1898-- . Monthly (except August). Cumulated quarterly, annually since 1969, and at least biennially since 1957.

Refer to item 2-8.

Consult: Divorce--fiction

11-11   FICTION CATALOG. Edited by Estelle A. Fidell. New York: H.W. Wilson Co., 1908-- . Annual, with quinquennial cumulations.

Experienced librarians select novels for inclusion in this work which are suitable for public libraries. Works of fiction on all subjects are included. Annotated entries are arranged by author, and since 1960 a title and subject index has been included.

Consult: Divorce   Stepfathers
Stepchildren   Stepmothers

11-12   FICTION INDEX. Compiled by Gerald B. Cotton, Raymond F. Smith, and Anthony J. Gordon. London: Association of Assistant Librarians, 1953-- . Cumulations.

Often referred to as the CUMULATED FICTION INDEX, this valuable work is a subject listing of works of fiction, including short story collections, written in English since 1945. There are no annotations but the works are described under some three thousand subject headings. The first cumulation, covering the period 1945-60, contains 25,000 titles; the second cumulation, for the years 1961-69, contains 18,000 titles; and the third cumulation, for the years 1970-74, has over 10,000 titles. While this work essentially has the same coverage as the FICTION CATALOG (item 11-11), it also includes materials not in that work.

Consult: Divorce

11-13   Lenrow, Elbert. READER'S GUIDE TO PROSE FICTION; AN IN-
TRODUCTORY ESSAY WITH BIBLIOGRAPHIES OF 1500 NOVELS
SELECTED, TOPICALLY CLASSIFIED, AND ANNOTATED FOR USE
IN MEETING THE NEEDS OF INDIVIDUALS IN GENERAL EDUCA-
TION . . . FOR THE COMMISSION ON SECONDARY SCHOOL
CURRICULUM. New York and London: Appleton-Century Co.,
1940. xi, 371 p.

> This topically analyzed guide to twentieth-century fiction
> is amply annotated and is written for the general reader.

> Consult: Divorce   Marriage and its problems
>   Love, psychology

Lists of novels may be identified in the future, as published, by periodically
checking subject headings such as the following in library card catalogs.
These listings may or may not be indexed by divorce as a subject, however.

American fiction--Bibliography
American fiction--20th century--
   Bibliography
Canadian fiction--Bibliography--Catalogs

B. SHORT STORIES ON DIVORCE

Of the following sources for identifying short stories on divorce, the FICTION
INDEX (item 11-16) is the most useful.

11-14   CANADIAN ESSAY AND LITERATURE INDEX, 1973-- . Toronto
and Buffalo: University of Toronto Press, 1975-- . Annual.

> Refer to item 11-31.

11-15   Cook, Dorothy Elizabeth. SHORT STORY INDEX; AN INDEX TO
60,000 STORIES IN 4,320 COLLECTIONS. New York: H.W.
Wilson Co., 1953. Quinquennial supplements.

> An index to short stories of less than 150 pages from
> the latter part of the nineteenth century to the present,
> this work contains more short stories than the title in-
> dicates. Both British and American works are indexed.
> This rich source for short stories on divorce also includes
> a list of the collections indexed. This work supersedes
> the INDEX TO SHORT STORIES, compiled by Ina Ten
> Eyck [Firkins] in 1923, and its supplements.

> Consult: Alienation of affec-   Divorce
>   tion   Divorcées
>   Alimony   Remarriage
>   Desertion and non-   Stepfathers
>   support   Stepmothers

11-16   FICTION INDEX. Compiled by Gerald B. Cotton, Raymond F.
         Smith, and Anthony J. Gordon. London: Association of Assistant
         Librarians, 1953-- . Cumulations.

         Refer to item 11-12.

To locate new listings of collections of short stories as they are published,
subject headings such as the following should be consulted periodically in library card catalogs. These listings, however, may not be indexed by divorce
as a subject.

    Short stories--Bibliography
    Short stories, American--Bibliography
    Short stories, English--Bibliography

C. DIVORCE DRAMA

Sources for finding dramatic works on divorce are described in this section.
The most comprehensive source is Koster's study of American divorce drama,
1871-1939 (item 11-22).

11-17   CANADIAN ESSAY AND LITERATURE INDEX, 1973-- . Toronto
         and Buffalo: University of Toronto Press, 1975-- . Annual.

         Refer to item 11-31.

11-18   CUMULATED DRAMATIC INDEX, 1909-1949: A CUMULATION OF
         THE F.W. FAXON COMPANY'S DRAMATIC INDEX. Edited by
         Frederick W. Faxon, Mary E. Bates, and Anne C. Sutherland.
         2 vols. Boston: G.K. Hall, 1965.

         A marginal source.

         Consult: Divorce
                   Divorcées

11-19   Drury, Francis K.W. DRURY'S GUIDE TO BEST PLAYS. Washing-
         ton, D.C.: Scarecrow Press, 1953. 367 p.

         Essentially an author index to over twelve hundred plays
         of continuing interest in English from the early Greek
         dramatists to the present time, this work also has a sub-
         ject and title index. The second edition, published in
         1969, lacks a subject index.

         Consult: Divorce

11-20   Firkins, Ina Ten Eyck, comp. INDEX TO PLAYS, 1800-1926. New
         York: H.W. Wilson Co., 1927. 307 p. Supplements.

         A selective list of over eleven thousand plays that have

received public recognition, this work has an author index and a title-subject index which is rather inadequate for a subject approach. A list of periodicals consulted and collections indexed is included.

Consult: Divorce

11-21   Ireland, Norma [Olin]. INDEX TO FULL LENGTH PLAYS, 1944 TO 1964. Boston: F.W. Faxon, 1965. 328 p.

Nearly twelve hundred plays published in English for the period are indexed in this work by author, title, and subject in a single alphabet. This work continues Ruth Thomson's indexes (items 11-25 and 11-26).

Consult: Divorce

11-22   Koster, Donald N. THE THEME OF DIVORCE IN AMERICAN DRAMA, 1871-1939. Philadelphia: Privately published, 1942. x, 117 p.

Thirty-nine American plays on divorce, that were written during the period, are analyzed in this dissertation. A good summary of divorce law and reform attempts as well as nineteenth-century public opinion about divorce as expressed in American periodicals is also included in this study.

11-23   Logasa, Hannah, and Ver Noy, Winifred, comps. AN INDEX TO ONE-ACT PLAYS FOR STAGE, RADIO, AND TELEVISION. Boston: F.W. Faxon, 1924-- . Irregular.

Over twenty-five thousand one-act plays published in English since 1900 are indexed in this work. It contains separate title, author, and subject indexes. This work was formerly entitled AN INDEX TO ONE-ACT PLAYS.

Consult: Divorce

11-24   PLAY INDEX, 1949/52-- . New York: H.W. Wilson Co., 1953-- . Irregular.

This index lists single plays and collections of plays published since 1949. Many pre-1949 plays are included in these collections. There is an author-title-subject index to all plays.

Consult: Divorce
        Remarriage

11-25   Thomson, Ruth G. INDEX TO FULL LENGTH PLAYS, 1895 TO 1925. Boston: F.W. Faxon, 1956. xi, 172 p.

This work indexes 562 English-language plays for the period and includes separate title, author, and subject indexes.

Consult: Marriage and divorce

11-26   . INDEX TO FULL LENGTH PLAYS, 1926 TO 1944. Boston: F.W. Faxon, 1946. ix, 306 p.

This work indexes 1,340 selected English-language plays published during the period by separate author, title, and subject indexes. It is continued by Norma Ireland's index (item 11-21).

Consult: Marriage and divorce

To keep up with new listings and indexes to plays as they are published, consult periodically library card catalogs under subject headings such as the following:

American drama--Bibliography
English drama--Bibliography--Catalogs
Drama--Bibliography--Catalogs
Drama--Indexes
Drama--20th century--Indexes

D. DIVORCE POETRY

Subject access to poetry is not as adequate as for other forms of literature, with the result that very few poems with divorce as a theme have been located. The references listed below contain to date only a few divorce poems.

11-27   Bruncken, Herbert, comp. and ed. SUBJECT INDEX TO POETRY: A GUIDE FOR ADULT READERS. Chicago: American Library Association, 1940. xix, 201 p.

This is a marginal source for divorce poetry.

Consult: Divorce

11-28   CANADIAN ESSAY AND LITERATURE INDEX, 1973-- . Toronto and Buffalo: University of Toronto Press, 1975-- . Annual.

Canadian poetry is indexed in this work. Refer to item 11-31.

11-29   Granger, Edith. GRANGER'S INDEX TO POETRY. Edited by William James Smith. 6th ed. New York: Columbia University Press, 1973. 2,260 p.

Over five hundred volumes of anthologies of poetry,

published before 1971, are indexed by title, first line, author, and subject. Previous editions of this work did not contain references to divorce.

Consult: Divorce

To keep up with any new listings or indexes to poetry that may appear in the future, consult periodically library card catalogs under subject headings such as the following:

American poetry--Indexes
Canadian poetry--20th century--
    Bibliography
Poetry--Bibliography
Poetry--Indexes

E. ESSAYS ON DIVORCE

Sources for identifying essays on divorce are described in this section. They may also be identified by consulting periodically library card catalogs under headings such as the following:

Divorce--Addresses, Essays, Lectures
Divorce--United States--Addresses,
    Essays, Lectures

11-30   American Library Association. THE "A.L.A." INDEX: AN INDEX TO GENERAL LITERATURE, BIOGRAPHICAL, HISTORICAL, AND LITERARY ESSAYS AND SKETCHES. By William Isaac Fletcher. 2d ed. Boston: 1905. Reprint. Freeport, N.Y.: Books for Libraries Press, 1971. Supplement, 1900-1910.

Selected English-language essays, historical works, reports from boards of social agencies, and other works from the last half of the nineteenth and the early twentieth century are indexed in this work. The most commonly held works are further analyzed. There is little overlap with the ESSAY AND GENERAL LITERATURE INDEX (item 11-32) for the period.

Consult: Divorce
          Marriage

11-31   CANADIAN ESSAY AND LITERATURE INDEX, 1973-- . Toronto and Buffalo: University of Toronto Press, 1975-- . Annual.

This recent work is an author, title, and subject index to essays, book reviews, poems, plays, and short stories published in Canada, in magazines, anthologies, and collections not already indexed.

Consult: Divorce
Marriage

11-32   ESSAY AND GENERAL LITERATURE INDEX, 1900-- . New York:
H.W. Wilson Co., 1934-- . Semiannual. Annual and quinquennial
cumulations.

This work indexes collections of essays and chapters in
composite books in the humanities and social sciences,
and to a lesser degree in the sciences. The disciplines
of philosophy, religion, political science, economics,
law, education, the arts, literature, and history are included. A good author and subject index is provided.

Consult: Children of divorced   Divorcées
            parents   Parent and child (law)
         Divorce   Paternal deprivation

F. JUVENILE LITERATURE ON DIVORCE

During the past decade, with the increased frequency of divorce, divorce as
a theme is being more often used in juvenile literature. Much of this
literature attempts to help the child or young person understand the family
situation which has changed because of divorce. The best sources for finding
juvenile literature with divorce themes are described in this section.

11-33   CHILDREN'S BOOKS IN PRINT. SUBJECT GUIDE. New York:
R.R. Bowker Co., 1970-- . Annual.

Over 39,000 titles of children's books currently in print
are listed under at least 8,300 subject categories annually.
This work should be used with care, as the lists are compiled from publishers' catalogs and not from an examination of the works themselves. This work was preceded
by CHILDREN'S BOOKS FOR SCHOOLS AND LIBRARIES.

Consult: Divorce
         Divorce--fiction

11-34   Johnson, Madelynne Billings. "Children's Fiction Involving Divorce
and Separation." Master's thesis, University of Chicago, 1974.
iv, 56 p.

All of the children's books that could be identified with
divorce as a theme are analyzed and annotated in this
work. Most of these thirty-three books were written
between 1966 and 1973. Photocopies of this thesis are
available from the University of Chicago.

11-35   Shaw, John MacKay. CHILDHOOD IN POETRY: A CATALOGUE,
WITH BIOGRAPHICAL AND CRITICAL ANNOTATIONS OF THE
BOOKS OF ENGLISH AND AMERICAN POETS. 5 vols. Detroit:
Gale Research Co., 1967. Supplements.

> The extensive children's poetry collection in the Robert
> Manning Strozier Library at The Florida State University,
> Tallahassee, is indexed in these volumes. Very few
> poems on divorce are included to date.

> Consult: Divorce

11-36   SUBJECT INDEX TO CHILDREN'S MAGAZINES. Edited by Gladys
Cavanagh. Madison, Wis.: 1949-- . Monthly (except June and
July), with semiannual cumulations.

> Over sixty magazines for children and teenagers are
> indexed by this publication. Only six of the maga-
> zines indexed are also indexed in the READERS' GUIDE
> TO PERIODICAL LITERATURE (item 4-31). Up to the
> present time, only a few articles on divorce have ap-
> peared in these magazines.

> Consult: Divorce

11-37   Wilson, H.W., Co., publishers. CHILDREN'S CATALOG. 13th
ed. New York: 1976. xii, 1,408 p.

> More than five thousand children's books, which were
> judged by specialists to be the best fiction and non-
> fiction books in print, are included in this work. Part
> 1 is a classified catalog which gives short summaries of
> each book. Part 2 contains a single author, title, sub-
> ject, and analytical index. This work, which is used
> for school and public library book selection, is just be-
> ginning to include books on divorce. Books described
> here are suitable for preschool through the sixth grade.

> Consult: Divorce--fiction

11-38   _____ . JUNIOR HIGH SCHOOL LIBRARY CATALOG. 3d ed.
New York: 1975. xii, 991 p. Annual with quinquennial cumulations.

> The third edition of this catalog contains an analysis
> of nearly 3,800 books that were judged by specialists
> to be suitable for grades seven through nine. The con-
> tents are analyzed in the same manner as in the CHIL-
> DREN'S CATALOG (item 11-37). This edition contains
> only a few books on the theme of divorce.

> Consult: Divorce--fiction

G. BIBLICAL AND PHILOSOPHICAL WRITINGS ON DIVORCE

Concern, controversy, and opinion regarding divorce have continued for many years, especially because of the variety of religious interpretations in this area. These interpretations continue to change rapidly. Biblical literature has been one of the basic value determinants of opinion and views on divorce. In this section, the most commonly used Bible concordances and commentaries are described. Consult chapter 2 and chapter 4 for books and articles on divorce from religious perspectives in general. At the end of this section, locating basic philosophical writings on the subject of divorce is treated briefly.

1. Bible Concordances

Concordances to the particular Bible at hand are used to locate passages in that version of the Bible on a given topic, such as divorce. Some of these standard concordances to some of the standard versions of the Bible are discussed here. In the various versions of the Bible, the words that are used for divorce may vary also. The concordances reflect these variations.

11–39   Ellison, John W. NELSON'S COMPLETE CONCORDANCE OF THE
         REVISED STANDARD VERSION BIBLE. New York: Nelson, 1957.
         2,157 p.

         Because this concordance was prepared with the help of
         a computer, the references are very complete. Thirty
         references on divorce in the Old and New Testaments are
         provided by the concordance.

         Consult: Divorce   Divorces
                   Divorced

11–40   Strong, James. EXHAUSTIVE CONCORDANCE OF THE BIBLE.
         New York: Hunt, 1894. 1,340 p.

         This comprehensive work is a concordance to the King
         James Version of the Bible.

         Consult: Divorce   Divorcement
                   Divorced   Put (away)

11–41   Young, Robert. ANALYTICAL CONCORDANCE TO THE BIBLE.
         22d American ed., rev. New York: Funk and Wagnalls, 1936.
         viii, 1,090 p.

         A comprehensive concordance to the King James Version
         of the Bible, this is slightly easier to use than that of
         Strong (item 11–40). This work includes the Greek and
         Hebrew words for each entry.

         Consult: Divorce   Divorcement
                   Divorced   Put away

2. Bible Commentaries

Bible commentaries are verse-by-verse explanations, prepared by scholars for the use of the clergy and other readers, that incorporate the recent findings of Biblical scholarship. The most generally used recent multivolume commentaries are cited below. To use these, one must first locate the Biblical texts in a particular version of the Bible by using the special concordance for that version. Then with these texts and passages in mind, the explanations and interpretations of the same can be found in the commentaries.

11-42   BIBLE. ENGLISH. 1964. ANCHOR BIBLE. 38 vols. Garden City, N.Y.: Doubleday, 1964-75.

> This commentary contains a new translation of the Bible with extensive comments by Protestant, Roman Catholic, and Jewish scholars.

11-43   THE BROADMAN BIBLE COMMENTARY. Edited by Clifton J. Allen. 12 vols. Nashville, Tenn.: Broadman Press, 1969-72.

> This work is a commentary on the Revised Standard Version of the Bible prepared by an international group of Baptist scholars.

11-44   HERMENEIA: A CRITICAL AND HISTORICAL COMMENTARY ON THE BIBLE. Philadelphia: Fortress Press, 1971-- . In progress.

> These commentaries on the Old and New Testaments, written by distinguished German Biblical scholars, are being translated from the German.

11-45   INTERNATIONAL CRITICAL COMMENTARY ON THE HOLY SCRIPTURES OF THE OLD AND NEW TESTAMENTS. Edited by Rev. Samuel R. Driver, Rev. Alfred Plummer, and Rev. Charles A. Briggs. 45 vols. Edinburgh: Clark; New York: Scribner, 1896-1937.

> A very scholarly exegisis of Biblical texts is combined in this work with an emphasis on the linguistic analysis of the texts by British and American scholars.

11-46   INTERPRETER'S BIBLE. 12 vols. New York: Abingdon Press, 1951-57.

> This important commentary was produced by Protestant scholars and contains the texts of both the Revised Standard Version and the King James (Authorized) Version of the Bible, interpretation of the texts and passages, and an exposition of the texts for homiletical purposes.

3. Philosophical Writings

11-47   GREAT BOOKS OF THE WESTERN WORLD. Edited by Robert
Maynard Hutchins. 54 vols. Chicago: Encyclopaedia Britannica,
1952.

> The easiest access to the writings of the classical philoso-
> phers on divorce is through the index of this reference
> set. Selected portions of the writings of the greatest
> thinkers of Western civilization are printed in these
> volumes. In volume 2, the SYNOPTICON, chapter 26,
> page 502, twenty-two references to philosophical thought
> about divorce are listed.

Chapter 12

ORGANIZATIONS

There are literally scores of organizations in the United States, Canada, and Great Britain, at national, state, and local levels, concerned with divorce. The goals of these organizations vary widely, from changing divorce laws, to information exchange, to self-help. Some of these organizations hold conferences and publish newsletters that reflect their interests and publicize their activities. The information sources listed in this chapter are useful for identifying these organizations, their conferences, and their publications.

A. IDENTIFYING DIVORCE ORGANIZATIONS

Directories of national associations are good sources for identifying national organizations concerned with divorce. These are updated at regular intervals. Special directories or lists of divorce organizations are good for information on regional or local groups, although they may not be kept as up-to-date as are the national directories, or they may have been published only once.

12-1   DIRECTORY OF ASSOCIATIONS IN CANADA. Prepared under the direction of Brian Land. Toronto and Buffalo: University of Toronto Press, 1974. 436 p.

> Over seven thousand associations, from the local level to international groups, functioning in Canada in the arts, business, trades, labor, and the professions are described in this book. The associations are listed alphabetically together with their addresses and telephone numbers but with no descriptions of their activities or publications. This work has a list of subject headings, and a subject index. There are no specific divorce groups listed but there are listings of single-parents organizations. The text is written in English and French.

12-2   DIRECTORY OF BRITISH ASSOCIATIONS AND ASSOCIATIONS IN IRELAND. Edited by G.P. Henderson and S.P.A. Henderson.

4th ed. Beckenham, Kent, Engl.: C.B.D. Research, 1974. xiv, 400 p.

This list of national organizations contains the address, date of formation, telephone number, number of branches, type of organization, activities, membership, titles and cost of publications, and previous name of the organization. A few divorce associations are listed.

Consult: Divorce

12-3   Doppler, George F. AMERICA NEEDS TOTAL DIVORCE REFORM-- NOW! New York: Vantage Press, 1973. xii, 165 p.

The appendix of this book lists, without description, the names and addresses of over fifty national and local divorce organizations in the United States.

12-4   ENCYCLOPEDIA OF ASSOCIATIONS. Edited by Mary Wilson Pair. 3 vols. 12th ed. Detroit: Gale Research Co., 1978. Annual, with quarterly supplements.

This guide lists nearly seventeen thousand national and international organizations operating in the United States, including trade, business, legal, governmental, educational, cultural, welfare, public affairs, religious, and citizen action groups. Data on each association includes the name, acronym, address, telephone number, chief official, founding date, number of members, staff, the number of state and local affiliates, a description of the purposes and activities of the organization, publications, name changes, time and place of future meetings. Organizations are grouped alphabetically by type of group. There is good subject access through keyword indexes. Keywords are provided in cases where the activity is not indicated in the title. Mostly nonprofit organizations are included. Some regional and local associations are listed when these groups may be of national interest. This is a basic reference work of American associations.

Consult: Alimony
        Divorce

12-5   McKenney, Mary. DIVORCE: A SELECTED ANNOTATED BIB- LIOGRAPHY. Metuchen, N.J.: Scarecrow Press, 1975. vi, 157 p.

The names and addresses of over thirty divorce organizations are included in appendix 1 of this work. The names, addresses, and extensive descriptions of the purpose and activity of each national or local group are given.

12-6   National Council on Family Relations. Task Force on Divorce and
        Divorce Reform. "Task Force Report: Divorce and Divorce Reform.
        1974 Report." Minneapolis, Minn.: 1973. vii, 70 p. Mimeo-
        graphed.

        The appendix of this report contains a list of twenty-five
        divorce-related organizations together with their addresses,
        telephone numbers, and brief descriptions of their activi-
        ties. Some professional organizations that have commit-
        tees on divorce are also included.

12-7   WOMEN'S ORGANIZATIONS AND LEADERS DIRECTORY. Edited
        by Myra E. Barrer and Lester A. Barrer. Washington, D.C.: To-
        day Publications and News Service, 1975. Biennial.

        This directory is a worldwide, geographical, and subject
        listing of ten thousand women's organizations, and leaders
        of women's organizations. It contains the addresses, tele-
        phone numbers, and descriptive information on groups of
        all types. This is an excellent guide to divorce groups,
        divorce research, and divorce counseling groups in the
        United States, Canada, and Great Britain. An excellent
        subject index is included.

        Consult: Alimony   Insurance, divorce
                  Child support   Law, divorce
                  Children, rights   Parents, single
                  Counseling, divorce Separation

B. CONFERENCES

Many national and professional organizations hold annual conferences with
sections pertaining to divorce. The best sources of information for finding
the time and place of these meetings are the ENCYCLOPEDIA OF ASSOCIA-
TIONS (item 12-4), the FAMILY LAW REPORTER (item 8-16), and the newsletters described in part D of this chapter.

C. CONFERENCE PROCEEDINGS

The proceedings of national and international meetings are often published,
and some are indexed by several sources that are described in this section.
It sometimes takes years, however, before proceedings are edited and published,
with the result that the time lag from the end of a conference to the point at
which its proceedings are cited in the indexes may be from two to ten years.
Therefore the investigator must be aware of this as he searches for the proceedings of a specific conference.

Two main sources for locating information on these conferences are described
in this section, although neither source contains many published proceedings of

conferences on divorce to date. The FAMILY LAW REPORTER (item 8-16) also summarizes proceedings of meetings that are held by various professional associations on the subject of divorce.

12-8   DIRECTORY OF PUBLISHED PROCEEDINGS. Series SSH-SOCIAL SCIENCES/HUMANITIES. Harrison, N.Y.: InterDok Corp., 1968-- . Quarterly, with annual cumulated index.

The published proceedings of congresses, conferences, symposia, meetings, seminars, and summer schools that have been held around the world are indexed in this directory. The contents are arranged in chronological order, giving the source, location, topic, and cost of the printed proceedings. There are indexes for the subject/sponsor, editor, and location of the published proceedings. The October issue contains the cumulated index.

Consult: Family disorganization
          Separation

12-9   PROCEEDINGS IN PRINT. Arlington, Mass.: 1964-- . 6 issues per year, with an annual cumulated index.

An index to the proceedings of conferences, symposia, lecture series, congresses, hearings, seminars, courses, colloquia, and meetings in all languages on all subjects, this work is arranged by title of the conference, and indexed by editor, subject, and sponsor. It also gives the source, address, and cost when available. Prior to 1967, this directory indexed only proceedings on aerospace technology.

Consult: Divorce

D. NEWSLETTERS

Newsletters are one of the best sources for up-to-date information on divorce. Some divorce organizations publish their own newsletters. These may contain information on new books, research, pamphlets, organizations, and changes in the law. The newsletters reflect the purposes and goals of their parent organizations. Some may be narrowly partisan, others broadly objective. However, newsletters on divorce are often difficult to find. In this section means for finding newsletters are described. Several of the most important newsletters are also described.

12-10   ENCYCLOPEDIA OF ASSOCIATIONS. Edited by Mary Wilson Pair. 3 vols. 12th ed. Detroit: Gale Research Co., 1978. Annual, with quarterly supplements.

The publications of national organizations are listed in
this up-to-date reference work. Most of the organizations are nonprofit organizations. Refer to item 12-4.

12-11   MARRIAGE AND DIVORCE TODAY NEWSLETTER. ATCOM, 2315
Broadway, New York, N.Y.: 1974-- . Biweekly. By subscrip-
tion.

This privately published newsletter reports on recent
and upcoming conferences, news features, new divorce
publications, resources, legislation, divorce counseling
clinics, and other information on divorce.

12-12   STANDARD DIRECTORY OF NEWSLETTERS. New York: Oxbridge
Publishing Co., 1972. 266 p.

Newsletters in over two hundred disciplines and interest
areas are described in this directory. Both professional
and trade newsletters are included. There is a title index only, and the contents are incomplete.

Consult: Social services and welfare
          Sociology

12-13   WOMEN'S ORGANIZATIONS AND LEADERS DIRECTORY. Edited
by Myra E. Barrer and Lester A. Barrer. Washington, D.C.: Today Publications and News Service, 1975. Biennial.

This extensive directory lists the publications of many
organizations. Refer to item 12-7.

Chapter 13

RESOURCES NEEDED FOR DIVORCE RESEARCH

This concluding chapter is devoted to consideration of information available, or lack of it, in regard to two kinds of resources needed for the facilitation of divorce research. In part A, divorce research centers and large research libraries, both with special collections of materials on divorce, are considered. In part B, special resources in terms of grants-in-aid and other special funding of divorce research are considered.

A. SPECIAL COLLECTIONS, CLEARINGHOUSES, AND RESEARCH CENTERS

As this information guide has revealed, information on divorce, both retrospective and current, is scattered throughout various types of literature, data banks, and nonprint media. At the same time, it is interspersed with the literature of numerous diverse subject areas. This information guide is a preliminary attempt to overcome these difficulties.

Research centers, clearinghouses for coordination and dissemination of information, and special library collections are very important for in-depth study and analysis of a specific subject such as divorce. To date, at least in the United States, the above mentioned special resources for divorce do not exist.

To find special collections of informational materials on divorce the researcher must locate these within the larger general library collections, some of which are mentioned in this guide, for example, the Center for Research Libraries in Chicago and libraries mentioned in chapter 2, parts A and C, in addition to more specialized centers such as the Office of Population Research at Princeton University (item 4-28 and 4-29). Also, the Educational Resources Information Center (ERIC), through its sixteen clearinghouses, is beginning to include more information on unpublished research and investigations on divorce in its data base (item 5-22).

Various ongoing reference works are available which the researcher can use to

locate special library collections and research centers which offer the possibility of considerable materials on divorce in their collections. These works
are described below. Although the authors, in searching through these works,
found none that were specifically on divorce, the researcher by looking under
headings such as "Family," "Population," "Marriage," and the like, may be
able to locate collections which may provide substantial specialized information on divorce. Future editions of these works should be watched for, as
they will probably provide more specific references for divorce information in
the future. To keep up with new editions of these, as well as completely
new similar works as they are acquired by libraries, consult library subject
card catalogs, under headings such as the following, which use the United
States as an example:

> Associations, Institutions, etc.--United States--
>   Directories
> Data libraries--United States--Directories
> Information services--United States--Directories
> Library resources--United States--Directories
> Research--United States--Directories
> United States--Learned institutions and societies--
>   Directories

13-1   Ash, Lee, comp. SUBJECT COLLECTIONS, A GUIDE TO SPECIAL
        BOOK COLLECTIONS AND SUBJECT EMPHASES AS REPORTED BY
        UNIVERSITY, COLLEGE, PUBLIC, AND SPECIAL LIBRARIES AND
        MUSEUMS IN THE UNITED STATES AND CANADA. 4th ed., rev.
        and enl. New York: R.R. Bowker Co., 1974. 908 p.

>   Approximately seventy thousand special collections are
>   listed under Library of Congress subject headings in
>   this directory. The address, number of volumes, budget,
>   and brief description of each collection is provided.

>   Consult: Family   Vital statistics
>   Marriage

13-2   ENCYCLOPEDIA OF ASSOCIATIONS. Edited by Mary Wilson Pair.
        3 vols. 12th ed. Detroit: Gale Research Co., 1978. Annual,
        with quarterly supplements.

>   It may be possible, by querying the national associations
>   listed which are interested in divorce, to locate any
>   special collections that these organizations may have.
>   Refer to item 12-4.

13-3   Gleiter, Karin. INTERNATIONAL DIRECTORY OF POPULATION
        INFORMATION AND LIBRARY RESOURCES. Preliminary 2d ed.
        Technical Information Service, Carolina Population Center, Uni-
        versity of North Carolina at Chapel Hill, 1975. xii, 331 p.

>   This work is a good source for information on population

research centers throughout the world, both governmental, private, and academic. It provides data on the publications of the various agencies and institutes, with a brief description of the books, government documents, census reports, and so forth, that are held in the libraries of the centers.

13-4   Kruzas, Anthony T. ENCYCLOPEDIA OF INFORMATION SYSTEMS AND SERVICES. 2d international ed. Ann Arbor, Mich.: A.T. Kruzas Associates, 1974. xii, 1,271 p.

This work describes and analyzes about 1,750 organizations, including approximately seventy Canadian and fifty English information services, such as information centers, clearinghouses, research centers, and micrographic firms. Legal services, traditional academic libraries, and special libraries are not included. Information on each entry includes name, address, telephone number of the organization, year organized, other sponsoring organizations, head of the unit, staffing, description of the service rendered, scope or subject coverage, data sources, information and type of holdings, publications, other services and use restrictions. The thirteen indexes include a subject index.

13-5   NATIONAL UNION CATALOG OF MANUSCRIPT COLLECTIONS: BASED ON REPORTS FROM AMERICAN REPOSITORIES OF MANUSCRIPTS, 1959/61-- . Washington, D.C.: Library of Congress, 1962-- . Annual. Publisher varies. Good subject index, with triennial cumulative indexes.

As of 1974, over 30,000 collections of manuscripts in 920 repositories in the United States are described. Of this number, approximately twenty-five have information on divorce. These are from the collections of lawyers and clergymen. The descriptions include dates of the manuscripts in each collection, the number of items comprising the collection, as well as access to and location of the collection.

Consult: Divorce

13-6   RESEARCH CENTERS DIRECTORY. Edited by Archie M. Palmer. 5th ed. Detroit: Gale Research Co., 1975. xi, 1,039 p. Biennial. Supplements between editions are titled NEW RESEARCH CENTERS.

A guide to over six thousand university-related and other permanent nonprofit research organizations in nearly all branches of learning in the United States and Canada, this directory has three indexes: an institutional or

sponsor index, a title index, and a subject index.
The information provided in each listing includes the
following: sponsor, address, telephone number, director,
date of founding, current status, sources of support, staff,
dollar value of research, principal fields of activity,
special research facilities, publications, educational
activities of the center, and any special library facilities of the center.

Consult: Demography   Public opinion
          Family relations

13-7   U.S. Library of Congress. National Referral Center. A DIREC-
        TORY OF INFORMATION RESOURCES IN THE UNITED STATES:
        SOCIAL SCIENCES. Rev. ed. Washington, D.C.: Government
        Printing Office, 1973. iv, 700 p. Subject index. LC1.31:D62/
        2/1973.

        This guide to nearly twenty-five hundred professional
        societies, historical societies, university and research
        bureaus and institutes, federal and state agencies,
        special collections in museums, and individual experts,
        as well as to technical libraries, information and docu-
        ments centers, and indexing and abstracting services is ar-
        ranged alphabetically by agency. Each organization is
        described briefly, with addresses and telephone numbers,
        areas of interest, holdings, publications, and information
        services provided.

        Consult: Public opinion
                  Vital statistics

13-8   Young, Margaret Labash; Young, Harold Chester; and Kruzas,
        Anthony T. eds. DIRECTORY OF SPECIAL LIBRARIES AND IN-
        FORMATION CENTERS. 4th ed. 2 vols. Detroit: Gale Research
        Co., 1977. Subject index. Irregular supplements, without indexes.

        This directory is a guide to special libraries, research
        libraries, information centers, archives, and data centers,
        managed by government agencies, business, industry, and
        newspapers, which provide information in the areas of
        social science, natural and physical science, humanities,
        business, and medicine. For each listing, it provides
        the address, telephone number, date founded, number of
        staff, name of the director, subjects and special collec-
        tions, number of items, subscriptions, services, publica-
        tions, special indexes, and staff names. A geographical
        index, covering the United States and Canada, is in-
        cluded.

        Consult: Family living
                  Marriage relations

B. SOURCES FOR FUNDING OF DIVORCE RESEARCH

Although much needed, it is very difficult to identify sources, either governmental or private, for obtaining grants-in-aid specifically for support of divorce research or for establishing the types of resources needed which were considered in part A above. The works listed below are the ones which are most widely used for locating sources of funding for research and demonstration projects in many fields. However, divorce as a specific subject listing in these works is virtually nonexistent. Therefore one must search under related listings, and actually must examine carefully and individually the organizations, foundations, and agencies listed in terms of their possible interest in funding research on divorce. For future editions of these works however, it is hoped there will be more interest indicated in funding research in this area. To find future new editions of these works, as well as similar works, consult headings such as those listed below (which use the United States as an example) in the subject card catalogs of the libraries.

Endowments--United States--Directories
Grants-in-aid--United States--Directories
Research grants--United States--Directories

13-9   ANNUAL REGISTER OF GRANT SUPPORT. 11th ed. Chicago:
         Marquis Academic Media, 1977-78. xxiii, 757 p.

> This work contains data on sources of support for research,
> travel and exchange programs, and publication support in
> a variety of fields, from government agencies, public and
> private foundations, and business, professional, and spe-
> cial interest organizations throughout the world. Informa-
> tion is arranged by disciplines with a subject index, an
> organization and program index, a geographic index, and
> a personnel index. The following information on each
> grant-making organization is provided: address, telephone
> number, date of founding, major field of interest, nature
> of support, qualifications required of individuals, amount
> or range of funds, total funding, cost-sharing stipulations,
> number of applicants and recipients, application require-
> ments and procedures, closing dates for application, and
> names of principal personnel.

13-10   Fondazione, Giovanni Angelli. GUIDE TO EUROPEAN FOUNDA-
         TIONS. Milan, Italy: Prepared by the Giovanni Angelli Founda-
         tions, distributed by Columbia University Press, 1973. 401 p.

> Listing foundations in the United Kingdom and on the
> Continent, this work contains information on the founding,
> purpose, activities, as well as reports on spheres of activ-
> ities, finances, and organization of each foundation.
> Arranged by country, it includes indexes with references
> to fields of activity, persons, and foundation names.

Consult: Social sciences   Sociology
         Social welfare

13-11   FOUNDATION DIRECTORY. Edited by Marianno O. Lewis. 6th ed. New York: Compiled by the Foundation Center, distributed by Columbia University Press, 1977. xxix, 661 p. Supplements.

> This guide to over twenty-five hundred foundations in the United States includes the address, date of founding, donor(s), purpose and activities, assets and expenditures, officers and directors for each foundation listed. The directory is arranged by states, with a subject index, a city and state index, and personnel and title indexes. Additional information includes a list of regional libraries that have individual foundation reports and also suggestions on how to write a proposal. A computer search of recent grants in excess of $5,000 can be made for the associate members. For further information on this refer to item 5-23. Refer also to item 13-12 below.

13-12   FOUNDATION GRANTS INDEX, 1970/71-- ; A CUMULATIVE LISTING OF FOUNDATION GRANTS. New York: Compiled by the Foundation Center, distributed by Columbia University Press, 1972-- . Annual.

> A computer-generated (refer to item 5-23) alphabetical listing of donating foundations by state, this work gives for each listing the amount granted, the recipient, the purpose of the grant, and the duration of the grant. There is also a recipients index, a foundation index, and a subject index by keyword. This index is cumulated from the Foundation Center's newsletter, FOUNDATION NEWS. Refer also to item 13-11 above.

13-13   GRANT INFORMATION SYSTEM. 3d ed. Compiled by William K. Wilson; edited by Betty L. Wilson. Scottsdale, Ariz.: Oryx Press, 1976. 4 cumulative vols. per year. Monthly FACULTY ALERT BULLETIN.

> This extensive and well-organized system for grant information covers quarterly over fourteen hundred grants in eighty-eight academic disciplines. Entries include full descriptive information about each grant and its sponsoring organization, total dollar value, restrictions, special requirements for applicants, including student or faculty status, number of grants available each year with their deadline dates; and renewability. All programs are indexed by grant name and sponsoring organization. The grants are

listed by deadline within each academic discipline.

Consult: Mental health   Social services
          Social sciences

13-14   GRANTS REGISTER. 5th ed. London: St. James Press; New York: St. Martin's Press, 1976. xxv, 764 p. Biennial.

Information on financial assistance for advanced training for graduate students and postgraduate scholars in the United States, Canada, and the United Kingdom, is provided by this source. Included are data on scholarships, fellowships, research grants, funding for research, grants-in-aid, and prizes. Information on each award includes the eligibility requirements. Besides a subject index, there is an index of awards and one by awarding body.

13-15   Great Britain. National Council of Social Service. DIRECTORY OF GRANT-MAKING TRUSTS. London, 1975. vx, 1,030 p.

This directory is an official listing of registered charities and foundations of Great Britain. The publisher varies.

13-16   INTERNATIONAL FOUNDATION DIRECTORY. Consulting editor, H.V. Hodson. Detroit: Gale Research Co.; London: Europa Publications, 1974. viii, 396 p.

Worldwide information on foundations is provided by this directory.

13-17   U.S. Office of Education. CATALOG OF FEDERAL EDUCATION ASSISTANCE PROGRAMS; AN INDEXED GUIDE TO THE FEDERAL GOVERNMENT'S PROGRAMS OFFERING EDUCATIONAL BENEFITS TO THE AMERICAN PEOPLE. Washington, D.C.: Government Printing Office, 1972-- . Annual. HE5.221:11035.

This directory is difficult to use. Access is by a keyword index. Although there is very little on divorce in this work, it is worth watching for future editions.

13-18   U.S. Office of Management and Budget. CATALOG OF FEDERAL DOMESTIC ASSISTANCE. Washington, D.C.: Government Printing Office, 1977. Annual. PrEx 2.20:976

This directory is easier to use than item 13-17 above. It has a good subject index. As with the above item, there is very little at the moment relating to divorce, but it is well worth watching for future editions.

13-19   Wilson, William K., and Wilson, Betty L. DIRECTORY OF RE-

SEARCH GRANTS, 1976–77. Scottsdale, Ariz.: Oryx Press, 1976. xvii, 235 p. Annual.

This is a well-organized and concise directory of 2,900 grant support programs, organized much as the GRANT INFORMATION SYSTEM (13-13). Information is provided on grants, contracted fellowships, and support programs available from federal and state governments, private foundations and associations, and corporations for research, training, and innovative efforts. Indexing is by grant name, sponsoring organization, and by subject abbreviation.

Consult: Mental health   Social services
Social sciences

ADDENDUM

The addendum updates this information guide through April 1978. The item numbers below indicate the appropriate location for the citations within chapters 4, 5, 6, and 8.

4-41A   ABSTRACTS OF POPULAR CULTURE. Bowling Green, Ohio: Bowling Green University Popular Press, 1976-- . Quarterly.

> Over 600 city, state, and regional periodicals are selectively abstracted in the fields of popular literature, folklore, television, films, theater, and the counter culture. A few foreign magazines, including British and Canadian, are abstracted. Copies of articles are available from the publisher. A marginal source at this time.

The numbers appearing after the citations in items 5-10A through 5-20A below are references to the volume and page number of DISSERTATION ABSTRACTS INTERNATIONAL (item 5-4) on which the dissertation cited is abstracted.

5-10A   CHILD CUSTODY

> Abarbanel, Alice R. "Joint Custody Families: A Case Study Approach." 1977. (38/06B, p. 2,840).

> Charnas, Jane F. "Interdisciplinary Practice Use of the Concept of Psychological Parenthood in Contested Child Custody Cases Resulting from Divorce." 1977. (38/05A, p. 3,054).

> Sanford, Jill L. "Contested Custody and the Judicial Decision-making Process." 1977. (38/09A, p. 5,746).

5-11A   CHILDREN OF DIVORCED PARENTS

> Beissinger, Tina P. "The Relationship of Parental Divorce, During Adolescence, to Self-concept." 1976. (37/07A, p. 4,220).

> Daniel, Ralph M. "Father-child Intimacy in Divorced Families." 1977. (38/06B, p. 2,854).

> Scott, Charles V. "The Effects of Family Structure on the Academic Status of Fifth Grade Students." 1974. (35/09A, p. 5,695).

Addendum

5-12A   DESERTION AND NON SUPPORT

Cassetty, Judith H.   "Child Support and Public Policy."   1977.
(38/09A, p. 5,714).

5-13A   DIVORCE

Darsa, Stephanie D.   "Initiation of Divorce as a Function of Locus
of Control, Self-actualization and Androgyny."   1976.   (37/09B,
p. 4,671).

Hampton, Robert L.   "Marital Disruption among Blacks."   1976.
(38/03A, p. 1,685).

Hayes, Maggie P.   "Divorce in the Middle Years."   1976.   (37/09A,
p. 6,093).

Laner, Mary R.   "Love's Labors Lost: A Theory of Marital Dissolution."
1977.   (37/11A, p. 7,350).

McCarthy, James F.   "Patterns of Marriage Dissolution in the United
States."   1977.   (38/07A, p. 4,392).

McKenry, Patrick C.   "A Comparison of Divorced and Married Dyads."
1976.   (37/11A, p. 7,350).

Melton, Willie III.   "Self-satisfaction and Marital Stability Among
Black Males: Socioeconomic and Demographic Antecedents."   1976.
(37/08A, p. 5,387).

O'Connor, Nancy D.V.   "An Exploration of the Effects of Antici-
patory Grief Versus Acute Grief on Recovery after Loss of Spouse
among Divorced and Separated Women."   1976.   (37/09A, p. 5,708).

Peskin, Tsipora R.   "Divorce and the Adult Life Span: A Longitudinal
Study."   1976.   (38/02A, p. 1,027).

Rosenman, Linda S.   "Marital Status Change and Labor Force Re-
adjustments: An Analysis of Female Heads of Families."   1976.
(37/12A, p. 7,975).

Shapiro, Terry H.   "A Comparison of Counseling MMPI Profiles of
Couples who Remain Married with Those who Divorce."   1977.
(38/07A, p. 3,965).

Sullivan, Wallace E.   "Some Personality Correlates of Marital Status."
1976.   (37/09B, p. 4,764).

5-13B   DIVORCE COUNSELING

Fisher, Bruce F.   "Identifying and Meeting Needs of Formerly-married

People through a Divorce Adjustment Seminar." 1976. (37/11A, p. 7,036).

Gillen, Frances C. "A Study of the Effects of Paraprofessionally Conducted Group Therapy on the Self Concept of Divorced or Separated Persons." 1976. (37/08A, p. 4,863).

Moerlin, Elinor B. "Competencies for the Divorced." 1977. (38/08B, p. 3,960).

Phillips, Carol A. "Interaction of Divorced and Single Females in a Group Setting." 1976. (37/11A, p. 7,048).

Wilkinson, Gary S. "Small Group Counseling with Elementary School Children of Divorce." 1976. (37/10A, p. 6,287).

5-14A   DIVORCED PERSONS

Fonte, Verona H. "Demographic Variables and Self-actualization for Divorced and Married Women." 1976. (38/09B, p. 4,452).

Grelf, Judith B. "Child Absence: Fathers' Perceptions of their Relationship to their Children Subsequent to Divorce." 1977. (38/09A, p. 5,714).

Herrick, Jeannette E. "An In-depth Study of Four Divorced Working-class Women." 1977. (38/03A, p. 1,835).

Newsome, Oliver D. "Postdivorce Interaction: An Explanation Using Exchange Theory." 1976. (37/12A, p. 8,001).

Patton, Robert D. "Sexual Attitudes and Behaviors of Single Parents." 1976. (37/02A, p. 820).

Sparks, Zoe A.D. "Socioeconomic Correlates of Divorce and Non-divorce among Professional Women in Arkansas." 1977. (38/05A, p. 2,471).

5-15A   DIVORCE IN LITERATURE

Gillis, Ruth J. "An Exploratory Study of Divorce, Religion, and Discipline in Family Relationships as Found in the Texts and Illustrations of Picture Books." 1977. (38/09A, p. 5,234).

5-15B   FATHER ABSENCE

Atkins, Shirley M. "Opacity and Clarity in the Play Styles of Four-year-old Father-absent and Father-present Male Children." 1975. (36/04A, p. 2,043).

Addendum

Badaines, Joel S. "Identification, Imitation and Sex-role Preference as a Function of Father-absence and Father-presence in Black and Chicano Boys." 1972. (34/01B, p. 403).

Baptiste, David A., Jr. "A Comparative Study of Mothers' Personality Characteristics and Childrearing Attitudes in Husband-present and Husband-absent Families." 1976. (37/10A, p. 6,263).

Bernhardt, Jeanne R. "The Young Child's Perception of the Father's Role Using a Comparison of Age, Sex, and Father-absent, Father-present Family Composition." 1975. (35/10B, p. 4,955).

Brightman, Lloyd A. "The Differential Use of Interpersonal Resources by Father-absent Adolescents as a Correlate of their School Achievement." 1971. (32/01A, p. 562).

Brodis, Nellie F.T.A. "Parent-child Relationship and Self-concept as Related to Differential Academic Achievement of Adolescent Siblings in Father-absent Families. 1969. (30/08A, p. 3,180).

Burns, Robert A. "The Effect of Father's Absence on the Development of the Masculine Identification of Boys in Residential Treatment." 1971. (32/07B, p. 4,179).

Cantey, Richard E. "The Relationship of Father-absence, Socioeconomic Status, and Other Variables to Creative Abilities in Fifth-grade Boys." 1973. (34/07A, p. 3,981).

Courtney, Dan E. "The Effect of Male Teachers on the Academic Achievement of Sixth Grade Father-absent Boys." 1977. (38/09A, p. 5,232).

Cox, Martha J. "The Effects of Father Absence and Working Mothers on Children." 1975. (36/07B, p. 3,640).

Dean, Katherine I. "Father Absence, Feminine Identification, and Assertive-aggressiveness--A Test of Compulsive Masculinity among Institutionalized Negro Juvenile Delinquents." 1970. (31/09A, p. 4,912).

Fowler, Patrick C. "Multivariate Assessments of the Effects of Early Father-absence on the Educational Preparedness and Academic Achievement of Black Children." 1977. (38/07A, p. 4,043).

Fox, Billy R. "Effect of Public Welfare Affiliation, Absence of a Father Figure and Other Selected Variable Factors on the Development of Socialization, Maturity, Responsibility and Intrapersonal Structuring of Values among Male High School Adolescents." 1972. (33/04A, p. 1,864).

French-Wixson, Judith. "Differences between Father-absent and Father-present Fifth-grade Boys in Political Socialization." 1976. (37/10A, p. 6,337).

Griggs, Shirley A. "A Study of the Life Plans of Culturally Disadvantaged Negro Adolescent Girls with Father-absence in the Home." 1967. (28/12A, p. 4,950).

Hull, Darrell M. "Examination of Three Maternal Characteristics in Relationship to Sex-role Development of Father-present and Father-absent Children." 1975. (37/02A, p. 807).

Imperio, Anne-Marie. "Ego Development, Father Status, and Perception of Parents in Psychopathic, Neurotic, and Subcultural Delinquents." 1975. (36/08B, p. 4,133).

Jones, Hugh E. "Father Absence During Childhood, Maternal Attitudes Toward Men, and the Sex-role Development of Male College Students." 1975. (36/06B, p. 3,047).

Kopf, Kathryn E. "An Exploration of Possible Relationships Between Selected Home Variables and School Adjustment of Father-absent 8th Grade Boys. 1967. (28/01A, p. 126).

Lewin, Philip. "Home and Self-concept Factors Related to Differential Academic Achievement of Teenagers in One-parent, Father-absent Families from Two Social Classes." 1969. (30-12A, p. 5,240).

Masingale, Eula M. "Father-absence as Related to Parental Role-play Behavior." 1971. (32/12B, p. 7,294).

Matthews, Graham P. "Father-absence and the Development of Masculine Identification in Black Preschool Males." 1976. (37/03A, p. 1,458).

Miller, Barbara A. B. "Effects of Father Absence and Mother's Evaluation of Father on the Socialization of Adolescent Boys." 1961. (22/04, p. 1,257).

Moran, Patricia A. "The Effect of Father Absence on Delinquent Males: Dependency and Hypermasculinity." 1972. (33/03B, p. 1,292).

Muir, Martha F. "Differential Effects of Father Absence on Sex-role Identity as a Function of Sex, Age at Time of Divorce, and Step-parent Availability." 1977. (38/09A, p. 5,744).

Nobers, Donald R. "The Effects of Father Absence and Mother's Characteristics on the Identification of Adolescent White and Negro Males." 1968. (29/04B, p. 1,508).

Oshman, Harvey P. "Some Effects of Father-absence upon the Psychosocial Development of Male and Female Late-adolescents: Theoretical and Empirical Considerations." 1975. (36/02B, p. 919).

Pearce, Doris P. "Familial Correlates of Father-presence and Father-absence." 1963. (24/11, p. 4,669).

Phillips, Judith. "Performance of Father-present and Father-absent Southern Negro Boys on a Simple Operant Task as a Function of the Race and Sex of the Experimenter and the Type of Social Reinforcement." 1966. (28/01B, p. 366).

Pipher, Mary B. "The Effects of Father Absence on the Sexual Development and Adjustment of Adolescent Daughters and Their Mothers." 1977. (38/02B, p. 913).

Schoolman, Benilu L. "The Relationship of the Development of Masculinity to Father Absence on Preadolescent Boys." 1969. (36/06B, p. 2,917).

Summers, George M. "Paternal Deprivation and Adaptation: A Study of Differential Loss Management in Latency Age Father-absent Boys." 1970. (31/10A, p. 5,524).

Vroegh, Karen S. "The Relationship of Sex of Teacher and Father Presence-absence to Academic Achievement." 1972. (33/10A, p. 5,569).

Wasserman, Herbert L. "Father-absent and Father-present Lower Class Negro Families: A Comparative Study of Family Functioning." 1968. (29/12A, p. 4,569).

5-16A   LEGAL ASPECTS OF DIVORCE

Combs, Elizabeth R. "The Development of a Set of Propositional Guidelines and Their Implementation for Use in Decision Making at Dissolution of Marriage in Indiana." 1977. (38/10A, p. 6,278).

Wallace, Arla S. "An Application of Attachment Theory to the Study of a Population of Court Referred Divorced People." 1977. (38/10B, p. 4,994).

5-17A   ONE- PARENT FAMILIES

Farley, Florence S. "Scholastic Ability and Birth Order, Family Size, Sibling Age Spacing, and Parental Absence in Eighth and Ninth Graders: An Empirical Study of the Confluence Model." 1977. (38/10A, p. 6,008).

Keshet, Harry F. "Part-time Fathers: A Study of Separated and

Divorced Men." 1977. (38/03A, p. 1,687).

LaPoint, Velma D.V. "A Descriptive Survey of Some Perceptions and Concerns of Black Female Single Parent Families in Lansing, Michigan." 1977. (38/03A, p. 1,231).

Loge, Betty J. "Role Adjustments to Single Parenthood: A Study of Divorced and Widowed Men and Women." 1976. (37/07A, p. 4,647).

Morris, Roger B. "Strengths of the Black Community: An Investigation of the Black Community and 'Broken Homes.'" 1977. (38/03A, p. 1,960).

Rasmussen, Dennis D. "Sex Role Differentiation in One-parent Families." 1974. (35/11B, p. 5,624).

Reinhart, Gail E. "One-parent Families: A Study of Divorced Mothers and Adolescents Using Social Climate and Relationship Styles." 1977. (38/06B, p. 2,881).

5-18A RELIGIOUS ASPECTS OF DIVORCE

Ruark, Katherine L. "Clergy Divorce and Subsequent Career Mobility." 1977. (38/09A, p. 5,746).

5-19A REMARRIAGE, STEPPARENTS AND STEPCHILDREN

Buhr, Kenneth S. "Stress, Marital Interaction, and Personal Competence in Natural-parent and Step-father Families." 1975. (36/01A, p. 564).

Keith, Judith A. "Child Rearing Attitudes and Perceived Behavior Patterns of Natural Parents and Stepparents." 1977. (38/07A, p. 4,396).

LaRoche, Shirley S. "The Role of the Stepfather in the Family." 1973. (34/05A, p. 2,792).

Medeiros, Julie P. "Relationship Styles and Family Environment of Stepfamilies." 1977. (38/09B, p. 4,472).

Nadler, Janice H. "The Psychological Stress of the Stepmother." 1976. (37/10B, p. 5,367).

Perkins, Terry F. "Natural-parent Family Systems Versus Step-parent Family Systems." 1977. (38/10B, p. 5,038).

Pritchard, James W. "Divorce-remarriage: An Investigation of the Effects of Divorce and Related Variables on the Communication Style of Reconstituted Marriages." 1976. (38/01B, p. 375).

Sardanis-Zimmerman, Irene. "The Stepmother: Mythology and Self-perception." 1977. (38/06B, p. 2,884).

Scarano, Thomas P. "Multivariate Informational Analysis: A Diagnostic Instrument for Measuring Social Interaction in Couples." 1977. (37/08B, p. 4,164).

Stern, Phyllis N. "Integrative Discipline in Stepfather Families." 1976. (37/10B, p. 4,991).

5-20A   SEPARATION

Gongla, Patricia A. "Social Relationships after Marital Separation: A Study of Women with Children." 1977. (38/09A, p. 5,742).

6-123A   116.--PERSONS HOSPITALIZED BY NUMBER OF EPISODES AND DAYS HOSPITALIZED IN A YEAR--UNITED STATES. 1972. (1977). HE20.6209:10/116.

> The number of hospital episodes and days hospitalized for divorced and separated persons is given in this report.

6-123B   117.--HOSPITAL AND SURGICAL INSURANCE COVERAGE--UNITED STATES. 1974. (1977). HE20.6209:10/117.

> The number and percentage of divorced and separated persons covered by hospital and surgical insurance is the focus of this report.

6-124A   204.--TUBERCULIN SKIN TEST REACTION AMONG ADULTS 25-74 YEARS--UNITED STATES. 1971-72. (1977). HE20.6209:11/204.

> The actual and expected rates of tuberculin positive results for divorced persons are reported in this study.

6-136A   27.--CHARACTERISTICS, SOCIAL CONTACTS AND ACTIVITIES OF NURSING HOME RESIDENTS--UNITED STATES. 1973-74. (1977). HE20.6209:13:/27.

> Data are reported on the number of divorced persons in nursing homes by age and sex.

6-155A   29.--DIVORCE AND DIVORCE RATES--UNITED STATES. (1978). HE20.6209:21/29.

> This report contains an analysis of divorce statistics from the early 1970s including divorce trend data through 1976.

6-169A   142.--ADMISSION RATES TO STATE AND COUNTY PSYCHIATRIC HOSPITALS BY AGE, SEX AND MARITAL STATUS--UNITED STATES. 1975. (1977). HE20.8116/142.

> The number and rate of separated and divorced persons ad-

mitted to psychiatric hospitals in 1975 are indicated in this study.

8-3A   Krause, Harry D.   FAMILY LAW IN A NUTSHELL.   St. Paul: West Publishing, 1977.   xxxiv, 400 p.

This short, non-technical treatment of family law is aimed at the general reader.   About one-half of the book deals with divorce and divorce related subjects such as alimony, custody, property settlements, and support.

NAME INDEX

This index lists all names associated with the items included in this information guide, with the exclusion of commercial publishers. It lists, therefore, personal authors, coauthors, editors, and compilers, as well as agencies, including government agencies, associations, libraries, organizations, and institutions. References are to entry numbers for the corresponding items in the guide. Entry numbers followed by the letter A or B are references to items in the addendum. A few references not associated with a specific item in the guide, but with a name in the introduction to the guide or in the text of a particular section of a chapter, are indicated by page number, e.g., p. ii or p. 204. Alphabetization is letter by letter.

Name Index

Name Index

D

Da Costa, Derek M. 5-13
Dahl, Nancy S. 1-3, 1-7
Daniel, Ralph M. 5-11A
Darsa, Stephanie D. 5-13A
Data Use and Access Laboratories
6-177
Dean, Gillian 5-13
Dean, Katherine I. 5-15B
Decker, John W. 5-18
de Mestier du Bourg, Hubert J.M.
5-13
Doppler, George F. 12-3
Dries, Robert M. 5-14
Driver, Samuel R. 11-45
Drury, Francis K.W. 11-19
DUALabs. See Data Use and Access
Laboratories
Duberman, Lucile 5-19

E

Economic Research Service 6-171
Educational Film Library Association
10-17
Educational Resources Information
Center. See U.S. Educational
Resources Information Center
Ellison, John W. 11-39
Emerson, James G., Jr. 5-18
Engemoen, Bonny L. 5-11
Erasmus, Desiderius p. v
ERIC. See U.S. Educational Re-
sources Information Center
Eubank, Earle E. 5-12
Evans, Charles 2-17
Evans, David S., Jr. 5-18

F

Fairbanks, James D. 5-16
Farley, Florence S. 5-17A
Faxon, Frederick W. 11-18
Feldblum, Meyer S. 5-18
Fidell, Estelle A. 11-11
Firkins, Ina Ten Eyck 11-20
Fisher, Bruce F. 5-13B
Fisher, Esther O. 5-13
Fletcher, William I. 4-26, 11-30

Fondazione, Giovanni Angelli 13-10
Fonte, Verona H. 5-14A
Foundation Center, The 5-23
Fowler, Patrick C. 5-15B
Fox, Billy R. 5-15B
French-Wixson, Judith 5-15B

G

Gallup, George H. 9-45
Gallup, Jennifer 10-18
General Register Office. See Great
Britain. General Register Office
Gerham, David 6-175
Gibbons, Marion L. 5-20
Gifford, Denis 10-2
Gillen, Frances C. 5-13B
Gillis, Ruth J. 5-15A
Gleiter, Karin 13-3
Glick, Paul C. p. 80
Gongla, Patricia A. 5-20A
Goode, William J. 3-21
Gordon, Anthony J. 11-12
Granger, Edith 11-29
Great Britain. Census Office 7-37
7-38
Great Britain. Central Statistics
Office 7-3
Great Britain. General Register
Office 7-39 - 7-52, 7-54
Great Britain. National Council of
Social Service 13-15
Great Britain. Office of Population
Censuses and Surveys 7-26 -
7-36
Great Britain. Stationery Office
7-56
Greif, Judith B. 5-14A
Griffin, Ernest R. 5-16
Griggs, Shirley A. 5-15B
Groves, Patricia H. 5-16
Gruen, Rhoda 11-8

H

Hackney, Gary R. 5-13
Haight, Willet R. 2-29
Halkett, John G. 5-15
Hampton, Robert L. 5-13A
Hamrick, Lillian A. 8-80

263

Name Index

Harrell, Pat E. 5-18
Hayes, Maggie P. 5-13A
Hellman, Florence S. 1-18
Henderson, G.P. 12-2
Henderson, S.P.A. 12-2
Heritage, Lena J. 5-13
Herman, Sonja J. 5-20
Herrick, Jeannette E. 5-14A
Hill, Reuben 1-10
Historical Commission of the Southern
  Baptist Convention 4-35
Hobart, James F. 5-13
Hodson, H.V. 13-16
Hopkins, Elizabeth 3-21
Horton, Pamela 9-48
Howington, Nolan P. 5-18
Huguelet, Theodore L. 5-15
Hull, Darrell M. 5-15B
Hutchins, Robert Maynard 11-47

I

Imperio, Anne-Marie 5-15B
Information Canada. See Canada.
  Information Canada
Institute for Scientific Information
  4-33, 4-58
Institute of Behavioral Research
  6-171
Institute of Mental Health. See
  U.S. National Institute of Mental
  Health
Internal Revenue Service. See U.S.
  Internal Revenue Service
International Political Science Asso-
  ciation 4-49
Ireland, Norma [Olin] 11-21
Israel, Stanley 1-4

J

Jacobstein, J. Myron 8-3, 8-133
Jaxel, Robert 6-174
Jenkins, William S. 8-77, 8-80,
  8-81
Johnson, Madelynne Billings 11-34
Jones, H.G. 7-4
Jones, Hugh E. 5-15B
Jones, Leonard A. 8-115

K

Kanely, Edna M. 8-6
Keckeissen, Rita G. 3-24
Keith, Judith A. 5-19A
Keller, Lillian M. 5-13
Kelly, James 2-24
Kent, Francis L. 5-8
Kephart, William M. 5-13
Keshet, Harry F. 5-17A
Kiernan, Irene R. 5-9
Kopf, Kathryn E. 5-15B
Koster, Donald N. 5-15, 11-22
Krause, Harry D. 8-3A
Kruzas, Anthony T. 13-4, 13-8

L

Land, Brian 12-1
Landgraf, John R. 5-20
Laner, Mary R. 5-13A
LaPoint, Velma D.V. 5-17A
LaRoche, Shirley S. 5-19A
Lee, David K. 5-13
Lenrow, Elbert 11-13
Levy, Robert J. 8-14
Lewin, Philip 5-15B
Lewis, Marianno O. 13-11
Library Association of the United
  Kingdom 4-26
Library of Congress. See U.S.
  Library of Congress
Library of Medicine. See U.S.
  National Library of Medicine
Lichtenberger, James P. 5-13
Lillywhite, John D. 5-13
Lloyd, David 8-2
Logasa, Hannah 11-23
Loge, Betty J. 5-17A
Loma Linda University Libraries 4-32
Long, Nathaniel T., Jr. 5-13

M

McCarthy, James F. 5-13A
McClure, Helen M. 3-21
MacDonald, Grace E. 8-74 - 8-76
McDonald, Michael 1-11
McIlvaine, Eileen 3-24

McKenney, Mary 1-5
McKenry, Patrick C. 5-13A
McNeal, Robert E. 5-11
March, Roman R. 9-49
Margolin, Frances M. 5-10
Masingale, Eula 5-15B
Matthews, Graham P. 5-15B
May, Elaine T. 5-13
Mazur-Hart, Stanley F. 5-13
Medeiros, Julie P. 5-19A
Melton, Willie III 5-13A
Mersky, Roy M. 8-3
Methodist Church. See Methodist
Publishing House
Methodist Publishing House 4-37
Meyer, Hermann H.B. 1-15
Meyers, Judith C. 5-20
Millar, John R., Jr. 5-16
Miller, Barbara A.B. 5-15B
Miller, Carrie E. 5-11
Mitchell, Brian R. 7-4
Moerlin, Elinor B. 5-13B
Mohler, Raymond D. 5-18
Moody, Lester D. 5-15
Moran, Patricia A. 5-15B
Morris, Adah H. 4-25
Morris, Roger B. 5-17A
Muir, Martha F. 5-15B
Munden, Kenneth W. 10-1

N

Nadler, Janice H. 5-19A
National Association of Social
Workers 3-7, 4-41
National Association of State
Libraries. Public Documents Clear-
ing House Committee 8-74 - 8-77
National Center for Health Statistics.
See U.S. National Center for
Health Statistics
National Conference of Commissioners
on Uniform State Laws 8-15
National Council on Family Relations.
Task Force on Divorce and Divorce
Reform 1-6
National Information Center for Edu-
cational Media 10-8 - 10-14
National Institute of Mental Health.
See U.S. National Institute of

Mental Health
National Library. See Canada.
National Library
National Library of Medicine. See
U.S. National Library of Medicine
National Library Service Corporation
2-39
National Office of Vital Statistics.
See U.S. National Office of Vital
Statistics
National Periodical Library 4-11
National Technical Information Ser-
vice. See U.S. National Techni-
cal Information Service
Newsome, Oliver D. 5-14A
New York (City) Public Library 1-12
NICEM. See National Information
Center for Educational Media
Niver, Kemp R. 10-3
Nobers, Donald R. 5-15B

O

Oberdorfer, Douglas W. 5-13
O'Brien, John E., Jr. 5-13
O'Connor, Nancy D.V. 5-13A
O'Farrell, Timothy J. 5-20
Office of Population Censuses and
Surveys. See Great Britain.
Office of Population Censuses and
Surveys
Office of Population Research 4-28,
4-29
Office of Vital Statistics. See U.S.
National Office of Vital Statistics
Olson, David H.L. 1-7
O'Neill, William L. 5-13
Oshman, Harvey P. 5-15B

P

Packman, James 11-6
Pair, Mary Wilson 12-4
Palmer, Archie M. 13-6
Pascal, Harold J. 5-13
Paskar, Joanne 6-179
Patterson, D.G. 1-17
Patterson, Margaret C. 11-4
Patterson, Samuel H. 5-12
Patton, Robert D. 5-14A

Name Index

Pearce, Doris P. 5-15B
Peddie, Robert Alexander 2-35
Perkins, Terry F. 5-19A
Peskin, Tsipora R. 5-13A
Petty, Charles V. 5-18
Phillips, Carol A. 5-13B
Phillips, Judith 5-15B
Pimsleur, Meira G. 8-78, 8-133, 8-134
Pineo, Peter C. 5-13
Pipher, Mary B. 5-15B
Plummer, Alfred 11-45
Polizoti, Leo F. 5-14
Pollack, Ervin H. 8-3
Pollard, Alfred W. 2-32
Poole, William Frederic 4-26
Population Association of America 4-28
Potts, James B., Jr. 5-15
Prewitt, Maryon P.W. 5-11
Pritchard, James W. 5-19A
Public Affairs Information Service 4-30
Pullen, William R. 8-79
Putney, Richard S. 5-20

R

Raschke, Helen J. 5-13, 5-25
Raschke, Vernon 5-25
Rasmussen, Dennis D. 5-17A
Redgrave, G.R. 2-32
Reinhard, David W. 5-11
Reinhart, Gail E. 5-17A
Ritchey, P. Neal 6-171
Rodis, Themistocles C. 5-13
Rodman, Karl M. 5-16
Roorbach, Orville A. 2-23
Rosenman, Linda S. 5-13A
Ruark, Katherine L. 5-18A
Rush, Bernard H. 5-13
Rutgers University. Camden Library 4-27
Ryder, Dorothy E. 3-23

S

Salem, James M. 10-22
Sanford, Jill L. 5-10A
Santrock, John W. 5-11

Sardanis-Zimmerman, Irene 5-19A
Scarano, Thomas P. 5-19A
Schoicket, Sally G. 5-14
Schoolman, Benilu L. 5-15B
Schroeder, Clarence W. 5-13
Scott, Charles V. 5-11A
Sear, Alan M. 5-13
Sell, Kenneth D. 1-8
Sellin, Johan T. 5-16
Sessions, Vivian S. 6-178
Seventh-Day Adventist Hospital Association 4-9
Shapiro, Terry H. 5-13A
Shaw, John MacKay 11-35
Shaw, Ralph R. 2-19
Sheehy, Eugene Paul 3-24
Shoemaker, Richard H. 2-19, 2-20
Shukri, Ahmed 5-18
Skaist, Aaron J. 5-16
Slade, W.A. 1-13
Smith, Raymond F. 11-12
Smithsonian Science Information Exchange 5-24
Snyder, Lillian M. 5-12
Society for Research in Child Development 4-44
Southern Baptist Convention. See Historical Commission of the Southern Baptist Convention
Sparks, Zoe A.D. 5-14A
Spinks, William B., Jr. 5-14
Statistics Canada. See Canada. Statistics Canada
Steinberg, David M. 8-100
Steinberg, Marvin A. 5-17
Stern, Phyllis N. 5-19A
Sterne, Richard S. 5-11
Stewart, Robert J. 5-11
Strong, James 11-40
Strunk, Mildred 9-50
Sullivan, Wallace E. 5-13A
Summers, George M. 5-15B
Superintendent of Documents. See U.S. Superintendent of Documents
Supreme Court. See U.S. Supreme Court
Sutherland, Anne C. 11-18

T

Task Force on Divorce and Divorce

Reform. See National Council on
Family Relations. Task Force on
Divorce and Divorce Reform
Taylor, Patricia A. 5-13
Thompson, Claud A. 5-15
Thompson, Kendrick S. 5-13
Thomson, Ruth G. 11-25, 11-26
Tod, Dorothea 2-30
Toronto. Public Library 2-27
Tremaine, Marie 2-28
Trumbull, Benjamin p. vii

U

UNESCO (United Nations Educational
Scientific and Cultural Organiza-
tion) 4-22, 4-23
United Methodist Church. See
Methodist Publishing House
United Nations 6-2, 7-2
United Nations Educational Scientific
and Cultural Organization. See
UNESCO
U.S. Air University, Library 4-38
U.S. Bureau of Labor Statistics
6-115
U.S. Bureau of the Census 6-5, 6-6,
6-10 - 6-38, 6-41 - 6-49, 6-51,
6-52, 6-53, 6-113, 6-180, 6-181,
7-5
U.S. Census Office 6-39, 6-40
U.S. Copyright Office 10-4, 10-5
U.S. Department of Agriculture
6-171
U.S. Educational Resources Informa-
tion Center 5-22
U.S. Internal Revenue Service 6-172
U.S. Library of Congress 2-5, 8-80,
8-81, 10-15
U.S. Library of Congress. Catalog
Publications Division 9-42, 9-43
U.S. Library of Congress. Census
Library Project 6-49
U.S. Library of Congress. Division
of Bibliography 1-13 - 1-18
U.S. Library of Congress. Division
of Documents 6-182
U.S. Library of Congress. Legisla-
tive Reference Service 8-10
U.S. Library of Congress. National

Referral Center 13-7
U.S. National Center for Health
Statistics 6-54 - 6-57, 6-116 -
6-158
U.S. National Institute of Mental
Health 6-159 - 6-170
U.S. National Library of Medicine
4-13
U.S. National Office of Vital
Statistics 6-58
U.S. National Technical Information
Service 5-21, 6-174
U.S. Office of Education 13-17
U.S. Office of Management and
Budget 13-18
U.S. Superintendent of Documents
6-183, 8-11
U.S. Supreme Court 8-93, 8-94
Urquhart, M.C. 7-6

V

Vanier Institute of the Family 1-9
Van Scoyoc, Marthellen R. 5-13
Ver Noy, Winifred 11-23
Vroegh, Karen S. 5-15B

W

Walford, Albert J. 3-25
Walker, Loretta 6-175
Wallace, Arla S. 5-16A
Waller, Willard W. 5-13
Walls, Howard Lamarr 10-6
Wasserman, Herbert L. 5-15B
Wasserman, Paul 6-179, 10-23
Watt, Robert 2-33
Webb, James B. 5-11
Whitaker, Joseph 3-12
Wilkening, Howard E. 5-13
Wilkinson, Gary S. 5-13B
Willcox, Walter F. 5-13
Williams, John W., Jr. 5-13
Willis, Gladys J. 5-15
Wilson, Betty L. 13-13, 13-19
Wilson, William K. 13-13, 13-19
Winchell, Constance M. 3-24
Wing, Donald G. 2-34
Wolodarsky, Meyer 5-18
Woody, Robert H. 5-10

TITLE INDEX

This index lists titles of all books, reports, documents, dissertations, sets, and series included in this information guide. Some titles are listed in their shortened form. References are to entry numbers for the corresponding items in the guide. Entry numbers followed by the letter A or B are references to items in the addendum. Entry numbers followed by the letter a or b are interfiled in the main body of the guide. A few references not associated with a specific numbered item in the guide, but with a title in the introduction to the guide or in the text of a particular section of a chapter, are indicated by page number, e.g., p. ii or p. 204. Alphabetization is letter by letter.

A

Abstracts for Social Workers 4-41
Abstracts of Popular Culture 4-41A
Abstracts on Criminology and Penology 4-42
Access 4-1
Accountants' Index 4-2
Achievement, Intelligence, Personality and Selected School-related Variables in Negro Children from Intact and Broken Families 5-11
Acts and Joint Resolutions of South Carolina 8-62a
Acts and Resolves of Massachusetts 8-42a
Acts--Indiana 8-35a
Acts--Iowa 8-36a
Acts of Alabama 8-21a
Acts of Assembly 8-68a
Acts of the Legislature of West Virginia 8-71a
Acts--State of Louisiana 8-39a
Adjustments of Women to Marital Separation, The 5-20

Admission Rates by Age, Sex, and Marital Status: State and County Mental Hospitals 6-160
Admissions Rates by Marital Status: Outpatient Psychiatric Services 6-161, 6-169A
Admissions to Outpatient Psychiatric Services 6-162
Affinal Relationships of the Divorced Mother 5-14
Age at First Marriage 6-27
Air University Library Index to Military Periodicals 4-38
Air University Periodical Index 4-38
"A.L.A." Index: An Index to General Literature 11-30
Alabama's Vital Events 6-59
Alaska Session Laws 8-22a
Alaska Statutes 8-22b
Alaska's Vital Statistics 6-60
Almanack, An . . . by Joseph Whitaker 3-12
Alternative Press Index 9-33
America, History and Life 4-43
American Bibliography. 1903-34 2-17

Title Index

G

H

Title Index

SUBJECT INDEX

All of the subject headings and subheadings listed in this index are in relation to divorce, even though the word "divorce" may not appear in the heading. Following each heading and subheading are entry numbers referring to the corresponding items in the information guide. Entry numbers followed by the letter A or B are references to items in the addendum. A few references are to specific chapters or sections of chapters. Some very broad subjects, along with formats, may be located from the table of contents. Alphabetization is letter by letter.

The user of this index should be aware that any very specific heading, e.g., Cancer, may refer to only the few hard-to-find items listed in the guide. This does not mean that this is the only information which can be secured on this aspect by means of this information guide. Following through on the systematic search procedures suggested throughout this information guide should provide not only more information, but also perhaps more appropriate information for each user, and, by means of the on-going sources cited, more up-to-date information at any time.

A

Abortion 6-86
Accidents. See Divorced persons--
  United States--Disabled
Age. See Divorced persons--Statistics;
  Divorced persons (all subheadings)
Aged. See Divorced persons--Great
  Britain--Homes for the aged;
  Divorced persons--United States
  --Homes for the aged
Alabama 6-59, 8-21. See also
  States (as a subheading)
Alaska 6-60, 8-22. See also States
  (as a subheading)
Alcoholism 5-20, 6-168, 6-169
Alimony 1-1, 1-8, 1-18, 3-8, 3-21,
  4-5, 4-30, 4-31, 4-33, 4-34,
  4-54, 6-85, 8-116, 9-35, 9-39,
  10-1, 11-15, 12-7
  Canada 8-114
  Great Britain 8-115
  United States 3-16, 6-51, 6-52,
    6-172, 8-7, 8-11, 8-88, 8-100,
    8-115, 9-3, 9-20, 9-22, 9-25,
    9-40
  See also Legal aspects
American Indians, divorced 6-20
Americans overseas 6-37
Annulment 3-12, 3-20, 4-31, 4-33,
  5-3, 5-4, 5-9, 8-116, 10-1
  Canada 8-114
  Great Britain 3-12, 7-3, 7-54
  United States 6-53, 8-7, 9-20,
    9-22, 9-24

Subject Index

Subject Index

Subject Index

Canada--education; Divorced
persons--United States--education;
Children of divorced persons
Elderly. See Aged
Employment. See Labor force
Ethnic groups. See Divorced persons
--Canada--national origin and
language; Divorced persons--
Great Britain--national origin
and language; Divorced persons
--United States national origin
and language; See also by name
of the group
Executive orders. See Regulations,
rules.

F

Family law. See Laws and statutes;
Court decisions; Regulations,
rules.
Family life cycle 5-20
Family services 4-21
Father absence 1-2, 1-8, 4-4, 4-30,
4-33, 4-34, 4-44, 4-45, 4-50,
4-54, 5-3, 5-4, 5-14A, 5-15B,
5-17, 5-22. See also Desertion;
One-parent family; Support; Chil-
dren of divorced parents
Father separated. See Father absence
Fiction. See Literature, divorce in
Filipino Americans, divorced 6-21
Films, educational 1-5, 10-7, 10-13,
10-15 - 10-22. See also Motion
pictures
Filmstrips. See Audiovisuals
Financial aspects. See Economic
aspects
Florida 6-68, 8-30. See also State
(as a subheading)
Foreign-born populations. See Ethnic
groups
French Americans, divorced 6-15
Funding of research. See Research,
funding of

G

Georgia 6-69, 8-31, 9-10. See
also States (as a subheading)

German Americans, divorced 6-15
Government regulations, rules.
See Regulations, rules.
Grants-in-aid. See Research, funding
of
Greek Americans, divorced 6-15
Grief (O'Connor) 5-13A
Grounds for divorce. See Legal
aspects

H

Hawaii 6-70, 8-32, 9-11. See also
States (as a subheading)
Health characteristics 6-122, 6-124,
6-134
Health insurance--United States
6-121, 6-123B, 6-157
Heart disease 6-126, 6-142
Historical aspects 3-8, 3-20, 4-25,
4-40, 4-48, 5-16, 5-18
bibliography 1-5, 1-8, 8-74,
8-75, 8-76, 8-77, 8-79, 8-80,
8-81
Canada 4-43, 7-5, 7-6, 7-16 -
7-25
Great Britain 5-13, 5-16, 7-37
- 7-52, 8-85, 8-112, 8-115
United States 4-43, 5-13, 6-5,
6-39 - 6-48, 6-51, 6-52, 6-53,
8-115
United States--States (laws) 8-74
- 8-77, 8-79, 8-80, 8-81
Homicide 6-141, 6-142
Homosexuality 3-19
Hospital patients. See divorced
persons--Great Britain--hospi-
talized; Divorced persons--United
States--hospitalized
Hospital staff 6-25, 6-28
Hospitals, mental. See Divorced
persons--Canada--psychiatric
care; Divorced persons--United
States--psychiatric care
Hotels 7-35, 7-41, 7-43
Hypertension 6-127
Hungarian Americans, divorced 6-15

I

Idaho 6-71, 8-33. See also States

Subject Index

also Divorced persons--United
States--psychological states;
Counseling
Puerto Ricans in the United States,
divorced 6-12, 6-17, 6-19
Puerto Rico 6-111, 8-60

Q

Quotations 3-17. See also Quotations as a subject heading in the
library card catalog

R

Race. See Divorced persons--United
States--race; Divorced persons--
United States--States--race
Rates of divorce. See Numbers and
rates of divorce
Reconciliation 3-12
Recordings, sound. See Audiovisuals
Reform, divorce 1-5, 12-3, 12-6
Reformatories 6-25, 6-28, 7-35
Regulations, rules.
Canada 8-116, 8-117, 8-123,
8-130
Great Britain 8-112, 8-113,
8-115, 8-116, 8-117, 8-123
United States 8-16, 8-80, 8-95,
8-102, 8-105, 8-115, 8-116,
8-117, 8-118, 8-120
United States--States 8-16, 8-80,
8-88, 8-110, 8-117, 8-118,
8-120
Religious aspects 1-4, 1-5, 1-8,
1-11, 1-15, 3-6, 3-10, 4-3,
4-7, 4-8, 4-11, 4-25, 4-51,
5-18, 518A, 6-104
Religious groups 4-32, 4-35, 4-37,
5-18. See Divorced persons--
United States--religious group
quarters; Religious aspects; Cath-
olics and divorce; Jews and divorce; Mormons and divorce
Remarriage 1-2, 1-8, 3-14, 3-15,
3-20, 3-21, 4-3, 4-10, 4-30 -
4-34, 4-46, 4-54, 5-3, 5-4,
5-19, 5-19A, 6-25, 6-26,
6-99, 6-104, 6-151, 6-155,
8-88

Research 1-3, 1-7, 1-8, 1-10, 2-5,
3-9, 3-20, 3-21, 4-10, 4-13,
4-21 - 4-24, 4-28, 4-33, 4-34,
4-41 - 4-50, 4-53, 4-54, 4-55,
4-58, 5-1 - 5-25, 12-8, 12-9
Research centers ch. 13
Research collections. See Collections,
research
Research, funding of 5-23, 5-24,
13-9 - 13-19
Research-in-progress, announcing and
reporting of 5-23, 5-24, 5-25
Residency requirements. See Legal
aspects
Resource persons 1-5, 5-25, 12-7
Resources. See Research, funding of;
Collections, research
Retirement 3-19, 7-33, 7-48, 7-52
Retrospective works. See Historical
aspects
Reviews 2-36, 2-37, 2-38, 2-39,
3-22, 3-23, 3-25, 4-1, 4-5,
4-6, 4-7, 4-9, 4-12, 4-15,
4-26, 4-31, 4-33, 4-34, 4-37,
8-114, 8-116, 10-16 - 10-22
Rhode Island 6-99, 8-61. See also
States (as a subheading)
Roles 5-13, 5-15B, 5-18. See also
Sociological aspects
Roman Catholic Church. See Catho-
lics and divorce
Rooming houses and hotels 6-25,
6-28, 7-35, 7-41, 7-43
Rural areas. See Divorced persons
--Canada--rural areas; Divorced
persons--Great Britain--rural
areas; Divorced persons--United
States--rural areas
Russian Americans, divorced 6-15

S

Second marriages. See Remarriage
Separation 1-3, 1-8, 3-12, 4-33,
4-50, 4-53, 4-54, 5-3, 5-4,
5-20, 5-20A, 8-116, 10-1,
10-15, 12-7, 12-8
Canada 1-3, 8-100
Great Britain 3-12, 7-3
United States 1-3, 1-8, 6-5,

Subject Index

V

Vermont 6-105, 8-67. See also
States (as a subheading)
Virginia 6-106, 8-68. See also
States (as a subheading)
Virgin Islands 6-13, 6-112, 8-69
Visitation 5-10. See also Child
custody
Vital statistics. See Statistics

W

Waiting period required for remarriage.
See Legal aspects
Washington (state) 5-13, 6-107,
8-70. See also States (as a
subheading)
Welfare 1-8, 3-7, 5-15B. See also
Social services

West Indian Americans, divorced
6-15
West Virginia 6-108, 8-71, 9-30.
See also States (as a subheading)
Wisconsin 6-109, 8-72, 9-31. See
also States (as a subheading)
Women 5-13, 5-13A, 5-14, 5-14A,
7-31, 8-5, 8-104, 12-7
Work. See Labor force; Occupation
Workers' dormitories 6-25, 6-28
Wyoming 6-110, 8-73. See also
States (as a subheading)

Y

Yugoslavian Americans, divorced
6-15